RIFLEMAN

The Untold Story
of Stevie Flemmi,
Whitey Bulger's Partner

HOWIE CARR

Frandel, LLC

Table of Contents

Acknowledgments

This type of book can never be produced in a vacuum, and I owe more people thanks than I can possibly list, or should, given the sensitive positions many of them still work in.

But let me start with my lovely wife Kathy, who handled much of the business involved in publishing a book outside the traditional routes. Also thanks to my three daughters, Carolyn, Charlotte and Tina, who helped their Luddite father with his technological problems.

Beyond my family, most thanks are due to my radio producer, Nancy "Sandy" Shack, who stepped in and tirelessly handled the compilation of the photographs, which was not easy, believe me, because I tried doing it before I turned the chore over to her.

At the *Boston Herald*, where I have worked for so many years, thanks to everyone, starting with publisher Pat Purcell, editor Joe Sciacca and managing editor John Strahinich for the use of many of the pictures in this book. The photo staff was awesome, running down archived photos, especially the mugshots, some of which I feared had been lost forever in our recent move to Fargo Street. Special thanks to Mark Garfinkel, Arthur Pollock and Matt Stone, as well as to *Herald* librarian Martha Reagan.

Connor Perry, a talented student at Cooper Union, did a fantastic job on the cover, and Jeff Walsh, a graphic artist for the *Herald*, produced a clear, easy-to-read map outlining the neighborhood bases of the competing (and cooperating) mobs.

Thanks also to Emily Sweeney, author of the great book "*Boston Organized-Crime*," for use of some of her best photos. I appreciate the invaluable assistance of Anthony Amore, director of security at the Isabella Stewart Gardner Museum. Much appreciation to Diane Wiffin at the Mass. Department of Correction for a number of previously-unseen mugshots, and to the Boston Police Department public-relations unit, for the Mullens Gang wanted poster which I obtained during the writing of my previous book, *Hitman*.

As to all the other sources whose names I haven't mentioned, you know I'm just doing it for your own well-being. In the bad old days that this book covers, that would mean your physical well-being. Now I just refer to your career prospects. In any event, you know who you are, and you know you have my profound gratitude.

WINTER HILL ORGANIZATION
CIRCA 1975

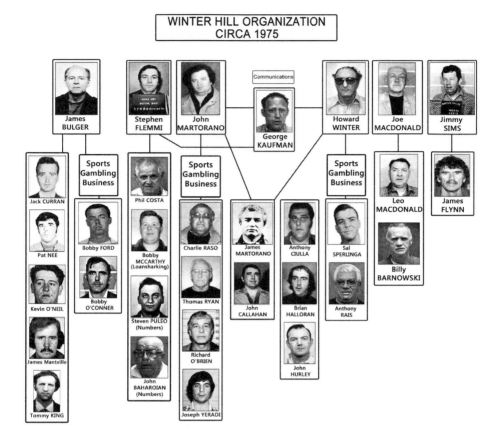

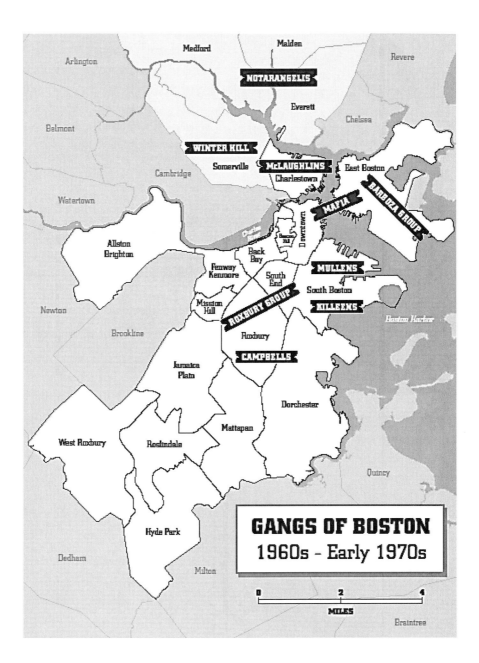

GANGS OF BOSTON
1960s - Early 1970s

0   2   4
MILES

Introduction

THIS IS STEVIE Flemmi's own story, dictated to the cops, in the presence of his own lawyers. The feds call it a DEA-6 and if it has a recurring theme, it's that nothing that ever happened was Stevie's fault. Whatever atrocities occurred, and there were many, Flemmi by his own account was not much more than a bystander. He was a victim of "ambiguous circumstances," to quote Whitey Bulger's brother during one Fifth Amendment-heavy Congressional hearing in Boston.

If somebody had to be killed, it was done "reluctantly." Or Whitey Bulger "talked him into it." One time Stevie was "under a great deal of stress." On another occasion, he and Whitey "had had enough." What choice did they have?

It wasn't murder, either. It was "elimination."

If there is ever a question about who was calling the shots, Flemmi's answer is something along the lines of: "Bulger was in control. He made all the decisions."

Stevie even knew why Whitey, originally a junior partner, took over the gang. It was his "management abilities," Flemmi explained to his interrogators over a period of weeks in 2003-04.

As Stevie told the federal and state law-enforcement handlers to whom he dictated this 146-page testament, "Things just developed." According to his own recounting of his life and crimes, Stevie was a font of practical, common-sense advice. In 1965, he warned his brother Jimmy he was going to get shot if he kept going home for dinner every night, and sure enough, he was. A few months later, he warned Winter Hill boss Buddy McLean that he was going to get shot if he kept going to the same bars every night, and sure enough, he was. In 1976, he ran into Patsy Fabiano who was on his way to dinner with a made member of the Mafia. Stevie says he knew exactly what was going to happen to Patsy, but he didn't bother to warn him. He didn't even say goodbye.

On other occasions, though, Stevie did save lives, if he does say so himself. The night of the Blackfriars massacre in 1978, he was at the Summer Street ginmill with his girlfriend Marilyn DiSilva. He had a strange hunch that "something was amiss," and if anyone should have known when something like this was amiss, it was Stevie. He convinced Marilyn to leave the barroom before the gunmen burst in and murdered the five men inside. He "probably saved her life," Flemmi modestly declares.

This book began as a document I received from a source several years ago. Once they have flipped, "top-echelon" organized-crime figures are routinely debriefed by federal law-enforcement about their life and crimes. In Flemmi's case, his career dated from the mid-1950's, shortly after the end of the Korean War, until his arrest in January 1995 at the age of 60. He wasn't just a violent criminal either. According to Flemmi, he and Whitey had "25 to 30" Boston police officers on the pad. As Whitey used to say of his annual holiday payoffs, "Christmas is for cops and kids."

As unreflective as Stevie Flemmi is in this autobiography of crime, he does tell a fascinating if horrific tale. At the beginning, gangs are swarming all over the city, squabbling—and murdering—each other over practically nothing. In 1968, three innocent people died over a $100 loan shark debt owed to Stevie. Needless to say, it wasn't his fault. As late as 1980, Mafia enforcer Larry Baione would be recorded on an FBI bug saying that Flemmi and Whitey Bulger "don't have two nickels to rub together."

But within two or three years, Stevie and Whitey had outmaneuvered their underworld rivals, both the Mafia and their own ostensible allies in the Winter Hill Gang. Everybody else was in jail or on the lam, and Whitey and Stevie were making up to a million dollars per shipload of marijuana being smuggled into Boston Harbor. Their only duty—providing "protection," which meant, basically, not informing their corrupt, bought cops of the drug ships' arrivals.

As Flemmi explained of his and Whitey's non-duties in a later deposition, "We weren't involved in the logistical end of it . . . if that answers your question."

For most of his time on the street as a gangster, Stevie was simultaneously an informant for the FBI, which is more than ironic, considering that another recurring theme in this brief report is how often people in his orbit were murdered because they, too, were informants—or rats, or snitches, as Whitey and Stevie often called the hoodlums who did the same thing they did, only not as successfully.

In fact, even though Whitey became the legend, Stevie Flemmi was the quintessential FBI gangland informant, just the sort of deep-inside hood J. Edgar Hoover had dreamed of developing in 1961 when he directed his men to start recruiting mobsters with the same determination that they courted Communist and fellow-traveler "double agents."

At the behest of his new boss, Atty. Gen. Bobby Kennedy, in 1961 the formerly reluctant (for whatever reasons) Hoover suddenly became obsessed with organized crime, or at least the Mafia. He wanted informants who were close to the LCN, but not directly of it.

In the early 1960's, the FBI in Boston—mainly H. Paul Rico and Dennis Condon—were doing their best to follow the Director's orders. They recruited a burglar named George Ashe, but Stevie's insane brother, Jimmy the Bear Flemmi, killed him the next day. Some have suggested that Rico recruited Buddy McLean, the founder of what became the Winter Hill Gang, as early as 1956, and that Buddy may have been the informant who gave Rico the tip about Whitey's fateful visit to the Reef Cafe in Revere, which turned out to be his last evening of freedom for nine years.

Rico and McLean definitely worked together during the Irish gang war. Unfortunately for the FBI, just as McLean was tightening his grip on the non-Mafia underworld, Stevie Hughes took him out on Halloween Eve 1965 from the darkened shadows of the shuttered Capitol Theater on Broadway. Hey, Stevie had tried to warn Buddy about not becoming a creature of habit. . . .

But the ideal FBI informants were Italians, who could move more easily among the Mafia. The feds even attempted to recruit Jimmy the Bear, but he was far too unstable, and as you will read, made too many jokes about the sexual preferences of the FBI, from Hoover on down.

Stevie, though, was more circumspect, which made him perfect for the job of informant. He'd grown up in a then-predominantly Irish neighborhood (the Orchard Park projects in Roxbury), he'd gotten his start with an Irish gang, and he had an Irish wife. Many years later, the *Globe* described him as "Irish gangster Stevie Flemmi." At first it seemed like a ridiculous howler, but once you got past the vowel at the end of his name, there was some truth to it. Still, he did have the Italian bloodlines, which meant he could move more easily among the Angiulos and the Baiones. But from the very beginning, he just plain didn't care much for the Mafia mumbo-jumbo, the ring-kissing, the cheek-kissing and the ass-kissing. If any money was going to be "whacked up," Stevie wanted to be taking, not giving.

Stevie was doing okay in the underworld, but until 1965, he was just another run-of-the-mill gunsel, one of Wimpy Bennett's bad boys. But in October 1965 at age 31 he looked George "Punchy" McLaughlin in the eye and shot him down at the Spring Street bus turnaround in West Roxbury.

Suddenly everybody knew that Stevie was "capable"—capable of murder, by himself. Not just riding around in a car with a bunch of other guys with Jimmy Sims at the wheel, firing machine guns at drunken Irish boyos, but capable of taking out a major player, one-on-one, in front of dozens of witnesses, and getting away with it. Of course, Punchy only had one hand by that time, which hampered his access to his gun more than somewhat, but that's quibbling.

Within a couple of years, Peter Limone was suggesting that both Stevie and Frank Salemme would be perfect candidates for the Mafia. Salemme swooned; it was his life's goal to be a made man. Stevie demurred. He still hung out sometimes on Hanover Street, but he'd always go home to Roxbury and meet Rico on the corner the next morning.

This balancing act could get delicate at times, as you will soon see. When Joe Barboza flipped, and began lying about who'd killed Teddy Deegan in 1965, in order to settle some old scores while putting away as many Mafia guys as possible, Stevie was put in a particularly tight spot. FBI agents Rico and Condon ordered him down to Norfolk to talk to his brother (one of Deegan's real killers) and tell him not to contradict Barboza's perjury.

Then the Mafia dispatched him back to Norfolk with instructions to tell the Bear he was expected to tell the truth. (The FBI's most famous fictional TV agent in those days, Inspector Lew Erskine, wouldn't have been able to comprehend such a tale of treachery. The FBI suborning perjury and the Mafia trying to get the true story out.)

As it turned out, Flemmi handled it with his usual aplomb. He told his brother, and Barboza's men who were in jail with him, Nick Femia and Patsy Fabiano, to stay the fuck out of it, that it wasn't their business, that there was no way to win getting in the middle of a pissing match between the Mafia and the FBI.

In the meantime, Flemmi kept feeding Rico a steady stream of information. After Walter Bennett was murdered and the rumor spread that he had fled to Florida, Stevie flatly told Rico to forget Florida, that "Walter won't be back."

Rico was too polite to ask Stevie how exactly he knew this. He just filed another 209.

Stevie went on the lam in 1969, but by 1974, everybody wanted him back—the FBI, the Hill, the Mafia. Jerry Angiulo gave him $50,000 to rebuild his loan sharking racket, but the Hill asked him to take the money from them. He gently rebuffed another attempt by Angiulo to get him to join LCN. No burning Mass cards for Stevie.

Back from Montreal, Stevie was even more valuable to the FBI. They were trying to prop up Whitey Bulger—when agents had to retire at age 50, it was quite convenient to have a friend at the State House who had power over state utilities. With Billy Bulger rising in the legislative leadership, soon there were opportunities for retired G-men beyond Boston police commissioner, always a thankless job. Now an old G-man could become, say. . . director of security at Boston Edison, a job held by at least three ex-Boston agents, including two of Whitey's friends, Zip Connolly and Doc Gianturco. Connolly began bringing newly-assigned agents to the State House to meet Billy in his plush offices; Billy would introduce Zip at his annual St. Patrick's Day breakfast as the world's greatest crime fighter. Everybody got it.

Beyond a friendship with J.R. Russo, Whitey had no sources in the Mafia. Almost all the reports that Zip Connolly wrote on "In Town" and attributed to Whitey actually came from Flemmi. Whitey ratted out small-time tailgaters in Southie; Stevie knew, and informed on, the heavy hitters on Prince Street. In 1980, when the feds wanted to add Whitey to the list of informants for the wiretap on Angiulo's headquarters (thus protecting him from indictment), they discovered he'd never been there. Not once.

FOR ALMOST all of his career, no one believed Stevie was an informant. The thought didn't even cross their minds. When the *Globe* wrote its famous 1988 series about Whitey's "special relationship" with the FBI, Bulger had to tap dance his way out of it, blaming it on the newspaper's alleged vendetta against his politician brother. But Stevie just sat back and watched. No one suspected Flemmi. They knew how many people he'd killed, how many rackets he juggled, how many girlfriends he had on the string.

He just didn't seem like. . . FBI material.

As it turned out, Flemmi got too complacent. He'd gotten the heads-up from Rico on when to skip town in 1969, ahead of the state indictments for murder and a car bombing. Then he got the heads-up when to return, in 1974. In between, he kept in touch with his FBI handlers as "Jack from South Boston."

But when the feds and the State Police began circling again in the early 1990's, Flemmi misread the situation. He underestimated his jeopardy. Whitey, having already done nine hard years, was determined to avoid any more time in prison. Stevie, who'd never spent more than a night or two in the jug, didn't realize the danger he was in. He figured his FBI friends would allow him to make a leisurely escape, as he had in the fall of 1969.

When Flemmi was arrested in January 1995, he didn't ask for a lawyer, he asked for an FBI agent. Times had changed, and Flemmi hadn't been paying nearly enough attention. Soon, as part of discovery, Flemmi and his codefendants, including Frank Salemme and the Martorano brothers, were being deluged in jail with ancient FBI 302's and 209's written in the 1960's by FBI agent H. Paul Rico among others. One day in the Plymouth County Correctional Facility, Salemme read something that the FBI calls "singular information," meaning that it could only have come from one source. It was about Salemme himself, and the only person who had known about the 1967 incident in the report was. . . Flemmi.

Salemme called Flemmi over and handed him the smoking-gun document, with the informant's name and ID number redacted. Salemme accused Flemmi of ratting him out to Rico. Flemmi shook his head and blamed their old boss, Wimpy Bennett.

"You know Wimpy was always talking to Rico," Flemmi said.

But Salemme shook his head. "Look at the date, Stevie," he said. "April 1967. You'd already killed Wimpy three months earlier."

The hearings continued in Judge Mark Wolf's courtroom until the day finally arrived when the judge had to decide whether to approve a motion by the defense attorneys to release the names of all the government informants in the case. A recess was called, and the marshals took the defendants upstairs to the holding pen. All of them except Flemmi. Everyone figured they'd seen the last of "the Rifleman," at least until he appeared as a government witness testifying against them.

The judge called Flemmi into his chambers and told him that at the next day's court hearing, he planned to out both him and Whitey Bulger as "top-echelon" government informants. Wolf asked Flemmi if he wanted to go with the government. Marshals were already waiting for him outside in the hall; did Flemmi really have a choice? Judge Wolf didn't have to say what future he envisioned for Flemmi—disappearing into the Witness Protection Program. But for some unknown reason, Flemmi declined the offer. He wanted to go back to Plymouth on the bus with the rest of them. That evening he summoned his codefendants together and said he had something very important to tell them. He and Whitey had been informants, he said. But don't take it the wrong way, he continued.

"They gave us gold," he said, "and we gave them shit."

The other defendants looked around at each another. They understood, even if Stevie didn't. They were the shit he and Whitey had given the feds.

In the end, Flemmi pleaded guilty to 10 murders. In various court proceedings, and related depositions, he took the Fifth Amendment when asked about at least 10 other slayings. Among those he murdered was a long-time girlfriend, Debbie Davis, whose underage sister he also raped, as well as one of his common-law stepdaughters. Actually, Whitey Bulger strangled Debbie Davis. Stevie was, in his own words, "emotionally distraught," so much so that at one point, he says, he actually considered killing

Bulger. Later, he told another of his Winter Hill partners, John Martorano, that he himself had "accidentally" garroted the woman.

"How do you 'accidentally' strangle somebody, Stevie?" Martorano asked him.

Later Stevie and Whitey decided they had to murder another of Flemmi's girlfriends, this one his common-law stepdaughter by longtime girlfriend Marion Hussey. As Flemmi elaborated a couple of years later, Deb was doing "a lot of things. . . which I didn't approve of."

For the record, though, he never murdered any of his own biological children. Deb Hussey was his stepdaughter.

"Take a DNA test if you like," he said in the 2005 deposition.

And as you will soon be reading, Stevie told his interrogators that he did not personally strangle the girl he raised, "although he may have twisted her light beige sweater around her neck, while stripping the body."

As the pace of the murders quickened, everyone developed their own specialties. Whitey Bulger did the killing. Kevin Weeks dug the graves. Phil Costa poured the lime around the bodies to hasten decomposition. And Stevie Flemmi's job was to extract the teeth, in order to make identification more difficult. After pulling out the teeth, he would grind them up and then flush them down the toilet. Eventually, Whitey had his dental-hygienist girlfriend order a set of state-of-the-art tooth extractors from her boss' catalogue, to expedite the process. It was Stevie's Christmas present that year.

When they murdered John McIntyre in 1984 (he was a "snitch," as they put it) according to other witnesses Bulger first tried to strangle him but couldn't. He grabbed a pistol and then, according to other witnesses, asked McIntyre, "Do you want to be shot in the head?"

"Yes please," McIntyre allegedly replied.

The McIntyre murder was brought up in some detail in the later depositions, with Flemmi's only reply, "Take the Fifth."

LAWYER: "In order to determine if Mr. McIntyre was dead, you put your ear to his chest and reported to Bulger that he is still alive?"

FLEMMI: "Take the Fifth."

LAWYER: "McIntyre was then shot several more times with the .22 caliber pistol while you held McIntyre's head up?"

FLEMMI: "Take the Fifth."

LAWYER: "While extracting his teeth, you also extracted his tongue?"

FLEMMI: "Take the Fifth."

Cadillac Frank Salemme probably knew Stevie Flemmi as well as anyone in the underworld, with the possible exception of Whitey Bulger and Stevie's younger brother, Jimmy the Bear Flemmi. By the time he was interviewed by Congressional investigators in 2003, Salemme understood completely how Stevie had played him for the fool for the better part of four decades. He was understandably bitter. Still, he had had the chance to observe his one-time "partner" over the years, and his summation of Flemmi's motivations seem uncannily on target.

"There's two things with Flemmi paramount to everything," Salemme said. "His money and his women. . . . That was his m.o. all along. That's what it was to him, his money and his women, not necessarily in that order."

He always had the women. During the FBI informant hearings of 1997, most of the defendants had their consorts in the courtroom. Cadillac Frank's second wife, Donna, was perhaps two decades younger than her husband. Rhode Island mobster Robert DeLuca's wife, Kimi—she was maybe 30 years his junior.

And then there was Stevie Flemmi's Asian girlfriend, the twentysomething he'd been with when he was arrested in January 1995. "What is this, a grandstand play?" he asked the State Police, in his best film-noir style. She was so young, so inappropriately young, even for a mobster's moll, that none of the other women wanted anything to do with her. It seemed unseemly. Maybe to have her as a girlfriend, but not sitting in there in the courtroom. . . .

On other days, one or more of his daughters by his first wife, the former Jeannette McLaughlin, would stop by. His children by Marion Hussey—they were no-shows. By then they knew that Stevie had not only murdered their sister, or had her murdered, strangled by Whitey Bulger and then buried in the basement of a small house in Southie, along with two other gang victims.

A few years later, when the house was sold, the bodies had to be disinterred and reburied. Among the details the usually unobservant Flemmi recalls is that some pieces of flesh were still hanging off the bones of his common-law stepdaughter.

There was yet another family—the Davises of Brookline Village. As you will read, Stevie met the married teenager Debbie when she was working for one of Boston's top fences. Debbie and Stevie were soon an item, and Stevie became a de facto father of sorts once the heavy-drinking Mr. Davis drowned under what the family (if few others) considered mysterious circumstances. Soon Stevie was also having sex with Debbie's dark-haired younger sister, Melissa. "My Ava Gardner," he called her, as if she had any idea who the 1940's Hollywood sexpot was.

Yet in these confessions, Stevie originally didn't even want to admit to having sex with Melissa Davis. He was too embarrassed to acknowledge to forcing his underage "stepdaughter" to fellate him.

"Stevie wasn't a planner," Salemme explained. "He would go if you took him by the hand, but he wasn't a planner at all. He had his own agenda, and he wasn't deviating from that. Money and women, I told you, he wasn't going to deviate from that."

If you took him by the hand. . . that's what Whitey did. Stevie didn't care, as long as he had plenty of money and women.

All of the partners in the Winter Hill Gang were "capable"—that is, capable of killing—but somehow they weren't as cold and calculating as Whitey and Stevie. After his return from the lam, in 1974, his old friends noticed a change in Stevie. Like Whitey, he was a bit of a hypochondriac; he didn't drink, or smoke pot, the way he used to in the Sixties.

In its original form, the document you are about to read ran 146 single-spaced pages. Misspellings have been corrected, and the prose style, standard cop-ese, has been edited with the intention of improving its readability. I have redacted names of people who are still alive, but have never been convicted of the crimes Stevie accuses them of. Throughout his now almost 20 years of incarceration, Stevie has often changed his accounts of the assorted crimes and other events in his life. Whenever possible, I have tried to point out the inconsistencies in the various versions. Perhaps the differences can be at least partially explained by the fact that in the beginning Stevie wasn't planning on spending the rest of his life in prison. For at least a few years he assumed that Whitey Bulger and Zip Connolly would soon be riding to his rescue.

"Maybe they still are," he told a federal prosecutor at the Wolf hearings in 1997.

Some of what Stevie says here is just plain untrue. For instance, he takes credit for recruiting crooked state trooper Richard Schneiderhan as a source. He didn't. Johnny Martorano did, at the old Enrico's in the Combat Zone. When Martorano went on the lam in 1978, he turned him over to Flemmi, much the way Connolly wanted to turn over his two "top-echelon" informants to another FBI agent when he retired in 1990.

One way that cops force confessions from criminals looking at lengthy prison sentences is to point out the ravages of time. Kevin Weeks was told that if he didn't flip, by the time he got out, if he got out, his then-teenage children would be in their 40's. Weeks didn't need much convincing; his nickname quickly became "Two Weeks," which was the length of time he languished in the lockup in Central Falls RI before he started singing.

In Flemmi's case, he was reminded that his father had lived to be 98. Flemmi wasn't getting out, but the odds were that even at his relatively advanced age at the time (68 or so), he might live another 20 or 30 years. He had a choice: he could do hard time, or he could do. . . not-so-hard time.

In Roxbury, or South Boston, Stevie cultivated the traditional mobster style—bad ass. As is noted on page one of this report, his parents were attacked by a gang of five blacks on Blue Hill Avenue. The feds ask him about his bragging that he later murdered all five. He denies it, but notes that at least two of them did come to violent ends. Around the same time, one of his rivals for Debbie Davis' affections is murdered in the Blue Hills reservation; Stevie knows nothing about it but speculates it may be related to a "problematic marijuana deal."

As part of his confession, Stevie has to detail all of his run-ins with the law, no matter how minor. Many involve barroom fights over women. He could become insanely jealous over almost anyone he considered a rival. Before her death from a drug overdose, Melissa Davis recalled how one spring day, when she was about 14, she was walking down the street with a young male classmate she liked. Stevie, who was already having sex with Melissa, pulled up in a brand-new car and offered them a ride.

The two teenagers climbed in the backseat, and the boy quickly noticed that despite the warm weather, Stevie was wearing leather gloves. The youth innocently asked Stevie why he was wearing the gloves.

"I always wear gloves when I'm planning to kill somebody in my car," Stevie said, a sinister smirk on his face. The boy looked over at Melissa pleadingly, as if to seek assurance that this strange man was kidding. Melissa just shook her head. The boy asked Stevie to pull over, and as soon as he did, the boy jumped out and took off running. Melissa never saw him again.

Of course, in his own mind, Stevie Flemmi was not a bad guy. He was, in fact, like King Lear, "a man more sinned against than sinning." Take Brian Halloran, later machine-gunned by Whitey Bulger on Northern Avenue in Southie.

"I thought he was a bully," Stevie said in a 2005 deposition. "In fact, he punched out, he killed a guy's horse. I thought that was a despicable act."

By his own accounting, Flemmi tried to keep a low profile.

"I never discuss my political views with anybody, sort of keep them to myself," he said in 2005. "That way I don't get into too many problems."

FLEMMI WAS tough, and so were the people he hung with. One of his early associates in crime was Red Conlin. In 1968, when Red's body turned up in a cemetery, the cops assumed that he'd been shot, at close range. But once they took a more careful look, they saw that he had been savagely beaten to death. His in-laws were arrested. . . and acquitted. It was a rough time. I once showed Johnny Martorano the February 1967 edition of Life magazine with the mugshots of more than 40 plug-uglies bumped off in the Boston gang wars.

"They needed another one of these," Martorano said, "for the Seventies."

As Frank Salemme told the Congressional investigators, "It's tough to walk up to a guy and snuff him right there." And Flemmi wasn't always available for a snuffing. From the killings of Stevie Hughes and Sam Lindenbaum in 1966 to that of horse-killer Brian Halloran in 1982, Flemmi had a way of being MIA if the murders weren't directly related to his own personal well-being.

Despite his volatile reputation in the underworld as a "spontaneous reactor," in Salemme's words, he could also turn on the tears in a tight spot. When Deb Davis went "missing," he enjoyed a good cry with her mother, Olga. After his return from Montreal, he visited the first wife of his old partner Frank Salemme, who was just beginning his 17-year state sentence for the car bombing of a mob lawyer.

"I'll never forget this," Salemme recalled, "strictly the dog-and-pony show, he's my man, he's this and that, he broke down crying. And there I was saying, he'll do the right thing, and (Raymond) L.S. (Patriarca) telling me he's a phony, you'll see it."

The old goombahs, they had Stevie pegged from the start. As early as 1965, in an FBI report by H. Paul Rico, Revere Mafioso Sammy Granito is quoted as saying that Wimpy Bennett has "a couple of bad kids" working for him—Stevie and Jimmy Flemmi.

Among the more fascinating characters in this story is H. Paul Rico, perhaps the most corrupt FBI agent in bureau history, certainly in Boston history. After the Rico-instigated murder of jai alai baron Roger Wheeler in Tulsa in 1981, Tulsa police detective Mike Huff was assigned to the case. As part of his investigation, Huff flew to Miami to interview World Jai Alai's director of security, the "decorated" retired FBI agent H. Paul Rico.

"I thought I was going in to interview a fellow law-enforcement professional," Huff recalled years later. "Instead, I sit down and find myself across the table from the Godfather."

Huff was neither the first nor the last person to assume Rico was a gangster, which in fact by most measures he was. In 1983, with the unsolved World Jai Alai murder investigation dying down, the FBI was looking for someone in Florida who could work an undercover sting on an allegedly crooked federal judge named Alcee Hastings. The person the feds needed had to pass cash to Hastings' bagman, and he had to pass himself off convincingly as a member of Santo Trafficante's Tampa Mafia family.

It took Washington about 10 seconds to come up with the perfect faux gangster. H. Paul Rico. He delivered his lines flawlessly; the bagman was convicted, and although Judge Hastings beat the rap, he was impeached and convicted in the U.S. Senate. Stripped of his robes, Hastings was immediately elected to Congress, where he serves to this day.

Rico died in 2004 in a Tulsa jail hospital bed. He had just been indicted in Oklahoma for first-degree murder in the death of Roger Wheeler. Days earlier, after more than 20 years on this case, Detective Huff had been given the honor of making the arrest. Wearing his World Jai Alai cardigan sweater when he came to the door of his suburban Miami condo, Rico had first refused to believe he was really about to be arrested. When Huff produced the handcuffs, Rico shat in his pleated madras pants.

THE BOSTON of the 20th century in which Stevie Flemmi lived, extorted, raped, murdered and corrupted no longer exists. It's become one of those "Faraway Places," as in the old Forties standard by Bing Crosby. When he was arrested in January 1995, Whitey's brother was still the president of the state Senate. Soon he would take over the presidency of the University of Massachusetts, while trying to pass the Senate seat on to his oldest son and namesake. With Whitey gone from the streets, the feckless Billy Jr. never had a chance. It was the end of the Bulger political dynasty.

In 2003, Flemmi pled guilty in the J. Joseph Moakley Federal Courthouse, named after Billy Bulger's late political mentor. It's a new building, built on Northern Avenue, just a couple of hundred yards west of where Whitey Bulger machine-gunned Brian Halloran and Michael Donahue 21 years earlier. At Moakley's funeral, Billy delivered the eulogy for his old pal, recalling how Moakley had made it a point to dine with Billy publicly after the stories of Whitey's serial murders began to dominate the city's newspapers.

Around the courthouse, posh new restaurants, craft beer gardens and high-rise condominiums now dot the once hard-scrabble cobblestone street. It is no longer "South Boston." Now it is the "Seaport District."

Stevie Flemmi and Whitey Bulger in undated surveillance photo from the 1980's.

Jimmy Kelly, the gang's go-to city councilor at City Hall, to whom Whitey allegedly paid $100 a week until his 1983 election to the Council, died in 2006. The new bridge connecting Southie to the rest of the city is now called the James M. Kelly Bridge.

All of the old Mafioso Stevie kept tabs on for the FBI are dead—Jerry Angiulo, Larry Baione, J.R. Russo. They don't even call it the Patriarca Crime Family anymore, not after the misrule of the Man's son, "Rubber Lips." What little remains of it is now known as the New England Mafia. Baione's old social club on North Margin Street has been turned into a doggy daycare center—The Dogfather.

As for Stevie and Whitey, they will meet one final time this summer, in a courtroom. H. Paul Rico's rat testifying against Zip Connolly's rat—ambiguous circumstances indeed.

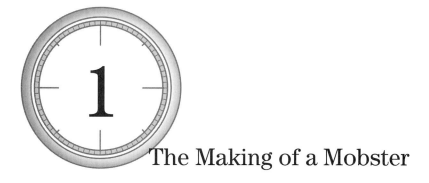

The Making of a Mobster

1. **FLEMMI** stated that he was born in Boston on June 9, 1934, the oldest son of Giovanni and Mary FLEMMI. FLEMMI's siblings were the late organized-crime figure, Vincent James "the Bear" FLEMMI, and former Boston Police officer (and convicted felon) Michael FLEMMI. FLEMMI further stated that his father, Giovanni or John, was an Italian immigrant who lived to the age of 98. Giovanni was a hard worker, quite frugal and operated a push cart, selling everything from quahogs to jewelry. Giovanni FLEMMI also worked as a bricklayer in the construction field. FLEMMI said that when his father died, he left his youngest son Michael some $70,000 that he had saved up over many decades. FLEMMI's mother Mary took care of her children and grandchildren, as well as

Stevie Flemmi, age 23, in 1957.

the household, first in Roxbury, then Mattapan and finally in South Boston. Mary FLEMMI also worked as a nurse's aide at Boston City Hospital. FLEMMI noted that his parents had been the victims of a robbery by five black juveniles in the late 1970's after a car accident. FLEMMI contended that he never attempted any type of retribution against the perpetrators of this crime against his parents. FLEMMI stated that he attended Boston English High School, but dropped out in order to fight in the Korean War. FLEMMI got his GED while in military service. After serving in the army, FLEMMI returned to Boston English High for some additional courses.

2. FLEMMI stated that he was too young to sign up for the military but entered the US Army, in January of 1952, using the name and identification of a childhood friend ███████. FLEMMI said that he was accepted into the paratroopers, and was assigned to the 187th Airborne Division. FLEMMI stated that he volunteered for his first eight-man combat patrol in Korea, which ran into a company of Chinese regulars. FLEMMI opened fire, and killed the first five enemy soldiers. The remainder of the American

Boston Police lineup, 1943. Second from left, Harry "Doc Jasper" Sagansky, preeminent Hub gambling czar of the 20th century.

patrol quickly reacted, and the majority of the opposing Chinese platoon was wiped out. FLEMMI stated that it was in this first encounter with the enemy, that he received the nickname "the Rifleman." FLEMMI added that after the war was over, friends from the service brought the nickname back to Boston. FLEMMI noted that soon after he arrived in Korea, he advised his first sergeant of his true name. FLEMMI straightened out the name issue after learning that his parents wouldn't be able to collect on his GI life insurance in the event he was killed in action.

3. FLEMMI stated that during the war he was involved in a lot of heavy combat action and as a result he killed many Chinese and North Korean soldiers. FLEMMI served two tours in Korea, and was honorably discharged at the rank of corporal on Feb. 1, 1955. FLEMMI returned to high school in an attempt to get enough credits for college, but had a difficult time making the transition to civilian life. FLEMMI supported himself during this time period by repairing roofs and the flashing on various area churches. FLEMMI had a few early scrapes with the criminal justice system in the mid-to-late 1950's, including a fist fight

Vincent "Jimmy the Bear" Flemmi.

over a missing coat. FLEMMI was found not guilty by a jury in this case. FLEMMI and a friend, Buddy WASHINGTON, were also arrested for unarmed robbery, when the pair attempted to grab a packet of money from a male victim. According to FLEMMI, this charge was adjudicated with each defendant receiving one year's probation. FLEMMI stated that he was involved in several businesses in the Dudley Street Roxbury area, first opening a small market called Jay's Spa. FLEMMI also owned several taverns in the area. Additionally, FLEMMI also operated a real estate office, a grocery store, rooming houses, and later a book store. FLEMMI also made money by occasionally picking up the mortgages on Roxbury-area buildings with very little money being initially invested.

4. FLEMMI stated that in approximately 1956, he met another Dudley Street area businessman, Edward "Wimpy" BENNETT, through his (BENNETT's) girlfriend ████████. Edward "Wimpy" BENNETT received his nickname because he hung around eating hamburgers at the Tremont Street White Castle Restaurant, in a fashion similar to the Popeye cartoon character. FLEMMI stated that he didn't like BENNETT's nickname, and often called him "the Fox." Like FLEMMI, BEN-NETT had also been in the military, and had served as a tail gunner in a B-29 dur-

Stevie's first underworld boss: Edward "Wimpy" Bennett.

ing World War II. At first BENNETT asked FLEMMI if some shylock customers could leave off payment envelopes for him at Jay's Spa. Later BENNETT offered to give FLEMMI cash to start his own shylock business. FLEMMI accepted BENNETT's offer, and began loaning small amounts of money to a neighborhood clientele. FLEMMI's 1961 arrest for extortion and loan sharking was a direct result of his illegal activities with BENNETT, and occurred after police found some records at Jay's Spa. FLEMMI paid a $500 fine in that case. FLEMMI recalled that during one of these searches by the Boston Police, he was told that he had been operating too flagrantly, and that there had been a lot of complaints from the local population.

5. FLEMMI stated that he continued to work as a shylock for BENNETT, and eventually the Boston Police returned with a search warrant on his real estate office at 224-226 Dudley Street (09/26/62). FLEMMI was not present during the raid, but contacted the police via telephone. FLEMMI gave the officers the combination to a safe that was in the office, and the law-enforcement officers opened the door and seized some evidence. The Boston Police also confiscated some rifles and a handgun. FLEMMI added that the police eventually returned the rifles, but failed to give back the handgun. FLEMMI stated that at a prior time, FBI S/A (Special Agent)

Rico, H. Paul   "**Ric**"
Football 2, 3
AMBITION: To come back and
         find everything the
         way I left it
PET PEEVE: Cards
"*A form more active, light and
strong
Ne'er shot the ranks of war
along*"

FBI agent H. Paul Rico graduated from Belmont High School in 1943.

H. Paul RICO had also visited FLEMMI at FLEMMI's home in Dorchester, and asked for permission to do a consent search. FLEMMI gave RICO consent, and RICO discovered a .45 caliber handgun from FLEMMI's time in military service. FLEMMI believes that no charges were brought against him as a result of RICO's search.

6. FLEMMI stated that when RICO first came around the Roxbury neighborhood in about 1958, he spoke with FLEMMI about FLEMMI's possible involvement in a bank robbery with Tommy TIMMONS and Beano ROSS. FLEMMI added that he was not involved in this or any other bank robbery. This first visit by RICO took place at approximately the same time as the consent search where the handgun was seized. FLEMMI also recalled another incident when RICO questioned him about aiding fugitive bank robber Richard CARIGNAN. CARIGNAN had been tracked down by law-enforcement officers to the Dudley Street Roxbury neighborhood. FLEMMI said that he had picked CARIGNAN up and driven him out to Los Angeles. FLEMMI believes that Walter and/or Wimpy BENNETT must have told RICO about his assistance to CARIGNAN. FLEMMI knew that Walter BENNETT, Wimpy's older brother, had supplied information to Boston Police in the past, and had helped them solve a liquor-store robbery

and murder. FLEMMI deduced that the BENNETT brothers must also be regularly speaking with RICO.

7. FLEMMI stated that his relationship with RICO developed slowly, but that these conversations with RICO eventually increased to the point where they were speaking almost daily. FLEMMI recalled that the discussion usually revolved around questions regarding La Cosa Nostra (LCN) in the North End of Boston, known locally as "In Town." RICO would also come by with various football cards to inquire

Dennis Condon of Charlestown, Rico's FBI partner.

which cards belonged to FLEMMI and the Roxbury group. FLEMMI noted that later in the relationship, RICO would swap information with FLEMMI and Wimpy BENNETT on the MCLAUGHLINs, a Charlestown organized-crime faction, during the gang wars of the early 1960's. FLEMMI recalled a couple of incidents that demonstrated the depth of his own relationship with RICO. On one occasion, RICO and his partner Dennis CONDON had been involved in a significant motor vehicle accident in a government car at Suffolk Downs. RICO and CONDON brought the vehicle to FLEMMI, who convinced George KAUFMAN, who operated the Roxbury gang's garage on Dudley Street, to repair the car within the space of a few hours. FLEMMI said that the repair job had to be completed prior to the end of the work day, so that the agents wouldn't get into any difficulties with their supervisors. RICO also claimed to have helped FLEMMI and "Wimpy" BENNETT avoid legal problems after a situation developed with Johnny FIUMARA. FLEMMI remembered getting in a fist fight with FIUMARA at the group's garage over a debt owed by a third party. FIUMARA was badly beaten up, and was also struck with the butt of a handgun by BENNETT. RICO later told FLEMMI that he had straightened out the matter, so that no legal action was taken against them.

8. FLEMMI stated that he did not realize that RICO had been writing up their conversations until his discussions with Department of Justice

attorney Paul Coffey in April 1997. FLEMMI also noted that much of the information on the reports that RICO attributes to him was either fabricated or did not come from him. FLEMMI also stated that RICO never paid him any money, nor did he sign any forms indicating money had been paid. FLEMMI added that his brother Jimmy also talked to RICO, but the relationship was not very good because of negative comments that Jimmy FLEMMI would make regarding J. Edgar Hoover's alleged homosexual relationship with his top deputy, Clyde Tolson. FLEMMI noted that Jimmy "the Bear" usually only talked to RICO about insignificant criminal matters.

9. FLEMMI stated that a dispute in the late 1950's significantly impacted his view of the LCN. FLEMMI said that he had a $3,000 numbers "hit," and went to see LCN enforcer Larry BAIONE (real name: Ilario M.A. ZANNINO) to collect the cash. FLEMMI stated that he had been taking numbers wagers, and passing the bets to the North End through an agent. FLEMMI's numbers agent was arrested while in possession of the winning wager slip, and the LCN refused to honor the bet, claiming that the winning wager was never officially placed. FLEMMI needed to pay off the winner,

Ilario Zannino, a/k/a Larry Baione, Boston Mafia enforcer.

Joseph "J.R." Russo, Mafia soldier from East Boston.

and went to BAIONE for the winnings. BAIONE, Rocco SANTONELLI and a third person met FLEMMI at Richie HAROLD's club. FLEMMI was given a hard time over the issue, and was told that the agent's arrest negated the winning wager. A fistfight erupted, and FLEMMI's friend, Richie HAROLD, joined in the brawl and saved FLEMMI. FLEMMI noted that because of the assistance HAROLD gave in the fight, the LCN began hunting HAROLD. FLEMMI said that in one confrontation HAROLD shot LCN soldier J.R. RUSSO in the leg. FLEMMI believes that he was eventually paid on the numbers hit, but that this incident forever changed his perspective of "In Town." FLEMMI also acknowledged that RICO was aware, from some unknown source, about this numbers hit incident with the LCN.

2

The "Irish" Gang War

10. FLEMMI stated that on the Labor Day weekend of 1961, George MCLAUGHLIN the youngest of Charlestown's MCLAUGHLIN brothers,

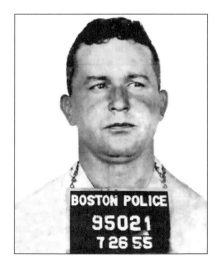

Bernie McLaughlin, Charlestown
gang boss, murdered 1961.

Buddy McLean, founder of the
Winter Hill Gang.

was badly beaten by a member of the MCLEAN Gang from neighboring Somerville when both groups were attending some type of function at Hampton Beach. The fight occurred after MCLAUGHLIN had drunkenly grabbed the breast of the wife of the MCLEAN gang member. FLEMMI added that George MCLAUGHLIN had to be hospitalized as the result of the beating. The other MCLAUGHLIN brothers, Bernie and Edward, also known as "Punchy," then approached Buddy MCLEAN, demanding that he set up the gang member who had beaten their younger brother. MCLEAN told the MCLAUGHLINs that he would deal with the offending gang member, but would not allow him to be killed by the MCLAUGH-LINs. Shortly thereafter MCLEAN observed MCLAUGHLIN gang members place a bomb underneath his vehicle as it was parked outside his house on Winter Hill in Somerville. FLEMMI noted that MCLEAN's car was usually used by MCLEAN's wife and children. At high noon the following day MCLEAN walked up to Bernie MCLAUGHLIN in City Square in Charlestown and fatally shot him (10/31/61) in front of dozens of witnesses. FLEMMI noted that he learned this information at some point later, directly from MCLEAN.

11. FLEMMI stated that the MCLEAN/ MCLAUGHLIN gang war resulted in numerous deaths on each side over the course of the next few years. FLEMMI added that many of the 60 deaths that are attributed to the gang war were "personal beefs" and crimes of opportunity, perpetrated by single individuals, as well as by the LCN, and other ethnic, non-Irish neighborhood groups. FLEMMI said that initially his Roxbury faction was more closely associated with the MCLAUGHLIN gang than the MCLEAN's, because of mutual friendships that existed with Roxbury associate Earl SMITH.

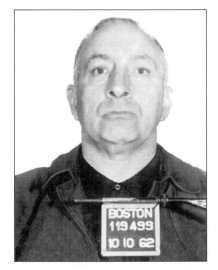

Earl Smith, member of Bennett's Roxbury Group.

Howie Winter, succeeded
Buddy McLean as boss of the Winter
Hill Gang.

Howie Winter removes
belongings from car bombed
by Stevie Flemmi, 1962.

FLEMMI further stated that on one occasion he and Wimpy BENNETT drove George MCLAUGHLIN to Somerville, where a bomb was placed under Howie WINTER's vehicle. The bomb exploded after the vehicle was driven by WINTER's paramour ███████. The explosion blew off the hood of the car, but caused no injuries to either ███████ or any bystanders. Later when the Roxbury group joined sides with the MCLEANs, FLEMMI admitted his involvement in the bombing to WINTER.

12. FLEMMI stated that he never really liked George MCLAUGH-LIN because MCLAUGHLIN was so dangerous. FLEMMI added that George MCLAUGHLIN was particularly vicious when he was drinking, which was often. FLEMMI said that one day his younger brother, Michael FLEMMI, told him that he was going to a local Roxbury party. FLEMMI knew that George MCLAUGHLIN also planned to go to the same party, and because of this, FLEMMI persuaded his brother Mike not to attend. During this Roxbury party, a fistfight occurred, and at that

Charlestown mobster George
McLaughlin under arrest.

William Sheridan, murdered by
George McLaughlin, 1964.

time or shortly thereafter, George
MCLAUGHLIN pulled out a gun, and
shot an innocent partygoer, 21-year-
old bank teller William SHERIDAN,
between the eyes. MCLAUGHLIN
committed this murder in front of
numerous witnesses, and became a
fugitive for almost a year. FLEMMI
noted that while a fugitive, George
MCLAUGHLIN and his brother Edward "Punchy" MCLAUGHLIN tried
to locate and kill some of the witnesses against George MCLAUGH-
LIN in this pending case. George
MCLAUGHLIN's fugitive status failed
to slow the gang war's carnage.

Punchy McLaughlin, murdered by
Stevie Flemmi, 1965.

Frank BENJAMIN murder (05/04/64)

13. FLEMMI stated that the first gang-war murder he was involved in was the killing of Frank BENJAMIN. FLEMMI recalled that "Wimpy" BENNETT was regularly lending money to ███████, who owned a local area restaurant. ███████ had some type of problem with BENJAMIN, and had been threatened by the ex-con. "Wimpy" BENNETT began instigating the other members of the Roxbury Group against BENJAMIN, including Jimmy "the Bear" FLEMMI, who had served prison time with BENJAMIN. FLEMMI understood that BENNETT's motive was to help ███████ with this problem with BENJAMIN, in order to become further involved in ███████ businesses. FLEMMI believed that one of the grudges "Wimpy" BENNETT held against BENJAMIN was that BENJAMIN had been siding with the MCLEANs. FLEMMI said that one night around closing time, while FLEMMI was cleaning up his tavern, the Dudley Lounge, BENJAMIN came inside and sat down at a booth with "Wimpy" BENNETT and Jimmy "the Bear" FLEMMI. FLEMMI stated at some point he

Frankie Benjamin, murdered by
Jimmy Flemmi, 1964.

Frankie Benjamin at MCI Norfolk.

heard a single gunshot, and observed BENJAMIN lying dead in the booth. FLEMMI was unsure if BENNETT or his brother Jimmy was the actual shooter of BENJAMIN.

14. FLEMMI stated that as a result of the shooting there was blood smeared all over that part of the bar, which was spread even further when the body was dragged from the booth, through the kitchen, and then to a storage room. Frank SALEMME, who was just becoming involved with the Roxbury group, was contacted. After SALEMME arrived, the group decided that the tavern had to be closed for a while so that the evidence of the crime could be destroyed. SALEMME, a master electrician by trade, determined that the business could be closed down because of an electrical problem. The following day "Wimpy" BENNETT contacted Edward "Punchy" MCLAUGHLIN, who picked up the body, and later, with the help of Earl SMITH, cut off BENJAMIN's head. FLEMMI added that SALEMME assisted in the removal of BENJAMIN's body. FLEMMI learned from MCLAUGHLIN, SMITH and "Wimpy" BENNETT that BENJAMIN's head was cut off as a sign to the

Jimmy Flemmi, Benjamin's murderer, at MCI Norfolk.

An early mugshot of Frank Salemme.

MCLEANs, and was intended to show how vicious Punchy's crew could be. SMITH later told FLEMMI that BENJAMIN's head was buried in a cemetery in West Roxbury.

A MORE LIKELY reason for the decapitation was later recounted by East Boston hitman Joe BARBOZA in his generally unreliable 1976 auto-biography, *Barboza*. BARBOZA said the gun used to kill BENJAMIN had been given to the Roxbury group by a Boston police officer. Not knowing whether the gun had been used in earlier crimes, the gang decided they could not risk allowing the bullet fired into Benjamin's head to undergo ballistics testing, so they disposed of the head, and thus the bullet. BENJAMIN left behind six children in South Boston.

15. FLEMMI stated that no matter what he did, he couldn't clean up all of the blood from the BENJAMIN murder. Eventually FLEMMI decided that he had to burn down the barroom in order to get rid of the evidence of BENJAMIN's murder. FLEMMI acquired a rubber-based accelerant through a friend of Bobby LABELLA, a North End associate of Wimpy BENNETT's, and began to spread the chemical around the interior of the bar. FLEMMI slipped during this process, and his clothes were covered

Frankie Benjamin's headless body in car trunk.

with the sticky, highly-flammable chemical. FLEMMI was then forced to leave the bar, shower and change his clothes, before resuming the task of torching the building. FLEMMI noted that this same accelerant was used to start another fire for Larry BAIONE, when BAIONE wanted his Franklin, MA residence burned for insurance purposes in the late 1960's. FLEMMI was asked by Frank SALEMME to do this particular arson for BAIONE.

Russell NICHOLSON murder (05/11/64)

16. FLEMMI stated he only knew limited details about the murder of the former MDC patrolman Russell NICHOLSON, who had recently been fired from his police job because of his association with the MCLEAN faction. NICHOLSON was widely believed to have been the driver for Buddy MCLEAN in the 1961 Bernie MCLAUGHLIN murder in Charlestown. FLEMMI added that ███████ ████████ killed NICHOLSON over some type of dispute involving "a score." ███████ shot NICHOLSON in a car, and the murder angered both MCLEAN and WINTER. They both told FLEMMI about the killing after the Roxbury group later joined forces

Russ Nicholson, former cop, murdered 1964.

with the MCLEANs. James "Whitey" BULGER, FLEMMI's future partner, was also aware of the details of the murder story, although he was still imprisoned for bank robbery at Leavenworth at the time. BULGER discussed the slaying with FLEMMI at a much later date. BULGER was prompted to tell FLEMMI the NICHOLSON murder story, because ███████ had failed to repay him a $5,000 loan.

Early photo of Whitey Bulger, second from left, circa 1940.

Harold Hannon and Wilfred Delaney murders (8/19/64)

17. FLEMMI stated H. Paul RICO and his FBI partner Dennis CON-
DON had a deep hatred for the MCLAUGHLIN gang, whose principals
shared Jimmy FLEMMI's distaste for
J. Edgar HOOVER's alleged sexual
predilections. Some of the Charlestown gangsters' disparaging remarks
had been picked up on a "gypsy" (i.e.,
illegal) wiretap on a telephone used by
"Punchy" MCLAUGHLIN. FLEMMI
added that some of this animosity was
also the result of Edward "Punchy"
MCLAUGHLIN having some type of
problem with CONDON's brother.
"Punchy" MCLAUGHLIN eventually
issued a death threat to CONDON's
brother. FLEMMI learned from
MCLEAN, and later saw for himself,
how RICO and to a lesser extent CON-
DON, assisted the Somerville group in
its efforts against the MCLAUGHLINs

Harold Hannon, murdered 1964.

during the gang war. One such situation where RICO gave aid to the MCLEANs resulted in the murders of Harold HANNON and Wilfred DELANEY. FLEMMI was told that the MCLEANs had been trying to locate key members of the MCLAUGHLIN gang so that they could be eliminated. RICO gave the Dorchester address of Harold HANNON and Wilfred DELANEY to MCLEAN. FLEMMI believed that MCLEAN had mentioned that the apartment may have been on Bowdoin Street. FLEMMI noted that this information was of a particular interest to the MCLEAN group because the Dorchester neighborhood was unknown territory for the gang, which would have made surveillance on these two MCLAUGHLIN associates very difficult.

Wilfred Delaney, murdered 1964.

18. FLEMMI stated that MCLEAN, ▓▓▓▓, Jimmy SIMS, Joe MC-DONALD and Tommy BALLOU, broke into the apartment and waited for HANNON and DELANEY to return home one day. The two arrived home, and were immediately secured. HANNON and DELANEY were then questioned about who else was helping the MCLAUGHLINs. HANNON and DELANEY were then given amphetamines to "relax" them before they were strangled. Their bodies were then

James Sims, orphan, future Winter Hill Gang wheelman.

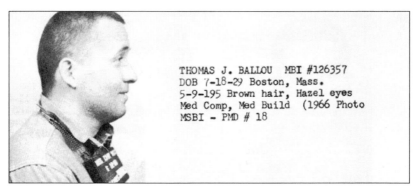

THOMAS J. BALLOU   MBI #126357
DOB 7-18-29 Boston, Mass.
5-9-195 Brown hair, Hazel eyes
Med Comp, Med Build (1966 Photo
MSBI - PMD # 18

Tommy Ballou, Winter Hill gangster, murdered 1970.

tossed into the harbor. Despite rumors that Winter Hill used an acetylene torch on the victims' private parts, FLEMMI stated that he didn't hear anything about the pair being tortured. FLEMMI added that the administration of the narcotics was a humane method intended to reduce the doomed pair's suffering. FLEMMI added that BALLOU was arrested a short time after the murders, and chose to remain in jail even when he became eligible for parole. BALLOU's reluctance to assist further in the gang war caused a lot of anger among the MCLEAN gang, and may be the reason that BALLOU eventually met his demise in Charlestown sometime after he came out of prison (02/11/70).

Leo Lowry murder (09/03/64)

19. FLEMMI stated that Leo "Iggy" LOWRY was also from Roxbury, but was not close to the BENNETTs or FLEMMI. FLEMMI added that on one occasion LOWRY had words with FLEMMI's wife Jeanette after making a pass at her. A third party notified FLEMMI of the encounter, and FLEMMI confronted LOWRY over the situation. According to FLEMMI, LOWRY never forgot the argument, and one day as he drove past FLEMMI at the corner of Eustis and Dearborn Streets, he fired several shots at FLEMMI. Lowry missed, but FLEMMI stated that he clearly saw that the shooter was LOWRY. LOWRY afterwards kept a low profile, until one day LOWRY ran into Jimmy the Bear FLEMMI while leaving a barroom. The Bear was well aware of the attempted shooting, and consequently assaulted LOWRY,

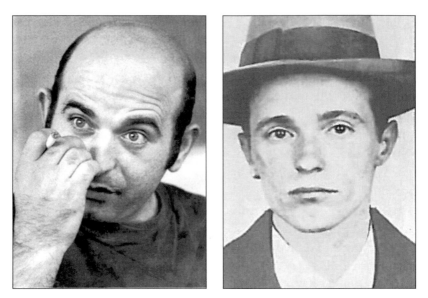

Jimmy the Bear Flemmi in custody.

Iggy Lowry, murdered by
Jimmy the Bear in 1964.

dragging LOWRY into his car. Jimmy FLEMMI then shot and killed
LOWRY inside the vehicle. Jimmy FLEMMI then drove around Roxbury
looking for his older brother Stephen, with LOWRY's body still inside the
car next to him. FLEMMI stated that the Bear pulled over in his car and
proudly showed him LOWRY's body. FLEMMI then followed his brother
Jimmy in his own car, and assisted in the dumping the body in Pembroke.
LOWRY's body was found by authorities a few days later. FLEMMI noted
that the Bear had also cut LOWRY's throat at some point. FLEMMI noted
that his brother's vehicle ran out of gas on the way home from dumping
LOWRY's body, and that the Bear may have dropped a pack of cigarettes in
the area where the corpse had been left. FLEMMI added that these mental
lapses of his brother concerned him, but did not appear to bother the Bear.

Ronald Dermody murder (09/04/64)

20. FLEMMI stated that after "Punchy" MCLAUGHLIN's murder, and
just prior to Buddy MCLEAN's own death in the fall of 1965, he met with
MCLEAN at Pal Joey's Lounge in Somerville. During this conversation,

MCLEAN told FLEMMI that Ronald DERMODY had some type of problem with the Somerville/Winter Hill mob at the time of his murder. DERMODY, whose father and brother were both murdered in prison, had been a member of the same bank-robbing crew as Whitey BULGER in the mid-1950's, and had finished his federal sentence a few months before Bulger's release in March 1965. MCLEAN also admitted to FLEMMI that he had a relationship with H. Paul RICO and Dennis CONDON. MCLEAN was also aware that DERMODY and RICO had developed a relationship after RICO arrested him on the bank robbery charges. MCLEAN said that on the day of the murder RICO had contact with DERMODY. (According to other accounts, DERMODY had been talked into trying to shoot MCLEAN by the MCLAUGHLINs. They had promised DERMODY that in return for shooting MCLEAN, the MCLAUGHLINs would make sure that one of DERMODY's rivals for the affection of local gun moll Dorothy BARCHARD, James "Spike" O'TOOLE, would be killed in the prison where O'TOOLE was then serving a sentence. DERMODY then went to Winter Hill where he shot and wounded the first blond-haired

Ronald Dermody, former member of Whitey Bulger bankrobbing gang, murdered by Buddy McLean in 1965.

H. Paul Rico at 1997 Congressional hearing: "Whaddaya want from me, tears?"

man he saw, who was not MCLEAN. Immediately realizing his peril, DERMODY reached out to his old FBI contact RICO, whom he assumed was an honest law-enforcement official. After receiving the call, RICO then phoned McLean and told him that DERMODY was waiting for him, RICO, in his car on the Watertown line near RICO's home in Belmont.) MCLEAN said he shot DERMODY to death in his car as the hard-luck ex-con waited for RICO to arrive. FLEMMI believed that after DERMO-DY's murder, MCLEAN went to RICO's home, and hid out there. FLEMMI recalled that some time after the murder, ████████ married Winter Hill associate ███████ .

Margaret SILVESTER (SILVESTRI) homicide and related murders (11/10/64)

21. FLEMMI stated that Margaret SILVESTER was dating ████████ at the time of her murder. FLEMMI added that the slaying took place in the after-hours section of the Martorano family's second-floor Combat Zone restaurant, Luigi's. FLEMMI added that Luigi's separate after-hours club had a reputation for trouble, and was frequented by many underworld figures. FLEMMI further noted that SILVESTER was the wife or daughter

The Martoranos: son John, father Andy, son Jimmy.

Robert Palladino, Johnny Martorano's
first victim, 1965.

Palladino's body, abandoned near
North Station.

of Buddy SILVESTRI, an associate of Boston LCN boss Gennaro "Jerry" ANGIULO. FLEMMI recalled that either "Wimpy" BENNETT or John MARTORANO advised him of the details regarding SILVESTER's murder. FLEMMI added that his brother "the Bear" never admitted to murdering her. FLEMMI stated that he was told that ███████ had badly beaten Margaret SILVESTER sometime during that night. The beating occurred because of the romantic relationship she had with ███████ . ███████ had been under the belief that SILVESTER was dead from the beating, but that later someone killed her when it was noticed that she was in fact still alive. FLEMMI does not know who actually murdered SILVESTER. FLEMMI noted that at some point during the evening, his brother Jimmy "the Bear" FLEMMI visited the club.

22. FLEMMI stated that it was possible that he told John MARTORANO that he and the Bear were suspects in the SILVESTER murder. FLEMMI added that he would have learned this information from his various Boston Police sources. (John MARTORANO was not in Luigi's the night of the

murder.) FLEMMI further added that at the time it was common practice that these law-enforcement sources would come by one or another of his businesses and discuss recent area murders with him. FLEMMI also stated that Robert PALLADINO had been a witness to the Margaret SILVESTER murder. FLEMMI was told by John MARTORANO that PALLADINO was murdered (11/15/65) while he (MARTORANO) and the victim were in a car on Blue Hill Avenue driven by ■■■■■■■. John MARTORANO, who was sitting in the rear seat, shot PAL-LADINO in the back of the head. (The body was then dumped near North Station.) According to FLEMMI,

John Jackson, bartender, murdered by Johnny Martorano and Tash Bratsos, 1966.

another witness to the SILVESTER murder, bartender John JACKSON was also killed by John MARTORANO (09/28/66). According to MAR-TORANO, he and Tash BRATSOS shot JACKSON through a fence in the Fenway where the victim lived. FLEMMI added that John MARTORANO was friendly with many of the hoodlums from the Roxbury group, but was not a member of the gang because he was not liked by "Wimpy" BENNETT or Frank SALEMME. FLEMMI noted that John MARTORANO was particularly close with his brother Jimmy the Bear FLEMMI.

William Treannie's murder (11/13/64)

23. FLEMMI stated that Johnny MURRAY was a South End hoodlum. MURRAY had a problem with William TREANNIE over monies from some kind of joint criminal activity. MURRAY killed TREANNIE, then chopped up his body into small pieces inside the bathtub of a local apartment. MURRAY then approached "Wimpy" BENNETT about assisting him in the disposal of TREANNIE's dismembered body. BENNETT

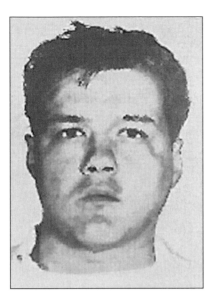

William Treannie, murdered and dismembered, 1964.

John Murray, murderer of Treannie, murdered two months later, 1965.

mentioned the situation to FLEMMI, who in turn hired Sonny SHIELDS and ▮▮▮▮▮▮ to handle the task. SHIELDS and ▮▮▮▮▮▮ were paid $1,000 by MURRAY to pack up the pieces of TREANNIE's body, and dump them somewhere. SHIELDS and ▮▮▮▮▮▮ disposed of the body pieces in a nearby vacant lot in the South End where the corpse was eventually found. FLEMMI noted that MURRAY was later killed by Jimmy "Spike" O'TOOLE (01/10/65), after being set up by "Wimpy" BENNETT. BENNETT told FLEMMI that he instigated the MURRAY murder because he didn't like MURRAY for some reason. FLEMMI also added that he had never personally met or had dealings with TREANNIE.

Edward "Punchy" MCLAUGHLIN's 1st shooting (11/23/64)

24. FLEMMI stated that Edward "Punchy" MCLAUGHLIN was first shot by Joe MCDONALD and Jimmy SIMS as part of the on-going feud with the Winter Hill Gang of Somerville, headed by Buddy MCLEAN. FLEMMI learned this information from MCLEAN in a conversation after

the FLEMMI's Roxbury group and MCLEAN's gang formed an alliance against the MCLAUGHLINs. FLEMMI learned that "Punchy" MCLAUGHLIN had been set up by a friend, fellow hoodlum Earl SMITH. FLEMMI was told that MCDONALD and SIMS fired a sawed-off shotgun at MCLAUGHLIN, the pellets striking the victim in the face.

George ASHE murder (12/28/64)

25. FLEMMI stated that George ASHE was a burglar from the South End and later Roxbury. ASHE also knew FLEMMI's brother Jimmy the Bear from time served together in MCI Walpole. FLEMMI stated that at some point ASHE had words with his brother, which resulted in "the Bear" shooting him inside of a car on Harrison Avenue in Roxbury. After shooting ASHE, Jimmy FLEMMI then walked away from the vehicle in full view of two Roxbury area patrolmen, ▇▇▇▇ and ▇▇▇▇▇▇ . After discovering ASHE's body, instead of taking some type of law-enforcement action, Officers ▇▇▇▇ and ▇▇▇▇ reported the incident directly to FLEMMI. FLEMMI promptly paid ▇▇▇▇ and ▇▇▇ $1,000. FLEMMI then chastised his brother, Jimmy the Bear and reminded him how lucky he was that he ran into two police officers who were friends. No arrests were ever made on this homicide. (In his 2003 testimony to Congressional investigators, Frank

Joe McDonald, Winter Hill, once on the FBI Ten Most Wanted List.

George Ashe, small-time burglar, murdered by Jimmy Flemmi in 1964.

Police examine car where Ashe's body was left.

SALEMME said that before ASHE's body was discovered, the two Boston police from District 4, Roxbury, pushed Ashe's car across an intersection into District 2, the Back Bay, so they would not have to deal with the homicide.)

Henry REDDINGTON murder (01/23/65)

26. FLEMMI stated that he was friendly with South Shore organized-crime figure Henry REDDINGTON, who had a real estate office on Dudley Street in Roxbury. FLEMMI added that just prior to the murder, REDDINGTON had gotten "Wimpy" BENNETT a $25,000 loan through shylocks ███████ and Nate COLSIA. REDDINGTON was ultimately responsible for this loan. BENNETT told Jimmy "Spike" O'TOOLE, who had just been released from prison, that REDDINGTON had taken up with O'TOOLE's longtime girlfriend Dorothy Barchard, by whom O'TOOLE had fathered two children. Enraged by the false information, O'TOOLE and the fugitive George MCLAUGHLIN then drove to Weymouth and shot REDDINGTON at his real estate office there. FLEMMI stated that he learned this information directly from BENNETT. BENNETT told FLEMMI that he made up the story about REDDINGTON and BARCHARD so that O'TOOLE would then murder REDDINGTON, thus freeing BENNETT from his obligation to repay the $25,000.

Loan shark Henry Reddington made the mistake of loaning $25,000 to Wimpy Bennett.

Dottie Barchard, gangster moll, had two children by O'Toole.

Spike O'Toole was told by Wimpy Bennett that Reddington had taken up with his girlfriend.

Before O'Toole, she'd been married to one of Whitey Bulger's bank-robbing gang, and later she took up with a lawyer whose car was blown up by the Mafia.

Nate Colsia, another loan shark who made the fatal mistake of loaning money to Bennett.

George McLaughlin was added to the FBI's Ten Most Wanted List after he murdered Sheridan.

FLEMMI ADDED that BENNETT later paid "Punchy" MCLAUGHLIN and Earl SMITH to kill COLSIA after Wimpy began getting loans directly from him. COLSIA was staying at a Sheraton Hotel in Quincy at the time of his murder. FLEMMI said that MCLAUGHLIN hid in COLSIA's van at the hotel and shot the victim in the head when he entered the vehicle.

George MCLAUGHLIN's arrest (02/24/1965)

27. FLEMMI stated that just prior to George MCLAUGHLIN's arrest on the SHERIDAN murder charge, H. Paul RICO and Dennis CONDON spoke to him at Dearborn and Dudley streets in Roxbury. During this conversation RICO asked FLEMMI for a throw-down handgun. RICO explained that the agents were about to arrest George MCLAUGHLIN, who had been an FBI Ten Most Wanted fugitive since the SHERIDAN murder in March 1964. RICO added that the arresting agents were planning on shooting MCLAUGHLIN as they took him into custody. The agents were going to plant the gun on a dresser next to MCLAUGHLIN and claim that

MCLAUGHLIN had reached for the weapon. The agents were planning on shooting MCLAUGHLIN and claiming self-defense. FLEMMI told RICO and CONDON to return a short while later, at which time he supplied them with a .38 caliber handgun. After MCLAUGHLIN's uneventful arrest, RICO explained to FLEMMI that there were five agents involved in the arrest, but that while four were in agreement to kill MCLAUGHLIN, the group was uncertain about a fifth agent on the arrest team, and the plan was dropped. FLEMMI added that RICO never returned the firearm to him.

Teddy DEEGAN murder (03/12/65)

28. FLEMMI stated that he was friendly with Teddy DEEGAN and had actually been involved in robberies from bookmakers' homes with him. FLEMMI was also aware, from some unknown source, that DEEGAN had killed Anthony SACRAMONE (10/17/64) for some long-forgotten reason that FLEMMI could not recall. DEEGAN's victim was the brother of Winter Hill associate and FLEMMI friend, Rico SACRAMONE. In the day following DEEGAN's murder, FLEMMI angrily confronted first his

Teddy Deegan, a few weeks before
his murder, 1965.

Anthony Sacramone, murdered by
Deegan in 1964.

Gennaro "Jerry" Angiulo, Boston Mafia underboss.

brother Jimmy, and later Joe BARBOZA over the slaying after each had admitted involvement.

JIMMY FLEMMI told his brother that DEEGAN had robbed a bookmaker connected with Jerry ANGIULO. Stephen FLEMMI explained to his brother that he and DEEGAN had also robbed another ANGIULO-connected bookmaker, as had George MCLAUGHLIN, and asked why they weren't next in line to be murdered. Jimmy FLEMMI explained that ANGIULO had pressed for retaliation against DEEGAN, and that New England LCN boss Raymond PATRIARCA had sanctioned the murder. Jimmy FLEMMI advised that ▮▮▮▮▮▮ and Henry TAMELEO

Henry Tameleo, framed by the FBI for the Deegan murder, died in prison.

had been present when PATRIARCA had given permission for the slaying. Jimmy FLEMMI further related that he and BARBOZA then recruited

Ronald CASSESSO, Romeo MARTIN and Roy FRENCH to assist in the murder plot, which involved luring DEEGAN to an alley outside a Chelsea credit union, which the conspirators told DEEGAN they were planning to rob.

FRENCH, DEEGAN'S friend, was then used to set up the victim for the execution. FLEMMI noted that in this conversation, which took place just a short time after the murder, neither Louis GRECO's nor Joe SALVATI's names were mentioned as being involved in the murder plot. A day or so later, in the North End, FLEMMI spoke with TAMELEO and ██████ and both admitted involvement in the murder plot. The pair also told FLEMMI that DEEGAN had to be killed.

Ronald Cassesso, one of the real killers of Deegan.

Deegan dead in the alley, the screwdriver he was planning to use in the burglary to his left.

29. FLEMMI stated that Romeo MARTIN, who played a role in DEEGAN's death, was himself later murdered by CASSESSO and BARBOZA (07/09/65). FLEMMI was told by both CASSESSO and BARBOZA that MARTIN was killed because they feared that he was weak, and might possibly cooperate with law-enforcement. FLEMMI stated that sometime after the DEEGAN murder, after BARBOZA was cooperating with the FBI against the Mafia, H. Paul RICO asked FLEMMI for some assistance in keeping the remaining members of the East Boston gang quiet about the identities of the real killers of DEEGAN. FLEMMI noted that this occurred after Attorney Joe Balliro had gone

Romeo Martin—Barboza feared he wouldn't stand up, so he killed him, 1965.

to MCI Walpole, and asked Jimmy FLEMMI to contradict BARBOZA's statements regarding the DEEGAN murder.

RICO THEN asked FLEMMI to go to MCI Walpole to convince the Bear not to discredit BARBOZA's testimony on the DEEGAN murder. RICO

Lou Greco was in Florida when Deegan was murdered, but he was still convicted and died in prison.

Joe Salvati refused to repay a debt he owed Barboza, so Barboza falsely put him in the death car. He served more than 30 years.

told FLEMMI that he had kept Jimmy the Bear from being prosecuted for his role in the murder. FLEMMI met with his brother, and advised him to mind his own business, and to tell Nick FEMIA and Patsy FABIANO to do

Raymond L.S. Patriarca, "the Man," the godfather of the
Patriarca Crime Family of Providence.

the same. FLEMMI warned "the Bear" that BARBOZA could implicate him and the others in several unsolved murders so that it was best to remain neutral—and silent.

30. AFTER being approached by the FBI, FLEMMI was then sought out by the LCN. FLEMMI stated that the LCN also sent him to MCI Walpole to speak with Jimmy FLEMMI about not assisting the DEEGAN prosecution team by corroborating BARBOZA's testimony. FLEMMI advised RICO of the LCN's overture to him. FLEMMI was of the belief that BARBOZA added GRECO to the names of the people involved in the murder plot because of a personal "beef" the pair had. FLEMMI understood that GRECO, a World War II hero, wouldn't back down from BARBOZA during some street confrontation the two had had. FLEMMI noted that he was aware that GRECO was out of town at the time of DEEGAN's murder. FLEMMI added that SALVATI must also have been falsely added to the murder plot by BARBOZA at some later point. FLEMMI was aware that SALVATI likewise had a personal problem with BARBOZA. This problem concerned SALVATI's failure to pay back a $4,000 loan made by the East Boston group. FLEMMI noted that neither Tommy DIPRISCO nor Tash BRATSOS could collect even a small portion of the loan from SALVATI while BARBOZA was in jail.

31. FLEMMI stated that shortly after the innocent men were convicted of murdering DEEGAN (07/31/68), he recalled RICO, CONDON and Boston Police Detective Ed WALSH walking into the group's Roxbury garage. FLEMMI recalled that SALEMME angrily confronted these law-enforcement officials over the conviction. SALEMME particularly complained that Louie GRECO had nothing to do with the DEEGAN murder whatsoever. FLEMMI noted that

FBI agent Dennis Condon later went to work for Gov. Michael S. Dukakis.

SALEMME's comment about GRECO was directed primarily at CONDON. FLEMMI stated that during the dispute, CONDON did not indicate that he knew that GRECO was innocent of the charges. CONDON did attempt to justify the conviction by mentioning that GRECO had been involved in a lot of other crimes. FLEMMI added that CONDON maintained that GRECO was not framed. FLEMMI also denied that he told SALEMME during a 1998 jailhouse conversation that the FBI convinced BARBOZA to make up the story to frame the defendants. It is FLEMMI's belief that "Wimpy" BENNETT had been the first to give information to RICO on the DEEGAN murder. FLEMMI noted that this initial information from Wimpy BENNETT had been inaccurate.

Roxbury's realignment with the McLean Gang

32. FLEMMI stated that while initially the Roxbury gang of "Wimpy" and Walter BENNETT, the FLEMMI brothers, SALEMME, ████████, Red CONLIN and George KAUFMAN, were aligned with the MCLAUGHLIN gang, at some point in early 1965, the group changed its allegiance. FLEMMI added that during this time period, Boston Police Detective Bill STUART, who was a close friend to the BENNETTs and Frank SALEMME, asked the Roxbury gang to come to a meeting with Buddy MCLEAN. FLEMMI further stated that STUART told him that H. Paul RICO had asked STUART to arrange this meeting. FLEMMI was aware that STUART and RICO were friendly, and often worked together. STUART would also pass on information to RICO which he had picked up from the BENNETTs and SALEMME. FLEMMI also knew that STUART was on Wimpy's payroll, and received $100 a week. At a later discussion, STUART told FLEMMI that Dennis Condon's brother, who was a heavy drinker, had a problem with Edward "Punchy" MCLAUGHLIN, and had been threatened with bodily harm. The brother had gone to CONDON, and advised CONDON of the threat. STUART asked that the Roxbury group split with the MCLAUGHLINs, and join up with MCLEAN's Somerville gang. FLEMMI noted that he personally did not like the MCLAUGHLIN brothers. FLEMMI recalled that George MCLAUGHLIN had once asked him to set Mickey REDDY up to be murdered. FLEMMI noted that this request had been refused.

Red Conlin, one of Stevie's early criminal associates.

Detective Bill Stuart, an important BPD source for Stevie.

33. FLEMMI stated that the Roxbury group agreed to speak with MCLEAN, and a meeting was set up at the Holiday Inn in Somerville. FLEMMI was of the belief that the switch of allegiance took place around the time of George MCLAUGHLIN's arrest. FLEMMI and Wimpy BENNETT attended from the Roxbury group. MCLEAN went to the meeting as the lone representative of his Somerville faction. STUART was present at the conference, but remained at the bar during the actual discussion. FLEMMI said that there was a second, more public meeting, which was also held on Winter Hill turf. The second meeting also had Joe

George Kaufman was with the gang from the start, until his death from cancer in 1996.

Cassesso on his way to court in a state car.

BARBOZA attending representing his East Boston gang, and BARBOZA friend and LCN associate Ronnie CASSESSO sitting in for the Mafia. At this second meeting, CASSESSO stated that the LCN would remain neutral in the fight. FLEMMI said that eventually after these and other meetings, both BARBOZA's East Boston gang and the Roxbury group agreed to unite against the MCLAUGHLINs.

Jimmy "The Bear" FLEMMI shooting (05/03/65)

34. FLEMMI stated that at some time after the Somerville meeting, Wimpy BENNETT had shots fired at him while he was in the vicinity of his personal residence in Mattapan. These shots were fired by Jimmy O'TOOLE (04/04/65). O'TOOLE and George MCLAUGHLIN had been the members of the Charlestown-based group who had most closely al-lied with the Roxbury gang. O'TOOLE and George MCLAUGHLIN had occasionally drunk in FLEMMI's Dudley Street tavern. Approximately

Wimpy Bennett usually wore a hat to cover his baldness.

Stevie Hughes, McLaughlin gunman and friend of Larry Baione.

one month later (05/03/65), Jimmy the Bear FLEMMI was shot 11 times while exiting the front doorway of his Dorchester home. FLEMMI added that he had warned the Bear about his pattern of regularly going home for supper each night. FLEMMI said that he actually predicted the way the shooting eventually took place. FLEMMI said that a doctor who lived nearby treated Jimmy FLEMMI at the scene, probably saving the Bear's life. FLEMMI said that he was transported to the hospital by the Boston Police after being notified of his brother's shooting. FLEMMI spoke with his brother and was told that Punchy MCLAUGHLIN, Stevie HUGHES and Jimmy O'TOOLE had been the shooters. FLEMMI later learned that ██████ had driven the get-away car during the failed murder attempt. Jimmy FLEMMI had also been able to return fire during the shooting. Jimmy FLEMMI was hit with buckshot and .38 caliber rounds, and several of the bullets struck on either side of his spine.

35. FLEMMI stated that Jimmy FLEMMI remained hospitalized for some time, and eventually John MARTORANO transported him to Vermont to recover from his wounds. FLEMMI noted that just prior to the Bear being shot, Jimmy FLEMMI had received a telephone call at his brother's market on Dudley Street. FLEMMI believes the caller was Jimmy O'TOOLE. FLEMMI also remembered that after his brother's shooting, several rounds were fired into his Dudley Street market. The shots were fired after the store was closed for the night. FLEMMI said that Wimpy BENNETT and Frank SALEMME later admitted that they had shot at the market in an attempt to arouse FLEMMI's anger so as to get him out of hiding, and back out on the street to fight the MCLAUGHLINs.

Edward "Punchy" MCLAUGHLIN's 2nd shooting (08/16/65)

36. FLEMMI stated that SALEMME and Wimpy BENNETT went out and conducted surveillance on Edward "Punchy" MCLAUGHLIN in an attempt to line him up for elimination. It was learned that MCLAUGH-LIN was living in Canton with his girlfriend ████████ , and was driving the same travel route into Boston most days. FLEMMI speculated that this information came from RICO to Wimpy BENNETT. The group chose a particular area near a traffic rotary in Dedham as the location where MCLAUGHLIN would be assassinated. FLEMMI recalled that the plan was to have Wimpy BENNETT pull out in front of MCLAUGHLIN's vehicle in order to pinpoint which automobile the group was to fire on. FLEMMI said that ████████ was armed with a high-powered rifle, and opened fire on MCLAUGHLIN's vehicle seconds after BENNETT's vehicle passed by. Some of the rounds fired by ████████ struck MCLAUGHLIN's steering wheel, and then hit the intended victim's hand. FLEMMI, who had a carbine, fired approximately seven rounds, but stopped after the weapon jammed. FLEMMI believes that SALEMME also shot at MCLAUGHLIN. FLEMMI recalled that MCLAUGHLIN drove on the wrong side of the roadway in order to get away from the assault.

37. FLEMMI stated that MCLAUGHLIN escaped, but had to have his right hand amputated as a result of the injuries from the attack. FLEMMI added

that the group had waited in the same location on several other earlier dates and had buried the weapons in the area so that they didn't have to drive around with them in their cars. FLEMMI also recalled mentioning the shooting to RICO. FLEMMI remembered that the group had also attempted to kill MCLAUGHLIN at Beth Israel Hospital in Brookline. FLEMMI stated that he dressed up like a rabbi and waited for MCLAUGHLIN in the hospital's lobby. FLEMMI said that Wimpy BENNETT remained outside in a get-away car. FLEMMI said that MCLAUGHLIN was scheduled to visit the hospital, but that Punchy never did arrive while he was present. FLEMMI added that after two hours had passed, a nurse came up to him in the waiting room and asked the "rabbi" if everything was all right. FLEMMI and BENNETT then left the hospital, and decided to drop this particular plan. FLEMMI does not recall SALEMME being involved in this attempt on MCLAUGHLIN's life.

Edward "Punchy" MCLAUGHLIN murder (10/20/65)

38. FLEMMI stated that one day he was standing on the sidewalk on Dudley Street, when H. Paul RICO walked up to him. FLEMMI added that Wimpy BENNETT and SALEMME may have been present for some or all of this meeting. FLEMMI noted that SALEMME was well aware that RICO gave information to FLEMMI and BENNETT regarding the MCLAUGHLIN gang. RICO told FLEMMI that Punchy MCLAUGHLIN could no longer drive since his hand had been amputated. So he had begun taking the bus every morning from the Spring Street, West Roxbury T station, traveling into the city to watch his brother George's murder trial in Pemberton Square. RICO said that prior to this, MCLAUGHLIN's girlfriend, ▇▇▇▇▇▇ , had driven "Punchy" directly to the courthouse. RICO then said that he wouldn't be working the following day, and was going golfing. FLEMMI recalled that RICO then took a make-believe golf swing. FLEMMI stated that he particularly wanted to kill Edward "Punchy" MCLAUGHLIN because of MCLAUGHLIN's involvement in the shooting of his brother the Bear. FLEMMI said that he and the others decided to take advantage of this information from RICO.

39. FLEMMI stated that the day of the murder, his girlfriend ▇▇▇▇▇▇ helped him dress in a disguise at his Dudley Street bookstore. FLEMMI recalled wearing a three-quarter length coat, gloves, clear glasses, and possibly a mustache. FLEMMI said that Ms. ▇▇▇▇▇▇ may have applied some type of makeup on his face, and also took some measures to change the look of his hair. FLEMMI does not remember Ms. ▇▇▇▇▇ accompanying him to any meeting with SALEMME on the day of the murder. FLEMMI also did not recall SALEMME wearing any type of disguise on that day. FLEMMI said that Wimpy BENNETT, ▇▇▇▇▇▇ , and ▇▇▇▇▇▇ were all in the area of the bus station, acting as surveillance and backup. SALEMME dropped FLEMMI off on a side street, and he then walked to the Spring Street bus station. FLEMMI stepped out from the side of a building, after MCLAUGHLIN had exited his girlfriend's vehicle, and begun walking to the bus. FLEMMI stated that he had a .38 caliber, long-barrel Webley handgun in his coat pocket. The gun was covered over by a folded newspaper. FLEMMI started walking toward MCLAUGHLIN and opened fire from 15 to 18 feet away, just as the victim was stepping onto the bus. FLEMMI said that he shot MCLAUGHLIN six times, centering the rounds in the victim's chest. FLEMMI added that MCLAUGHLIN had looked FLEMMI directly in the eye as the pair walked from different directions toward the bus. MCLAUGHLIN had been holding a brown paper bag in his one remaining hand, which FLEMMI later learned contained a handgun. As he fell, MCLAUGHLIN handed the bag to a female passenger on the bus. After the shooting, FLEMMI quickly walked away, but later learned from Buddy MCLEAN that he had been clearly observed by a teenage male witness.

40. FLEMMI stated that he and SALEMME immediately left the Boston area after the shooting and stayed away for a week or so. FLEMMI added that when he next saw RICO, the FBI S/A made the comment, "Good shooting" or "Nice shooting," when the discussion turned to the MCLAUGHLIN murder. Upon FLEMMI's return, he also met with MCLEAN at Pal Joey's Lounge in Somerville for a lengthy conversation. MCLEAN told FLEMMI that the teenage boy who witnessed FLEMMI run from the

scene of the MCLAUGHLIN shooting was no longer a problem. MCLEAN said that RICO had given him the witness's name and telephone number. MCLEAN then called the boy's father, and told him that the shooting was a personal matter, and "had nothing to do with you." MCLEAN then made a veiled threat to both the teen and his father, telling them to stay out of the situation. FLEMMI believes that this conversation with MCLEAN may have been the same one in which MCLEAN revealed details about RICO's involvement in the DERMODY murder. FLEMMI also stated that MCLEAN

A Punchy mourner tries to hide her face.

was drinking heavily at this meeting. FLEMMI warned MCLEAN that he was likely to get "hit" coming out of Pal Joey's or one of the other Somerville-area clubs that he frequented. FLEMMI noted that he even mentioned the Capitol Theater across Broadway from Pal Joey's as a likely spot for an ambush.

James "Buddy" MCLEAN murder (10/30/65)

41. FLEMMI stated that MCLEAN was killed in a way similar to the scenario that he had predicted. FLEMMI was unsure who exactly told him the details of the murder, but heard that MCLEAN had been out drinking, and was walking to his car, from Pal Joey's. MCLEAN was accompanied by Tony "Blue" D'AGOSTINO and Rico SACRAMONE, the brother of Teddy Deegan's 1964 murder victim. FLEMMI's understanding was that Stevie HUGHES and Jimmy O'TOOLE did the shooting, but that contrary to common belief, Connie HUGHES was not present. MCLEAN was hit with shotgun blasts to the side of his head, as well as some to the body. FLEMMI noted that MCLEAN's two bodyguards were also wounded. Sacramone's parole was immediately revoked and he was sent back to MCI Walpole.

Buddy McLean's last mugshot;
he had aged considerably
during the gang war.

McLean bodyguard Rico Sacramone
on his way back to MCI Walpole
after being wounded by
Stevie Hughes, 1965.

Raymond DISTASIO and John O'NEIL murders (11/15/65)

42. FLEMMI stated that Raymond DISTASIO and John O'NEIL were killed by Joe BARBOZA at the Mickey Mouse Lounge in Revere, where DISTASIO was tending bar. FLEMMI learned from an unknown source, possibly BARBOZA, that he was the shooter in this murder, and that possibly Nick FEMIA was with him. FLEMMI understood that DISTASIO may have been aligned with the MCLAUGHLINs, but that the other victim O'NEIL was not a hoodlum, but a construction worker from New Hampshire with three children who had stopped by the bar to buy cigarettes. (In his autobiography, BARBOZA said O'NEIL was shot because he panicked when the shooting began.) FLEMMI believed that the reasons for the murders may have been of a personal nature rather that anything to do with the gang war. BARBOZA did admit to FLEMMI that he killed boxer Rocco DISEGLIO (06/16/66). FLEMMI was not aware of the reason for this murder, but noted that Jerry ANGIULO was eventually indicted and went to trial on

Raymond DiStasio, bartender at the Mickey Mouse Lounge, murdered by Barboza, 1965.

John O'Neil, innocent bystander, was buying cigarettes from DiStasio when Barboza burst in.

O'Neil left behind a widow and three small children.

the DISEGLIO homicide. (DISEGLIO, a former boxer, had reportedly been robbing LCN card and barbooth games.)

Anthony VERANIS murder (04/26/66)

43. FLEMMI stated that former professional prize fighter Anthony VERANIS was killed by John MARTORANO. FLEMMI added that VERANIS was a heavy drinker, and not very bright. After his release from prison, VERANIS had taken to robbing people as a way to support himself. FLEMMI said that one night VERANIS badly beat ▮▮▮▮▮▮ and another person, possibly Tash BRATSOS. At some point later, VERANIS was confronted by John MARTORANO at FLEMMI's after-hours lounge located at Humphrey and Dudley Streets. John MARTORANO then shot VERANIS in front of numerous witnesses at the club. (MARTORANO says the shooting took place at Billy O'SULLIVAN's nearby after-hours club, on its opening night, which also turned out to be its closing night.) VERANIS' body was then transported to the Blue Hills, and dumped

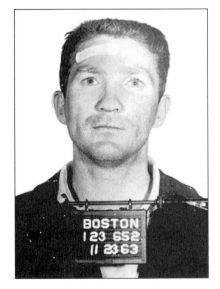

Anthony Veranis, murdered by Johnny Martorano, 1967.

Boxers like Veranis often drifted into the underworld, and many ended up dead.

by ▬▬▬ and a third person, possibly Rickie GRASSO. FLEMMI indicated that he learned about this murder from Phil COSTA who was a witness to the shooting. FLEMMI claimed that he had to pay the Boston Police some additional bribe money because of the attention the murder drew to the after-hours club.

Connie Hughes was in the Stork Club in Charlestown, looking for Howie Winter.

Connie HUGHES murder (05/25/66)

44. FLEMMI stated that the day MCLAUGHLIN gang member, Connie HUGHES was murdered, he was drinking at the Stork Club in Charlestown.

Winter Hill found Connie first, 1966.

HUGHES was observed at the bar by Brian HALLORAN who quickly contacted others in the Winter Hill gang. ███████ and Jimmy SIMS then followed HUGHES out onto the Expressway and shot HUGHES fatally using a rifle. FLEMMI learned this information concerning the murder through conversation with ███████ . FLEMMI noted that earlier in the year (03/15/66), HUGHES' brother, Stephen, was also shot and critically wounded. FLEMMI stated that it was his understanding that this shooting was not committed by the Winter

The Hughes brothers being brought into BPD headquarters for questioning.

Hill gang, or any other associated group. FLEMMI learned that Stephen HUGHES was actually shot by own his brother Connie. The reason for this shooting was that Stephen HUGHES was having an affair with ███████ .

Kathleen MURPHY murder (06/26/66)

45. FLEMMI stated that he is unsure who was responsible for Kathleen MURPHY's murder, but indicated that the main suspect in the case Jimmy KEARNS, denied involvement in her death. FLEMMI stated that he didn't know Ms. MURPHY very well, having met her only a few times, but was aware that her boyfriend was in the armed forces. FLEMMI added that he was more friendly with Ms. MURPHY's girlfriend Anne LNU (last name unknown). On the night of the murder, Ms. MURPHY and Anne

Kathleen Murphy's murder remains unsolved to this day.

were drinking at FLEMMI's after-hours club. At approximately one to two in the morning, Ms. MURPHY told FLEMMI and Anne (LNU) that she was going to get a bite to eat with Jimmy KEARNS. FLEMMI and Anne LNU remained together, at the after-hours club. The next day FLEMMI learned that Ms. MURPHY was dead.

The leading suspect in the Murphy slaying: Jimmy Kearns of the Barboza Gang.

46. FLEMMI stated that Jimmy KEARNS told him that he had dropped Ms. MURPHY off at the Sahara Club, and that Johnny MAR-TORANO and others had been at that location. FLEMMI heard talk from an unknown source that KEARNS had forced himself on Ms. MURPHY, and had killed her because of this sexual assault. FLEMMI admitted that he had been interviewed by the Boston Police regarding Ms MURPHY's murder. FLEMMI did not recall ever loaning Ms. MURPHY money, but indicated that it was possible. It should be noted that a receipt for a money order made out to FLEMMI was found on Ms. MURPHY's body. FLEMMI did not also recall any information regarding Ms. MURPHY having had an abortion shortly before her murder.

Stephen HUGHES and Sam LINDENBAUM murders (09/23/66)

47. FLEMMI stated that he, Wimpy BENNETT, SALEMME and Peter POULOS all worked as a surveillance team which was attempting to learn the activities of both Stephen HUGHES and Sam LINDENBAUM. FLEMMI added that surveillance was established on the pair in order to set them up to be murdered. FLEMMI added that with Punchy MCLAUGHLIN and Con-nie HUGHES dead, the Winter Hill and Roxbury groups were focusing on killing the two most dangerous remaining members of the MCLAUGHLIN

gang, Jimmy O'TOOLE and Stephen HUGHES. FLEMMI said that Larry BAIONE, like most of the Boston LCN, played to both sides during the gang war, and had given HUGHES $5,000 to operate with. At first the Winter Hill and Roxbury gangs' efforts revolved around O'TOOLE. FLEMMI said that ▆▆▆▆▆ using a friend in the New England Telephone Co. named ▆▆▆▆▆ , set up a wire tap on O'TOOLE's telephone. FLEMMI added that during ▆▆▆▆▆ company work hours, he ▆▆▆▆▆ would patch all of O'TOOLE's telephone calls through to a line in an apartment in South Boston which was used by the group. FLEMMI noted that this apartment had been rented by Peter POULOS

Sammy Lindenbaum was in the wrong place at the wrong time.

A Winter Hill hit car caught up with Hughes—and Lindenbaum—in Middleton, 1966.

and ███████ . This telephone tap on O'TOOLE's line produced little useful information, and the two groups decided to focus their attention on Stephen HUGHES.

48. FLEMMI stated that the gangs were aware that HUGHES was involved with 66-year-old loan shark and abortionist Sam LINDENBAUM. The group then decided to tap LINDENBAUM's telephone. FLEMMI said that Wimpy BENNETT and SALEMME climbed a telephone pole and located LINDENBAUM's line. Using BENNETT's equipment, the group found that LINDENBAUM spoke openly on the telephone. During one conversation, LINDENBAUM told a female party that he was going to make the rounds of his shylock business, and would be accompanied by HUGHES. This trip was scheduled for the following day, a Friday. FLEMMI was unavailable to participate that day, but ███████ /SIMS and SALEMME decided to try to take advantage of the information. FLEMMI learned that ███████ was in one car with SIMS driving, with SALEMME in a back-up "crash car."

49. FLEMMI stated that ███████ , armed with a rifle, opened up on the car containing LINDENBAUM and HUGHES just after the two vehicles had passed each other in Middleton. ███████ and SIMS' vehicle turned around and then closed in on the LINDENBAUM-driven auto from behind. ███████ shot HUGHES first and then fired on LINDENBAUM. FLEMMI was told that LINDENBAUM and HUGHES' car then crashed. (LINDENBAUM's two Chihuahuas, riding in the backseat, survived the crash and jumped out of the broken windows and were playing in the roadside grass when the State Police arrived.) The vehicle used by ███████ and SIMS was then dumped in a shopping mall parking lot in nearby Danvers. FLEMMI stated that ███████ , SIMS and SALEMME all related details about the double murder to him. FLEMMI added that after the story of the shooting was told to him, he and SALEMME drove back to Danvers and cleaned the rifle shells and any other evidence out of the "hit" vehicle.

Charles VON MAXCY murder (10/03/66) and Andrew VON ETTER murder (02/02/67)

50. FLEMMI stated that John SWEET (a/k/a Robert TOWK) was friendly with Walter BENNETT. SWEET began a romance with VON MAXCY's wife while in Sebring FL. VON MAXCY's wife decided that she wanted to have her husband killed in order to collect on his life insurance policy. SWEET then offered the murder contract to BENNETT for $25,000. Walter BEN-NETT in turn asked FLEMMI if he was interested in the contract, but the offer was declined. FLEMMI admit-ted the reason he refused the offer was because he knew Walter BENNETT

Andrew "the Count" von Etter was in over his head.

was an informant for various law-enforcement organizations. FLEMMI also was angered at being asked in the first place and thought that the amount of money being offered to murder a legitimate person was far too low. FLEMMI mentioned his anger about the offer to Wimpy BENNETT. FLEMMI said that against Earl SMITH's wishes, the contract was offered to Andrew VON ETTER, a local "loudmouth" who hung around Walter BENNETT's tavern. VON ETTER and his wife, along with Billy Kelley and his girlfriend, drove to Florida to scout out the situation. After the couples returned to Massachusetts, VON ETTER and KELLEY again traveled to Sebring FL and killed VON MAXCY.

51. FLEMMI stated that he learned that KELLEY and VON ETTER com-mitted the VON MAXCY murder from Earl SMITH and Wimpy BEN-NETT. After the VON MAXCY murder, Walter BENNETT became concerned whether VON ETTER would stand up. He decided to elimi-nate VON ETTER and convinced his friend Earl SMITH to handle the murder. FLEMMI was told by SMITH that he and VON ETTER were out together, and the pair stopped in an isolated area. SMITH asked VON

ETTER to get out of the vehicle and check to see if there was a problem with a rear tire. While VON ETTER was examining the tire, SMITH struck VON ETTER on the head with a small sledge hammer. VON ETTER's body was then placed inside the trunk of his car. Upon SMITH's return to the Dudley Street area, SMITH asked FLEMMI to accompany him out to Mattapan Square, where SMITH had left the car. FLEMMI said that SMITH wanted to check on VON ETTER's body and asked for his assistance. FLEMMI agreed to go, and the pair drove out to

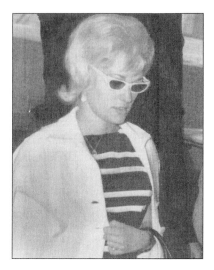

The grieving widow, Antoinette von Etter.

Von Etter's body ended up in the trunk of his car; note the vanity license plate, 1967.

the car and examined the body, which had been dumped inside the vehicle's trunk. FLEMMI did not actually observe the body, and therefore could not actually say that VON ETTER was dead. At this point FLEMMI saw SMITH swing the hammer again at something within the trunk. FLEMMI noted that this action by SMITH must have been done in a spontaneous fashion, because he had been told that VON ETTER was already dead. FLEMMI assumed that the hammer struck VON ETTER's person in some fashion.

Billy Kelley, the other shooter in the von Maxcy murder.

Joe BARBOZA's transformation into an FBI witness

52. FLEMMI stated that eventually the LCN faction in the North End became disillusioned with BARBOZA. (BARBOZA, a Portuguese-American,

Jerry Angiulo hated cops and reporters.

Barboza is brought into court to testify.

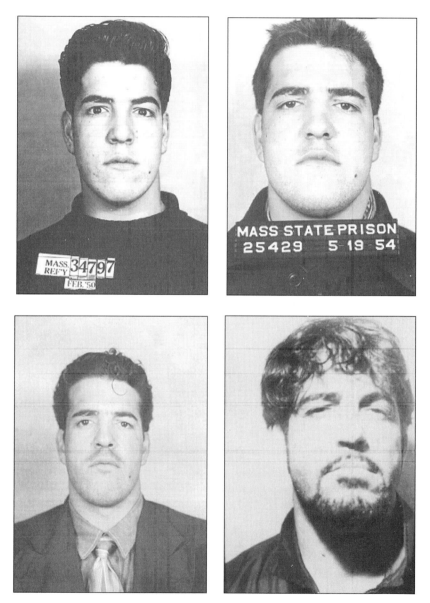

Joe Barboza down through the years.

dreamed of becoming the first non-Italian in the Mafia, but did not know that behind his back, the Mafia members referred to him as "the nigger.") At some point after the DEEGAN murder, FLEMMI learned that BAR-BOZA was being set up for elimination by the North End. FLEMMI told his friend BARBOZA to meet LCN underboss Jerry ANGIULO at his North End headquarters, the Dog House, and address the problem. FLEMMI cautioned BARBOZA not to tell anyone where the warning had come from. BARBOZA went to ANGIULO and told ANGIULO exactly what FLEMMI had said to him, including the fact that FLEMMI had warned him about the threat. FLEMMI was later questioned by ANGIULO about the situation, and FLEMMI replied that he had only told BARBOZA to go to Prince Street to work out the problem. Sometime later BARBOZA was arrested after being stopped in his car in the Combat Zone by Boston Police. FLEMMI noted that the police found a handgun in BARBOZA's motor vehicle. Bail was set in BARBOZA's case at an impossibly high $100,000 in order to keep him in jail. FLEMMI added that it was his belief that BARBOZA's arrest was orchestrated by the LCN as another way to eliminate BARBOZA as a problem. FLEMMI added that ANGIULO and the LCN had numerous contacts within both the Boston Police Department and the Suffolk County District Attorney's office at that time, and could have easily arranged to have BARBOZA set up for the arrest.

Tash BRATSOS and Tommy DIPRISCO murders (11/15/66)

53. FLEMMI stated that Larry BAIONE, in particular, expressed many concerns about BARBOZA. BAIONE claimed that BARBOZA was a loose cannon and much too aggressive. BAIONE was also concerned that BARBOZA's East Boston-based crew was getting too large, and that Tash BRATSOS was taking a significant role in the decision making process. FLEMMI noted that BAIONE had killed BRATSOS' brother Jimmy in the 1950's and that there was a great deal of animosity between the two South End hoodlums. FLEMMI

Tash Bratsos, Barboza gang member; his brother was murdered by Larry Baione in 1954.

added that he had personally heard many of these negative comments made by BAIONE and other LCN members, and knew that this type of talk usually meant that the individual(s) discussed would soon be on "the Hit Parade." FLEMMI stated that after BARBOZA's arrest, BRATSOS and Tommy DI-PRISCO began collecting some of the outstanding loan shark debts in order to raise BARBOZA's $100,000 bail money. FLEMMI said that BRATSOS had approached SALVATI to recover some or all of the $4,000 he owed, but the request was rebuffed, which angered BARBOZA.

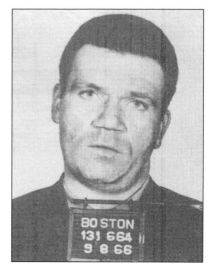

Tommy DiPrisco, Bratsos' partner.

54. FLEMMI stated that eventually the East Boston group raised $80,000 of the $100,000 needed for BARBO-ZA's bail. BRATSOS then approached the North End for the remaining $20,000. According to Wimpy BEN-NETT, BRATSOS was told to bring all of the $80,000 bail money to the Nite Lite Tavern on Commercial Street, which would prove that the request was not a scam. The remaining

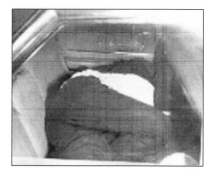

Last stop for Bratsos and DiPrisco, murdered by the Mafia in 1966.

$20,000 would then be provided by the LCN. FLEMMI said that BRAT-SOS and DIPRISCO went to the Nite Lite after the 1:00 a.m. closing time with the $80,000 cash. FLEMMI added that the pair was then murdered at the club in the presence of eight mobsters, and that all of the BARBOZA bail money was stolen. FLEMMI stated that he was not sure of the identities of all of the people who were present when the murders took place, but noted that BAIONE, Nick GISO, Ralphie "Chong" LAMATTINA and ███████ were there.

55. FLEMMI stated that at some point that night, while returning from Bobby LABELLA's place, "Wimpy" BENNETT observed Tash BRATSOS'

Ralphie Chong, right, in an undated surveillance photo.

Cadillac parked outside the Nite Lite. Later when the bodies of BRATSOS and DIPRISCO were found in the back seat of the car abandoned in South Boston, BENNETT relayed his observations to Boston Police Detective Bill STUART. FLEMMI noted that he was present for the discussion with STUART. FLEMMI said that STUART then advised FBI agent H. Paul RICO of this information. A search warrant was quickly issued and a bullet hole located in the wall of the Nite Lite was found. Investigators also determined that a rug in the club had been changed immediately after the shooting. Eventually Ralphie "Chong" LAMATTINA

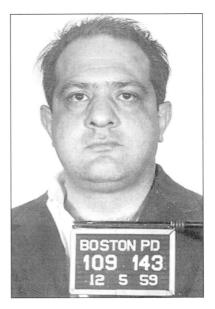

Nick Giso, Mafia soldier.

was arrested for accessory after the fact on the murders, and was sentenced to four-to-seven years in prison.

Chico Amico murder (12/07/66)

56. FLEMMI stated that Wimpy BEN-NETT met in Providence with Raymond PATRIARCA after the Nite Lite murders and told the LCN boss that the Roxbury gang was not going to back BARBOZA's now-depleted East Boston crew in a war with the Italian mob. FLEMMI added that without the backing of the Roxbury gang, the BARBOZA crew became easy targets

Chico Amico, Barboza protégé.

Chico Amico, murdered in East Boston 1966. Jimmy Kearns survived with multiple wounds.

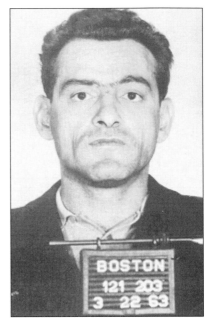

Richie the Pig DeVincent, one of Amico's killers.

Guy Frizzi, switched allegiance from Barboza to the Mafia.

for elimination. FLEMMI said that one night the LCN developed information that East Boston gang members Chico AMICO and Jimmy KEARNS were in a club in Revere. J.R. RUSSO and Richard "the Pig" DEVINCENT located AMICO's vehicle and waited for the pair to leave the establishment. After the vehicle drove away, with KEARNS driving, RUSSO opened fire with a carbine and struck AMICO, a dishwasher-turned-gangster, in the back of the head. FLEMMI said that KEARNS was also wounded. KEARNS recovered and was arrested for accessory after the fact, for failing to assist police in identifying the shooters. While in jail, KEARNS contacted FLEMMI and asked him to straighten out the problem KEARNS had with the LCN.

57. FLEMMI stated that he spoke to BAIONE and promised that KEARNS would not retaliate against the LCN for the murder of his friend

Johnny Martorano at age 22.

Jimmy Martorano attended
Boston College.

AMICO. BAIONE agreed to allow KEARNS to live, and also instructed
FLEMMI to keep control of his brother the Bear so that he wouldn't have
a problem with the LCN. FLEMMI was also aware that East Boston gang
member Guy FRIZZI was also left alone because his brother Connie's ties
to the North End. FLEMMI noted that other BARBOZA associates Nick
FEMIA and Patsy FABIANO were in prison at the time and would be dealt
with later by the LCN, as they were. FLEMMI further added that Wimpy
BENNETT assisted two other BARBOZA associates, Jimmy and Johnny
MARTORANO, in obtaining "a pass" from Raymond PATRIARCA, in ex-
change for a promise not to come to the aid of the remaining East Boston
gang members.

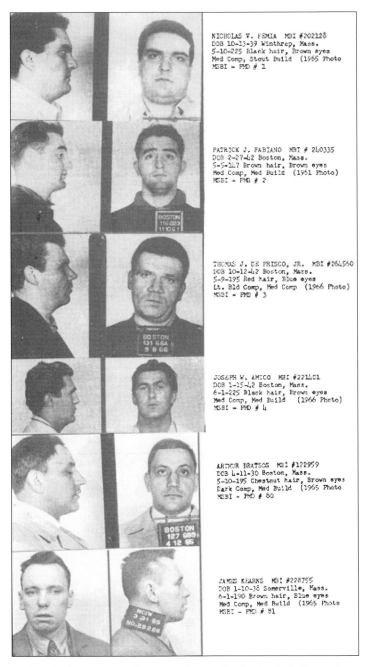

The Barboza gang—five were shot to death, the sixth (Kearns)
died in federal prison.

Edward "Wimpy" BENNETT 01/19/67) murder

58. FLEMMI stated that Wimpy BENNETT had a good working relationship with Raymond PATRIARCA, also known as "the Man," but was hated by the Boston-area LCN. He was considered the Man's "spy" in the Boston underworld. FLEMMI and SALEMME were well aware that Larry BAIONE had a particular dislike for Wimpy BENNETT, and that these feelings were mutual. FLEMMI recalled that SALEMME had told BAIONE that BENNETT was looking to kill him. SALEMME said that BENNETT had planned to park a truck across from BAIONE's Jamaica Plain home and then shoot the Boston LCN's number-two man as he exited the residence. FLEMMI eventually became aware that BAIONE wanted both Walter and Wimpy BENNETT eliminated. FLEMMI said that SALEMME also sowed the seeds of discord between himself and Wimpy BENNETT. SALEMME told FLEMMI that Wimpy BENNETT had wanted to kill Jimmy the Bear but was concerned how Stevie FLEMMI would react. FLEMMI noted that Wimpy BENNETT and the Bear didn't always get along, so the information had a ring of truth to it.

Peter Poulos, murdered in Nevada by Stevie Flemmi in 1969.

AFTER A while FLEMMI came to the conclusion that Wimpy had to be killed and began planning the murder with SALEMME. The pair decided to kill BENNETT at the next available opportunity. FLEMMI also recalled that some time prior to the murder, the group had a problem regarding the gang's numbers operation. FLEMMI confronted Peter POULOS over the problem in the presence of Wimpy BENNETT, but the situation was eventually resolved.

59. FLEMMI stated that one evening Wimpy BENNETT walked into the garage on Dudley Street that FLEMMI owned with George KAUFMAN and SALEMME. BENNETT was in the garage for approximately five minutes when he abruptly decided to leave. As Wimpy was walking out of the office, FLEMMI ran up and shot BENNETT in the left side of his head with a .38 caliber handgun. BENNETT was shot in front of the office doorway which led to the garage area. BENNETT's dead body fell into the office after being hit by the single gunshot. KAUFMAN, who had been unaware of the plan to kill BENNETT, ran out the door of the garage in a state of panic. SALEMME ran after KAUFMAN and assured him that he didn't have "anything to be concerned about." FLEMMI cleaned up the blood and then wrapped the clothed body and placed it in the trunk of BENNETT's car. The body was then transported to the other garage the gang operated on Hancock Street in Dorchester. BENNETT's remains were then placed in the trunk of a stolen car housed there, and his car was brought back to the Dudley Street garage. KAUFMAN then sold BENNETT's car the next day for $6,000.

60. FLEMMI stated that ▬▬▬▬ was aware of the plan to kill "Wimpy" BENNETT, and ▬▬▬▬ was contacted and came by the Dorchester garage the following day. FLEMMI believes that it was his idea to bury BENNETT's body at the Hopkinton Gun Club. FLEMMI noted that they had used the range in the past and suggested it to the group as a possible burial site. FLEMMI said that he, SIMS and MCDONALD dug the grave, which was circular and about six feet deep. ▬▬▬▬ and SALEMME were assigned to drive Wimpy's body out to Hopkinton. Just prior to the arrival of the body, a local police officer pulled into the range and questioned FLEMMI about why he was in the area. FLEMMI told the officer that he was just preparing to go shooting. During this discussion ▬▬▬▬ and SALEMME arrived with the body. ▬▬▬▬ and SALEMME observed the police car and turned around and left the range. After the policemen left, SALEMME and ▬▬▬▬ returned with the body. The pair drove past the shed that covered the shooters at the range, and stopped a short distance away after backing in. FLEMMI then took the body out of the trunk and

dragged it some 80 paces to the grave, which was situated on the range side of a stone wall. ███████ and SALEMME immediately left the range after FLEMMI removed BENNETT's body from the trunk. FLEMMI, SIMS and MCDONALD departed later after covering the body with dirt. FLEMMI noted that the burial was conducted during daylight hours.

Walter BENNETT murder (04/07/67)

61. FLEMMI stated that after the disappearance of "Wimpy" BENNETT, his brother Walter no longer trusted him. Walter BENNETT believed that the LCN had killed "Wimpy," but assumed that FLEMMI was involved in some fashion. FLEMMI noted that for some unknown reason, Walter BEN-NETT still trusted SALEMME. Later, when it was decided that Walter must also be eliminated this task fell to SALEMME. FLEMMI further stated that he was not present when Walter BENNETT was murdered, but learned the details regarding the crime directly from SALEMME. SALEMME told FLEMMI that he was able to convince Walter BENNETT to get into the back seat of a motor vehicle being driven by Peter POULOS. SALEMME occupied the front passenger seat in the same vehicle, and had previously secreted a handgun in his groin. Shortly after picking Walter BENNETT up, SALEMME wheeled around and shot Walter BENNETT. The single fatal gunshot fired by SALEMME struck BENNETT in the mouth and chipped off several teeth. After BENNETT was dead, FLEMMI was contacted and went to the Dudley Street garage. FLEMMI noted that Walter BENNETT's body was already inside the trunk of a stolen car when he arrived. FLEMMI added that he washed out the blood that had spilled inside POULOS' car and that this cleaning took place at George KAUFMAN's Brookline home. Walter BENNETT left behind a wife and 13 children.

62. FLEMMI stated that ███████, who was also aware of the plan to kill Walter, was called, and arrived at the garage the next day, to again assist, along with Jimmy SIMS and Joe MCDONALD. FLEMMI said that SIMS and MCDONALD again dug the grave, and ███████ and SALEMME transported the body to the range in the stolen car. FLEMMI, in his own

car, followed the vehicle with the body out to the Hopkinton range. FLEM-MI's "crash car" was used to protect the stolen motor vehicle with the body in it, and to guard the rifle range from unwanted visitors. FLEMMI never saw the burial site but was told by SIMS that Walter BENNETT was interred on the other side of the stone wall from his brother Wimpy in the same general area. FLEMMI's memory is somewhat vague regarding the burial, but believes that he may have again dragged the body out to SIMS and MCDONALD. FLEMMI noted that this burial was also conducted in the daytime. (Decades later, Salemme tried to direct investigators to the two burial sites. But the dumping of tons of fill from the Big Dig excavations had changed the topography, and the Bennetts' bodies have never been found.)

63. FLEMMI stated that he did not recall that after the murder a story was circulated that Walter BENNETT had left Boston for Florida. FLEMMI stated that this type of story would not have been credible, because it was

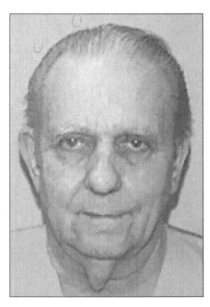

Billy Kelley is still on Death Row in Florida.

Junior Patriarca, a/k/a Rubber Lips.

well known that Walter BENNETT did not like traveling from the Boston area. FLEMMI did recall driving to Providence to tell Raymond PATRIARCA about the murders. FLEMMI further added that SALEMME had concocted a false rumor that Walter BENNETT had been planning on kidnapping PATRIARCA's son Junior. FLEMMI also admitted that ███████ picked up Walter's BENNETT's loan shark records from ███████ after Walter's murder. ███████ gave the records to FLEMMI and SALEMME and received a percentage of the money he collected from the outstanding debts. FLEMMI also said that neither ███████ nor Andrew VON ETTER's widow were ever threatened to keep them from testifying in the VON MAXCY murder trial which occurred several years later. FLEMMI added that ███████ began dating ███████ and passed on money to her from himself and SALEMME.

William BENNETT murder (12/23/67)

64. FLEMMI stated that Billy BENNETT was not really a criminal like his two brothers, and primarily made his living as a bartender. FLEMMI added that Billy BENNETT began vocalizing his belief that FLEMMI had murdered both his brothers. Billy BENNETT told Phil COSTA and

Hugh "Sonny" Shields, acquitted of the murder of Billy Bennett.

Billy Bennett dead in the snow in Mattapan in 1967.

others about his suspicions concerning FLEMMI's complicity in the deaths. FLEMMI said that Billy BENNETT was not as convinced that SALEMME had a role in the murders as he was about FLEMMI's involvement. FLEMMI noted that Red CONLIN became so enraged over BENNETT's talk against FLEMMI that he tried to stab BENNETT in the cellar of Walter's Lounge. FLEMMI added that Billy BENNETT did not trust anyone within the Roxbury group, and recruited Hugh "Sonny" SHIELDS and Ricky GRASSO to assist him in attaining revenge for the murder of his brothers. Soon after being recruited, GRASSO and SHIELDS began passing information concerning William BENNETT's plans to FLEMMI.

65. FLEMMI stated that eventually, he, SALEMME and POULOS reluctantly decided that Billy BENNETT had to be killed. FLEMMI and SALEMME then convinced GRASSO and SHIELDS to actually do the murder for them, as the pair were the only ones who Billy BENNETT trusted enough to get into a car with. On the night of the murder, GRASSO and SHIELDS picked up BENNETT at his home in Mattapan. FLEMMI, SALEMME, ███████ and POULOS followed in POULOS' car. GRASSO was driving with SHIELDS in the front passenger seat and BENNETT in the rear seat. After approximately five minutes, SHIELDS turned around and shot BENNETT twice, the second round striking the victim as he attempted to dive out of the right rear door. FLEMMI said that he observed a taxi cab traveling on the opposite side of the same street towards the GRASSO-driven vehicle as the murder took place. It was clear to FLEMMI that anyone in the taxi had to have seen BENNETT's body as it rolled out of the car onto the street. The body came to a stop against a snow bank. FLEMMI observed the taxi cab make a U-turn and drive back towards the body after first passing it. GRASSO then panicked, pulled over and left his car running in the driveway of a nearby residence. POULOS then stopped and picked up both GRASSO and SHIELDS and after a short drive the pair was instructed by FLEMMI to meet at the Greek Club on Tremont Street in the South End. FLEMMI then went back to GRASSO's car, and drove the vehicle a few blocks away. FLEMMI also recalled digging out a bullet from a seat cushion in the back seat.

66. FLEMMI stated that SALEMME called Boston Police Detective Bill STUART, who went to the crime scene and reported back to the group the status of the investigation. FLEMMI added that STUART was immediately told that he and SALEMME had been involved in the murder of BENNETT. FLEMMI and SALEMME then attempted to locate GRASSO and SHIELDS, who had initially left the area on foot. FLEMMI stated that the group had already decided to eliminate GRASSO because of the panic he had exhibited at the murder scene. Upon returning to the Greek Club, FLEMMI observed GRASSO in the front passenger side seat with ███████ in the back of the same car. FLEMMI then observed ███████ shoot GRASSO in the back of the head. A second shot was fired, and the round went through the windshield of POULOS' vehicle. FLEMMI added that he was very surprised that ███████ shot GRASSO, having observed some Boston Police officers standing across the street a short distance from the vehicle where the murder took place. FLEMMI stated that these officers did not react to the gunshots, nor did they respond when FLEMMI jumped into the vehicle, and accidentally hit the siren that POULOS had installed in the car. FLEMMI speculated that the officers may have been under the impression that POULOS' vehicle was a police car, because the Ford resembled a typical detective's unmarked cruiser. FLEMMI added that POULOS later replaced the windshield, and sold the car. FLEMMI noted that POULOS was unhappy about having to sell his vehicle, which had other expensive equipment installed inside, such as "kill switches," a siren, and a device which turned off different head or tail lights.

67. FLEMMI stated that after getting into POULOS' car and driving away he covered GRASSO's body with a blanket and drove over to the Castle Gate housing project. ███████ then left the area and FLEMMI took the .38 caliber handgun that was used to kill GRASSO and disposed of it. SALEMME came out to assist, and POULOS' vehicle, with GRASSO's corpse inside, was taken to the Dorchester garage. FLEMMI said that he retrieved GRASSO's vehicle from Roxbury and it too was brought to the Dorchester garage. SALEMME then transferred GRASSO's body from the POULOS vehicle and placed it into the trunk of GRASSO's own car. FLEMMI noted that SALEMME dropped his wallet in GRASSO's vehicle at some point

during the transfer. FLEMMI later located the wallet before GRASSO's vehicle was dropped off in Brookline. FLEMMI stated that GRASSO's car was angle-parked near some trolley tracks, and the body was located a few days later by police. SHIELDS never came back to the Greek Club on the night of the murders, but a few days later met with FLEMMI and SALEMME and was given cash so SHIELDS could leave the area.

Herbert Smith, Elizabeth Dixon, Douglas Barrett murders (01/06/68)

68. FLEMMI stated that "Woody" LNU (last name unknown), the son-in-law of Carioca LAMATTINA owed him approximately $100 from a shylock loan. FLEMMI added that "Woody" wasn't paying the debt and action had to be taken. FLEMMI said he pointed a gun at "Woody" while on Dudley Street, but this still did not motivate the debtor to pay. FLEMMI then went down to BASIN STREET SOUTH, which was being operated at the time by Carioca LAMATTINA, to ask about the money. LAMATTINA argued with FLEMMI and a scuffle ensued. LAMATTINA pulled a gun out, and he, the African-American doorman and another black male joined in and a fight continued out onto the street. FLEMMI stated that he was struck several times in the back of the head with a blackjack, but he was finally able to pull away and escape. Sometime later, FLEMMI and Red CONLIN again brawled with LAMATTINA's associate, Henry TAGLIARDI, and two others. FLEMMI and CONLIN successfully defended themselves on this occasion. FLEMMI said the dispute continued with yet another fist fight, this time with him alone at The Mayflower Club in the South End.

Trio Found Slain in Car At Roxbury

BOSTON SUNDAY ADVERTISER JANUARY 7, 1968

A go-go dancer, the assistant manager of a South End nightspot and another man were found shot to death early Saturday in a station wagon parked on Normandy st., Roxbury. One victim was identified as Herbert Smith, 47, of 11 Crestwood pk., Roxbury, employed at Basin Street South on Washington st. at Northampton.

Hours after the shootings the girl, who was wearing a go-go costume, and the other victim remained unidentified.

★

Their bodies were discovered by Sgt. Michael Donnelly of District 9. The rear window of the vehicle appeared to have been shattered by a shotgun blast.

One victim was slumped over the wheel, the girl against the dashboard and the other across the rear seat. A cigaret was still burning in the girl's fingers when the bodies were found.

Neighbors in the vicinity told police they heard nothing unusual during the night and investigators said it looked like the work of one person.

★

The vehicle was registered to a Roxbury woman, who said she let Smith borrow it several days ago.

A trail of blood led from the car to a nearby home and detectives feel there may have been a fourth wounded person, who left to seek treatment.

Medical Examiner Richard Ford scheduled autopsies for all three victims.

In 1968, the murder of three blacks rated a one-column headline on page 47 in the Hearst-owned *Sunday Advertiser*.

Ralphie Chong served time as
an accessory in the
Bratsos-DiPrisco murders.

Peter Limone, another Mafia
soldier convicted on Barboza's
perjury.

69. FLEMMI stated that a meeting was called to de-escalate the conflict. In attendance were FLEMMI, WINTER, Peter LIMONE and Jerry AN-GIULO. ANGIULO told FLEMMI that he couldn't kill Carioca LAMAT-TINA because his brother Ralphie "Chong" was connected with the LCN. ANGIULO did not mention ▮▮▮▮▮▮▮ in the conversation. But FLEMMI believed that ▮▮▮▮▮▮▮ too was untouchable because ▮▮▮▮▮▮▮ had been involved in the LCN-approved murder of Joey LESTER in the 1950's. FLEMMI added that ANGIULO did okay the murder of the black doorman (Herbert SMITH). FLEMMI noted that after LIMONE and ANGIULO left the meeting, WINTER told FLEMMI that it didn't matter what the LCN wanted, the Winter Hill gang would do whatever he wished to do. FLEMMI then told WINTER that he wanted to drop the entire matter.

70. FLEMMI stated that one snowy night John MARTORANO showed up at his new home in Milton. MARTORANO told FLEMMI that he had just

killed the black doorman from BASIN STREET SOUTH in the doorman's car on Normandy Street in Roxbury, along with two other younger blacks who had been with the doorman. FLEMMI observed blood on MAR-TORANO's coat, which was quickly washed. MARTORANO was given a replacement jacket and driven home. FLEMMI stated that he believed that MARTORANO was just looking to do him a favor by killing the doorman, but indicated that the murders were not done at his request. (MARTORANO says FLEMMI had been complaining bitterly to him about the beating he had suffered at the club, which was sometimes controlled by the MARTORANOs. So MARTORANO sought out SMITH at the club, seeking an apology. When SMITH brushed off the incident, MAR-TORANO decided to kill him, not knowing that SMITH had been fighting under orders to protect his employer or that the two teenagers would be in the car.) FLEMMI does not recall much about ▮▮▮▮▮▮ involvement in the murder, but did note that soon after these killings, ▮▮▮▮▮▮ moved to Cape Cod.

BARBOZA becomes a witness for the FBI (1967-1968)

71. FLEMMI stated that BARBOZA became increasingly angry as his crew was eliminated, but that the Nite Lite murders and the loss of his bail money pushed BARBOZA over the edge. FLEMMI added that Larry BAIONE asked FLEMMI to speak to his brother the Bear, who in turn could contact Nick FEMIA in jail. BAIONE didn't want FEMIA to testify in any way that would corroborate BARBOZA's false statements. FLEMMI did speak to the Bear but told Jimmy FLEMMI to neither help nor discredit BARBOZA. FLEMMI stated that he did not recall ever telling Raymond PATRIARCA that BARBOZA was trying to get Patsy

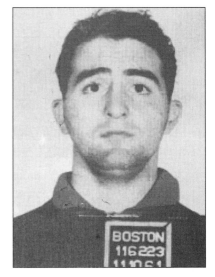

Patsy Fabiano—Barboza wanted him in jail, so the Mafia wouldn't kill him.

FABIANO to testify about the Nite Lite murders, and any FBI document claiming otherwise would be false (03/27/67). FLEMMI added that he only directly met with PATRIARCA on a couple of occasions. FLEMMI was aware that the LCN was concerned about FABIANO's possible testimony.

Nick Femia, future drug addict, future employee of Whitey Bulger.

72. FLEMMI stated that during this time period (10/02/67), he was driving in a car behind SALEMME and Frank BALLIRO, when LCN associate Fifi SILVESTRI was attacked. FLEMMI said that SALEMME stabbed Fifi SILVESTRI in the back, in an attempt to kill him. The stabbing was the result of an "old beef" between Joe LOMBARDO and SILVESTRI. After the stabbing, SILVESTRI was allowed to leave SALEMME's vehicle. FLEMMI also denied that he and SALEMME made an attempt to take over the gaming activities in South Boston, which eventually resulted in the South Boston gang war of the late 1960's. FLEMMI admitted that the Roxbury group may have tried to get some of the gaming business from nearby South Boston, but denied that they ever had much success, or that any violence was involved in their efforts. FLEMMI added that he once got into a fist fight with a friend of the KILLEENs named NICHOLS but noted that the brawl was over the affections of a female, and not for any gang activities. FLEMMI also

Joe Lombardo, old-time Mafia boss.

recalled he and SALEMME assaulted another bookmaker named ███████ , over a dispute regarding a competing Roxbury-controlled gaming contact. ███████ was struck in the jaw but not seriously injured.

John FITZGERALD bombing (01/30/68)

73. FLEMMI stated that as Joseph BARBOZA's cooperation with the FBI increased, the LCN became more and more concerned with the activities of BARBOZA's attorney John FITZGER-ALD. FLEMMI said that Raymond PATRIARCA decided to make an ex-ample of FITZGERALD, because the lawyer was acting more like a partner of BARBOZA than his attorney. FLEMMI cited some of the troubling behavior of FITZGERALD that bothered both PA-TRIARCA and his LCN underlings. With his jailhouse access to BARBOZA, FITZGERALD was passing messages from BARBOZA to his surviving crim-inal associates. The lawyer was also

Phil Waggenheim, Jewish hitman for the Mafia.

dating organized-crime groupie Dorothy BARCHARD and he was driving BARBOZA's souped-up "James Bond" motor vehicle. FLEMMI added that a meeting was called by the LCN regarding BARBOZA and FITZGERALD. The meeting was held at a restaurant in the North End. FLEMMI recalled that he, SALEMME and Larry BAIONE attended this North End discussion. FLEMMI added that J.R. RUSSO was never involved in any of these discus-sions concerning the potential BARBOZA/FITZGERALD murders.

74. FLEMMI stated that at first the discussion centered around murder-ing BARBOZA. The LCN wanted to send a message to future snitches by killing BARBOZA and BAIONE suggested going into the Barnstable

House of Correction and killing him in his cell. As the subject changed to FITZGERALD, BAIONE suggested that FITZGERALD should be killed in a dramatic bombing. FLEMMI noted that PATRIARCA had previously expressed a desire that FITZGERALD be shot. FLEMMI said that Earl SMITH, Frank BALLIRO and Phil WAGGENHEIM were assigned to watch FITZGERALD's movements, and on one occasion, the group had FITZGERALD lined up at his residence in Everett. WAGGENHEIM then traveled to pick up the firearms to be used, but was late in returning, and the opportunity was lost when FITZGERALD left the area.

75. FLEMMI stated that SALEMME was desperate to become a made member of the LCN, even though he was half-Irish. (His middle name was Patrick.) As he became closer and closer to BAIONE, SALEMME even began to speak like him. FLEMMI stated that at some point Peter LIMONE talked to both him and SALEMME about becoming made LCN members, and indicated that the usual requirement that a LCN member observe the candidates commit a murder would be waived. LIMONE added that the pair had already killed enough people to qualify. FLEMMI noted that neither he nor SALEMME were initiated into the LCN at that time and that SALEMME eventually initiated himself into the Mafia after his release from state prison in 1989.

76. FLEMMI stated that he felt he had no choice but to become involved in the plot to kill FITZGERALD, but was not convinced that the idea was in anyone's best interest. FLEMMI said that SALEMME insisted that he involve himself in the murder plot. FLEMMI noted that he quickly warned RICO that FITZGERALD was in danger. FLEMMI believed that he only told RICO that FITZGERALD was "on the Hit Parade" but not about the plan to use a car bomb. FLEMMI stated that he was unsure how the dynamite was obtained once it had been decided that this was the method to be used to accomplish the murder. FLEMMI did not recall asking ███████ for the dynamite, but had a vague memory that it was obtained in New Hampshire.

77. FLEMMI stated that SALEMME practiced wiring the blasting caps to the bomb at KAUFMAN's Intercity Garage. FLEMMI recalled SALEMME experimenting with the caps, using a tire with a wooden board on top. FLEMMI noted that KAUFMAN and KAUFMAN's good friend Bobby DADDIECO observed SALEMME practicing these bomb-wiring activities at the garage, but were not at the actual scene in Everett when the bomb was planted in FITZGERALD's car. KAUFMAN also obtained a car similar to the BARBOZA/FITZGERALD vehicle to aid SALEMME in his practice. FLEMMI noted that SALEMME conducted between 8 to 10 experiments with the blasting caps, in an effort to get the timing correct. FLEMMI added that some of these experiments even took place outside in the garage's yard.

Bobby Daddieco, witness against Frank Salemme, but not Stevie Flemmi.

78. FLEMMI stated that it was determined that the best place to conduct the bombing was outside FITZGERALD's law office in Everett, and to wire the explosive in place during the daylight morning hours. FLEMMI added that on the day of the blast, he drove SALEMME and BAIONE to a street perpendicular to where FITZGERALD had parked the car. FLEMMI noted that he used his own motor vehicle for this transportation. SMITH, WAGGENHEIM, and Frank BALLIRO were in automobiles conducting surveillance for the operation. FLEMMI said that BAIONE and SALEMME were dressed in overalls and that SALEMME completed the wiring while BAIONE functioned as a lookout. SALEMME and BAIONE returned to FLEMMI's vehicle after about 15 or 20 minutes and reported that at least one witness had seen the pair working on the intended victim's car. FLEMMI and his companions then left Everett and drove to the Greek Club in the South End where they remained for the rest of the day. FLEMMI

John Fitzgerald's car after the bombing.

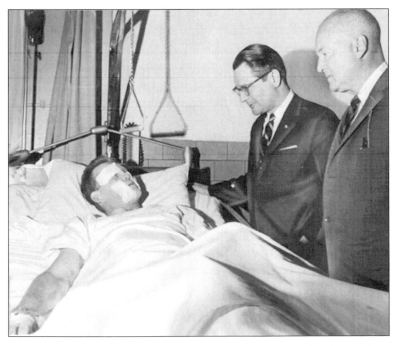

Fitzgerald is visited in the hospital by Atty. Gen. Elliot Richardson and
Middlesex County District Attorney John Droney.

stated that BAIONE's and SALEMME's coveralls were placed inside a floor "hide" that had been built into the club, and that later someone disposed of the clothing. FLEMMI, BAIONE, SALEMME, POULOS and John VIGLAS along with other regular members of the club were present when the group heard a radio news broadcast regarding the detonation of the bomb.

79. FLEMMI stated that BAIONE was upset that the bomb hadn't killed FITZGERALD, but shortly thereafter PATRIARCA sent word that the group had done a good job and that the message had been delivered. FLEMMI added that SALEMME had used four to six sticks of dynamite, but the reason that the blast wasn't more effective was that a low-strength formula explosive had been used. FLEMMI noted that the group had been concerned during the practice phase of the operation that BARBOZA's/ FITZGERALD's motor vehicle was equipped with a burglar alarm, but that the equipment was not in use on the day of the blast. FLEMMI stated that he was never paid for his efforts in the FITZGERALD bombing. FLEMMI did not recall telling RICO about his knowledge of the bombing after the fact, but added that it was possible that he did. FLEMMI further added that RICO did mention to him that FITZGERALD had asked for RICO by name immediately after the bombing. FITZGERALD told RICO that he was only half-way inside the motor vehicle when the blast occurred. FLEMMI got the impression that RICO was aware that the order for the murder had come directly from PATRIARCA and BAIONE.

Tommy TIMMONS murder (04/27/68)

80. FLEMMI stated that Tommy TIMMONS and ▬▬▬▬ had recently kidnapped LCN-connected bookmaker Abe SARKIS. This action angered BAIONE, who asked SALEMME, Red CONLIN and ▬▬▬▬ to kill TIM-MONS in order to settle this infraction. FLEMMI added that early one morning he was awakened by a telephone call from SALEMME, and told to go to Tommy TIMMONS' bar at Hyde Park Avenue and River Street to assist with a problem there. FLEMMI arrived at the tavern and went to the basement where he found a beaten and bloodied TIMMONS. FLEMMI learned that ▬▬▬▬ and CONLIN, who were still present at the bar,

Tommy Timmons kidnapped the wrong man.

Gambling boss Abe Sarkis had Mafia protection.

Red Assad, South End gangster, fingered by Stevie Flemmi as Tommy Timmons' murderer in 1968.

had done the beating. FLEMMI and SALEMME then took TIMMONS to SALEMME's home at 14 Marie Drive in Sharon, and dragged TIMMONS inside the residence. TIMMONS was then strangled by Red ASSAD with assistance from FLEMMI, BAIONE and SALEMME.

81. FLEMMI stated that ASSAD then dropped off SALEMME and BAIONE at a spot where a grave was dug. This grave, chosen by SALEMME, was a short distance away from his home, somewhere in the town of Sharon. FLEMMI estimated that the burial spot was no more than a mile and a half from the SALEMME residence. After the hole was dug, ASSAD and FLEMMI took the body to the burial site. FLEMMI stated that they drove to a small parking area adjacent to the roadway which was parallel to where two sets of commuter-rail tracks ran. The body was taken from the vehicle by FLEMMI and carried across the two sets of tracks. SALEMME then took the body from there, and dragged it to the burial spot a short distance away. FLEMMI stated that while he didn't walk up to the grave, he could easily see it from the parking area and noted that it appeared to be about waist deep. FLEMMI said that he left Sharon a short time after dropping off the body.

82. FLEMMI stated that he did not recall SALEMME making any threats on the life of Suffolk County District Attorney Garrett Byrne after the guilty verdicts in the DEEGAN murder trial (07/31/68). FLEMMI was aware that the LCN wanted to kill Byrne. FLEMMI did remember a significant amount of police surveillance on the remaining Roxbury gang members around the time of the FITZGERALD bombing and the end of the DEEGAN murder trial. FLEMMI noted that the surveillance teams consisted mostly of Boston Police, occasionally accompanied by FBI agents. FLEMMI also recalled that on New Year's Eve 1968, his friend and criminal associate, Frank BALLIRO, was killed in an automobile accident. FLEMMI said that BALLIRO had been drinking heavily on the night of the accident and was driving

Frank Balliro, drunk and dead in a
car crash, New Year's 1969.

FLEMMI's car. FLEMMI added that BALLIRO was speeding in a raging snow storm when the accident occurred, but insisted that the episode was not a suicide. FLEMMI also recalled that sometime in 1969 he was drinking in the Party Lounge in Roslindale and got in a fight with a large fellow over a woman. FLEMMI struck this man with a chair and badly injured him. FLEMMI said that the police came to the scene but that he was not arrested.

Additional LCN murders in the 1960's

83. FLEMMI stated that the LCN were involved in several other homicides that were considered part of the gang war in the 1960's. FLEMMI was told that BAIONE had killed Benny ZIMMERMAN in the early 1960's, and had buried ZIMMERMAN's body. FLEMMI added that BAIONE had bragged that he and ▆▆▆▆ had buried and burned some bodies on BAIONE's late mother's pig farm in Franklin MA. BAIONE had built a homemade crematorium on the property. BAIONE was also longtime friends with ▆▆▆▆ . FLEMMI said that ZIMMERMAN was killed over a

Wady David, South End gambler and drug dealer, murdered 1965.

Bernie Zinna, Revere hoodlum, murdered 1969.

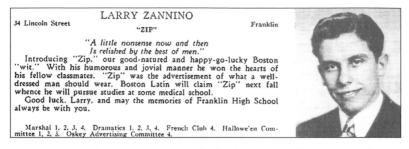

Larry Baione a/k/a Zannino went to high school in Franklin, where he later constructed a crematorium at his mother's pig farm to dispose of his victims.

personal problem with Jerry AN-GIULO. FLEMMI recalled that while eating and drinking in a restaurant, BAIONE had admitted to him that he had Jewish bookmaker and drug dealer Wady DAVID killed (08/23/65). FLEMMI also believed that Mel KROSIER, who owned a South End credit union with his father, was killed by the LCN after large loans were run up by associates of BAIONE. BAIONE and Jerry ANGIULO also killed FNU (first name unknown) CRISTOFORO. FLEMMI noted that he believed that CRISTOFORO's body was found somewhere in the North End. Also, Bernard Zinna was found murdered in his Cadillac in Revere (12/20/69). Zinna had been tried and acquitted of the murder of Rocco DiSeglio before he was shot in the head at the age of 39. DiSeglio was a welterweight boxer from Newton who had been sticking up LCN-protected card and barbooth

Rocco DiSeglio, murdered for sticking up Mafia card games in 1966.

games with, among others, Bernard Zinna, before he was shot in the head by Joe BARBOZA and others at the age of 27 (04/03/66).

N.E.G.R.O. multiple murders (11/13/68) and Ronald HICKS murder (03/20/69)

84. FLEMMI stated that he was told by Deke CHANDLER that he and ███████ had committed the notorious N.E.G.R.O. murders in Roxbury. These three murders occurred inside the offices of the New England Grass Roots Organization (N.E.G.R.O) on Blue Hill Avenue. The victims included the N.E.G.R.O. founder and leader, a blind ex-con named Guido St. Laurent. Two other individuals, including Ronald HICKS, were wounded. FLEMMI further added that John MARTORANO also advised him that CHANDLER, Alvin CAMPBELL and ███████ were the shooters in this murder. FLEMMI noted that CHANDLER, who was shot to death in 1976,

Alvin and Arnold Campbell, Roxbury gangsters and friends of Johnny Martorano.

Guido St. Laurent, ex-con and
founder of N.E.G.R.O., murdered 1968.

Deke Chandler, enforcer for the
Campbells, murdered 1976.

had been a childhood friend of his in Roxbury. FLEMMI learned that the murders were the result of an argument over control of the federal "War on Poverty" grants in Roxbury. CHANDLER told FLEMMI that he and ▇▇▇▇▇▇ started shooting as soon as they entered the offices of the organization, which were located above a pizza parlor. HICKS and another witness survived the shooting. HICKS was able to identify the shooters and CHANDLER and the CAMPBELL brothers were subsequently arrested and held in custody at the Charles Street Jail.

85. FLEMMI stated that MARTORANO was friendly with much of the African-American community in Boston, and must have known Alvin and Arnold CAMPBELL, whose reputation for criminal activity was well established. (Originally bank robbers, the CAMPBELLs had served time in federal prison with Whitey BULGER.) FLEMMI said that Alvin CAMPBELL's wife Bert went to a bar and asked HICKS to come outside the club and speak with MARTORANO. HICKS met with MARTORANO and was

immediately shot and killed. (Actually, Martorano befriended HICKS before eventually shooting him in HICKS' car in the Fenway while HICKS was snorting a line of cocaine. CHANDLER and the CAMPBELLS were subsequently acquitted of the three murders by a Suffolk County jury.) FLEMMI was asked if MARTORANO was involved in drug trafficking, with or without the CAMPBELLS and CHANDLER. FLEMMI responded that MARTORANO was a drug user but to the best of his knowledge was never involved in drug dealing.

Ronald Hicks, potential witness against the Campbells and Chandler, murdered by Johnny Martorano in 1968.

On the Lam

FLEMMI, SALEMME fugitive status and POULOS murder

86. FLEMMI stated that one morning in 1969 he was awakened at 7:30 by a telephone call. The male voice on the line did not identify himself, but FLEMMI recognized the speaker as H. Paul RICO. RICO stated to FLEMMI "indictments on the (William BENNETT) murder are coming down, I suggest you and your friend leave town." FLEMMI immediately called SALEMME and the pair agreed to meet in Dedham. FLEMMI then called John MARTORANO and handed the keys to his car to MARTORANO. FLEMMI then left for Dedham, where he met SALEMME, Peter POULOS and Phil WAGGENHEIM. FLEMMI noted that it had been SALEMME's idea to contact POULOS and WAGGENHEIM. Together the group drove to Peoria, IL in WAGGENHEIM's motor vehicle. FLEMMI, POULOS and WAGGENHEIM then boarded an airliner for Los Angeles, while SALEMME flew to New York. FLEMMI said that the West Coast-bound group stayed for a few days in Los Angeles in a home belonging to WAGGENHEIM's friend, ▬▬▬▬▬. SALEMME moved into an apartment belonging to Rhode Island LCN member Billy CANDELMO located on 46th Street

in New York City. FLEMMI and POULOS then took separate apartments in Los Angeles for several weeks, while WAGGENHEIM returned home to Boston. FLEMMI added that WAGGENHEIM remained the conduit for communications between the fugitives and Jerry ANGIULO and the LCN.

87. FLEMMI stated that even before going on the lam, SALEMME had been concerned that POULOS might fold under pressure if questioned about the BENNETT murders. After arriving in California, FLEMMI also became concerned that POULOS' will was weakening. FLEMMI often had to search for POULOS, who would miss scheduled meetings. FLEMMI stated that WAGGENHEIM eventually returned to Los Angeles with a .38 caliber snub-nose handgun. WAGGENHEIM told FLEMMI that SALEMME had communicated his concerns about POULOS to Jerry ANGIULO. WAGGENHEIM indicated that he had returned to the West Coast in order to assist FLEMMI in eliminating POULOS. FLEMMI then concocted a story that he and POULOS needed to travel to Las Vegas in order to meet WAGGENHEIM. FLEMMI tried to cover up the pair's approximate two-month stay in Los Angeles by thoroughly cleaning both of their apartments in an attempt to remove the pair's fingerprints. FLEMMI then convinced a reluctant POULOS to get into a car that he had purchased under an assumed name in order to drive together out to Las Vegas.

88. FLEMMI stated that while driving out to Las Vegas, he and POULOS were stopped by the California Highway Patrol because their vehicle had only a paper license plate. After checking the paper work on the car, the officer allowed the vehicle to proceed. FLEMMI noted that during the trip he turned off the highway onto a smaller roadway, which caused an already-leery POULOS to question the move. Approximately 25 miles from Las Vegas, FLEMMI announced to POULOS that he was tired. FLEMMI then asked POULOS to drive the remainder of the trip and pulled the car over to the side of the roadway to switch positions. FLEMMI got out of the car and shot POULOS in the chest as POULOS approached the driver's side of the vehicle. FLEMMI said that after being shot POULOS immediately fell to the ground. FLEMMI then fired one or two additional rounds into

the back of the victim's head to insure that POULOS was dead. FLEMMI added that he tried to bury POULOS but found that the ground was so hard-packed that it was impossible. FLEMMI then simply covered the body up with brush and left the area. FLEMMI noted that the badly decomposed body was found intact a few days to a week later. FLEMMI had removed all identification from the body along with $300 in cash, but somehow missed a receipt from POULOS' Los Angeles apartment while searching POU-LOS' body. FLEMMI was aware that POULOS' body was later identified by dental records, a lesson he took to heart in a number of later homicides, always extracting his victims' teeth whenever possible before burying their bodies. FLEMMI discarded the handgun approximately 20 miles from the murder scene.

89. FLEMMI stated that after murdering POULOS, he drove for the next six days to New York City in an effort to see SALEMME. FLEMMI told SALEMME the story of how POULOS had been eliminated. SALEMME

Jackie Salemme, Frankie's
younger brother.

Marion Hussey, longtime Stevie
Flemmi girlfriend and mother of three
of his children, as well as Debra Hussey,
murdered by Whitey Bulger in 1985.

indicated his pleasure but questioned FLEMMI why the body hadn't been buried. FLEMMI gave Joe RUSSO the car that had been purchased out in California and it was demolished at a Brooklyn junk yard. FLEMMI stayed in SALEMME's apartment for approximately two weeks and then got his own place across from the Improv Comedy Club at 46th Street and 9th Avenue. FLEMMI noted that SALEMME worked at a watch shop, next to FLEMMI's apartment. FLEMMI reported that he had approximately $5,000 saved up when he left Boston, and that Jackie SALEMME would regularly travel to New York and pay him some $800 a month. FLEMMI noted that this money came directly from Jerry ANGIULO and was from FLEMMI's share of the numbers business ANGIULO took over when the Roxbury group became fugitives. FLEMMI said that Danny ANGIULO actually conducted the day-to-day operations of the business with the assistance of Earl SMITH. FLEMMI further added that in spite of this regular income he received, Marion HUSSEY and his children had to go on welfare for several years. FLEMMI also added that Jackie SALEMME controlled the Roxbury shylock business for the group, but he did not receive any money from this.

90. FLEMMI stated that by the fall of 1971, he and SALEMME were not getting along. FLEMMI said that he objected to SALEMME's condescending attitude towards him and complained to Jerry ANGIULO about the behavior during several telephone conversations. FLEMMI was also concerned that SALEMME was "too flashy" and drew attention to himself. FLEMMI said that after his girlfriend ███████ arrived in New York, he decided to get away from SALEMME. FLEMMI and ███████ traveled to Florida for a few weeks and then the couple drove to Montreal. FLEMMI noted that he did not contact H. Paul RICO in Florida while visiting there. FLEMMI stated that while in New York, he did meet Marion HUSSEY and the couple's children out in Montauk on Long Island on at least one occasion. FLEMMI initially did not recall Boston Police Detective Bill STUART visiting him when HUSSEY and the children were around but later remembered seeing the Boston detective there at Montauk.

Angiulo brothers at the grand jury; Jerry is second from right.

91. FLEMMI stated that he was still in New York with SALEMME, when he received the unfortunate news that Boston organized-crime figure Billy O'SULLIVAN was murdered near his Dorchester home (03/28/71). FLEMMI noted that O'SULLIVAN had been known by just about everyone involved in the rackets, but had aligned himself during the Boston gang war with the Roxbury group. It was FLEMMI's understanding that O'SULLIVAN was killed by Tommy KING from South Boston. FLEMMI also said that at some point while they were fugitives, SALEMME traveled to a Greek community in West Virginia, in an attempt to find and kill ▆▆▆▆▆▆ who had become a witness in the cases against the pair. SALEMME returned to New York after a flood or some other type of natural disaster struck the town, which prevented ▆▆▆▆▆▆ from being located.

92. FLEMMI said that after arriving in Montreal, he sent ▆▆▆▆▆ home to Boston. FLEMMI said that he took a furnished apartment in the Mount Royal section of the city and attended photography school. FLEMMI then accepted a job up in North Bay taking publicity photos for Skidoo. After the Skidoo job was over, FLEMMI found work at the Montreal Gazette,

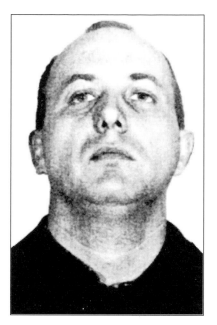

Billy O'Sullivan, murdered 1971, a month after he shot Mullen boss Buddy Roache, paralyzing him.

Tommy King, murderer of O'Sullivan, slain by Johnny Martorano in 1975.

operating the four color offset printing machine on the night shift. FLEMMI added that this night job paid well, between $300 and $400 a week. At the newspaper, FLEMMI used the alias of Robert Leombruno, which he had obtained with supporting identification from a female party named FNU (first name unknown) Hamilton before going "on the lam." FLEMMI further stated that he obtained a driver's license under the Leombruno name and got Canadian land and immigrant status. FLEMMI noted that he accidentally bumped into Jimmy SIMS in Windsor Park while a fugitive. FLEMMI also recalled being struck by a car while riding a motorcycle in Montreal. FLEMMI was injured but was treated at a hospital and released.

KILLEEN/MULLENS Gang War in South Boston

93. FLEMMI stated that while "on the lam" in New York and Canada, and later upon his return, he was filled in on the goings-on in the Boston underworld. Among the events that FLEMMI learned about was the South

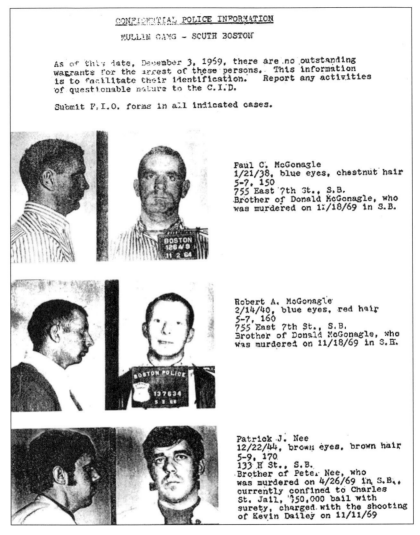

1969 BPD wanted poster for the "Mullin" (sic) gang of South Boston.

Boston gang war, between the Mullens and the older faction controlled by the KILLEEN brothers, led by Donald KILLEEN. This was the same war which had taken the life of O'SULLIVAN. FLEMMI later learned from Whitey BULGER, that prior to O'SULLIVAN's death, O'SULLIVAN had shot and paralyzed the Mullens' leader, Buddy ROACHE during a meeting at the tavern owned by Bobby FORD. (ROACHE was the brother of future

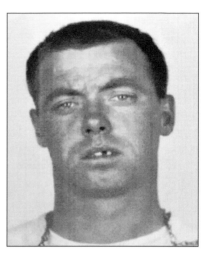

Donald Killeen ran the Lower End crew Whitey joined after getting out of prison in 1965.

Bobby Ford—Buddy Roache was shot in his West Broadway barroom.

Boston Police Commissioner Francis "Mickey" ROACHE.) FLEMMI also learned from BULGER that Donald KILLEEN was killed at his Framingham home by ▮▮▮▮▮▮, Tommy KING, Paul MCGONAGLE, and Jimmy "the Weasel" MANTVILLE (05/13/72). FLEMMI does not believe that BULGER had any involvement in his KILLEEN's murder. (In fact, KILLEEN was murdered after BULGER met secretly with the Mullens in a meeting he asked John MARTORANO to set up through Howie WINTER.) FLEMMI did note that KILLEEN's widow sold the Transit Cafe to BULGER associate Kevin O'NEIL a short time after her husband's death, and that the sale occurred only after a conversation with BULGER. The café was subsequently renamed Triple O's, and BULGER later murdered at least one person there.

94. FLEMMI stated that BULGER also told him that he had mistakenly shot and killed Donald MCGONAGLE (11/18/69). BULGER said that he shot MCGONAGLE between the eyes after pulling up in a vehicle one evening across from the victim's car. BULGER told FLEMMI that O'SULLIVAN was in his vehicle at the time of the shooting. BULGER said that he had been trying to locate the victim's brother, Mullens gang member Paul MCGONAGLE.

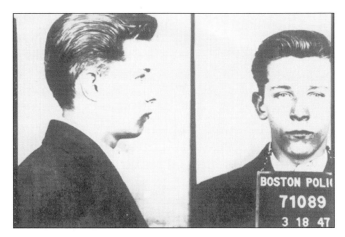

Whitey Bulger at 17.

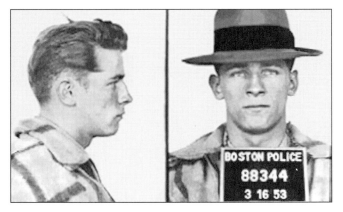

Whitey Bulger at 23, shortly after his discharge from the Air Force.

It wasn't until later that BULGER learned that he had killed the noncombatant Donald MCGONAGLE. FLEMMI noted that according to BULGER, he soon began dating MCGONAGLE's widow Catherine GREIG shortly after the murder. (NOTE: Catherine GREIG was actually married to Robert MCGONAGLE, the younger brother of Paul and Donald.)

95. FLEMMI stated that after Donald KILLEEN's murder (circa 5/13/72), Howie WINTER and John MARTORANO negotiated a peaceful merger of the remaining members of the two South Boston gangs. FLEMMI learned

Catherine Greig, future Whitey Bulger girlfriend, in the 1970's with her then-husband Robert McGonagle, both of whose brothers were murdered by Whitey.

that WINTER had been friendly with most or all of the warring parties and convinced them a merger would mutually benefit all, particularly financially. FLEMMI stated that he was unsure why BULGER became the head of this combined gang, but speculated that BULGER emerged as the leader because of his management abilities. FLEMMI said that BULGER also became a major figure within the Winter Hill gang, along with WINTER, SIMS, MCDONALD, and John MARTORANO. They were the original five partners of the Winter Hill Gang. FLEMMI said that BULGER got a one-third share of Winter Hill's profits because he had to split it with the rest of the reconstituted South Boston gang.

The end of the 1960's gang wars

96. FLEMMI stated that when the South Boston gang members were added to Winter Hill, this formidable outfit began reaching out and extorting more Boston-area bookmakers. FLEMMI said that the Winter Hill gang was also involved in other violent crimes and were, according to either ███████ or

John Robichaud, prison escapee,   David Glennon, missing 1971. Foul play
murdered by Winter Hill in 1972.   suspected. Only suspect: Winter Hill.

John MARTORANO, responsible for the death of prison escapee and murderer John ROBICHAUD (05/22/72). FLEMMI recalled that ROBICHAUD had been paid by "Wimpy" BENNETT to kill George ROONEY back in the late 1950's. ROONEY was shot in the head by ROBICHAUD but didn't die from the wound. FLEMMI also speculated that Winter Hill was responsible for the murders of Tommy BALLOU (02/11/70) and David GLENNON's disappearance (01/11/71). FLEMMI has no specific information on these murders but believed that Winter Hill had the most to gain by the deaths of these individuals.

NOTARANGELI Gang War murders 1972-74

97. FLEMMI stated that he was aware that the Winter Hill gang was involved in the murder of several individuals during a one-sided war with the smaller NOTARANGELI faction. FLEMMI said that he learned about

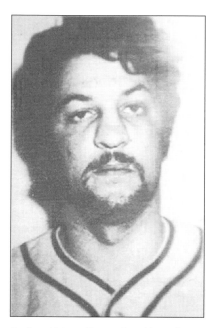

Indian Al Angeli, murdered by Johnny Martorano in 1974.

Tommy Callahan—Stevie bought his machine gun when he retired from the rackets.

the elimination of NOTARANGELI gang primarily after his return from Canada, from ▆▆▆▆▆▆ and John MARTORANO, as well as during infrequent contact while "on the lam." FLEMMI learned that the violence began when Al ANGELI, an aspiring hoodlum from the Somerville-Medford area, killed one of Jerry ANGIULO's bookmakers, Paulie FOLINO (08/24/72). ANGIULO then asked the Winter Hill gang to assist the LCN in avenging FOLINO's death. FLEMMI said that John MARTORANO contacted him through George KAUFMAN and asked about obtaining a machine gun he had prior to becoming a fugitive. FLEMMI stated that he had originally obtained the machine gun from Tommy CALLAHAN, and had passed it on to Bobby LABELLA during the gang war of the 1960's. FLEMMI contacted LABELLA and okayed the release of the machine gun to MARTORANO.

98. FLEMMI stated that John MARTORANO then used the machine gun in several shootings, (Michael MILANO murder 03/08/73 and Al

PLUMMER murder 03/18/73). In the MILANO murder, a motor vehicle was hit on Sparhawk Street in Brighton with machine gun fire and several innocent people were wounded, one fatally. (The bullet holes are still visible in a stone wall on the corner of Sparhawk and Market Streets.) FLEMMI said that the Winter Hill group, in the persons of ████████, BULGER and John MARTORANO, killed William O'BRIEN (03/23/73) in his car on Morrissey Boulevard in Dorchester. (O'BRIEN was a stevedore who had served several years in prison for killing George O'BRIEN in a South Boston barroom in a chance meeting. William O'Brien was driving north to pick up his daughter in South Boston for her 10th birthday, and was accompanied by NOTARANGELI associate Ralph DEMASI, who was wounded.) FLEMMI's understanding was that O'BRIEN was more of a target of opportunity. FLEMMI believed that BULGER had told him that O'BRIEN had been an informant for some law-enforcement official and that this was at least part of the reason O'BRIEN was killed. BULGER also told FLEMMI that Joe MCDONALD and Jimmy SIMS had traveled to Fort Lauderdale, FL and murdered NOTARANGELI associate James LEARY (04/03/73).

99. LEARY had been a protégé of MCDONALD's prior to the war. FLEMMI said that LEARY was chased around a trailer by MCDONALD before being shot to death. FLEMMI was told by MARTORANO that WINTER had arranged for Joe NOTARANGELI (Al ANGELI's brother) to call him about making peace. The gang was given the number of a pay phone where ANGELI could be reached. MARTORANO traced the number to the Pewter Pot restaurant in Medford Square. Accompanied by MCDONALD, who drove the get-away car, MARTORANO then went to the restaurant and shot NOTARANGELI at a pay phone near the entrance (04/18/73).

Indian Joe Notarangeli, Al's brother, murdered by Johnny Martorano in 1973.

FLEMMI STATED that he had some involvement in the Jimmy O'TOOLE murder. FLEMMI learned that one day O'TOOLE had strolled into the Somerville gang's garage and asked if peace was possible between himself and Winter Hill. WINTER was upset that O'TOOLE had brazenly walked into the garage without notice and could have easily killed him. After the peace offer from O'TOOLE was made, MARTORANO telephoned FLEMMI about FLEMMI's feelings on the matter. FLEMMI told MAR-TORANO not to trust O'TOOLE, but to kill him instead. FLEMMI added that O'TOOLE couldn't be trusted and that while drinking had even shot his good friend, John FLANNERY, with a .45 caliber handgun. FLEMMI said that Winter Hill decided to take his advice and tracked O'TOOLE down with some help from Eddie CONNORS, the owner of the Bulldogs bar in Dorchester. FLEMMI added that MCDONALD, MARTORANO, ███████ and BULGER caught up with O'TOOLE one night as O'TOOLE was leaving Bulldogs Tavern on Savin Hill Avenue. BULGER told FLEMMI that MARTORANO and ███████ opened up on O'TOOLE with a machine gun. O'TOOLE tried to duck behind a mail box, but was killed after the shooters' car made a U-turn, and MCDONALD jumped out of the vehicle and fired at the victim from close range (12/01/73). FLEMMI also had

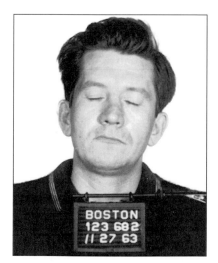

Spike O'Toole, wanted peace with Winter Hill, was shot to death by Joe McDonald in Dorchester in 1973.

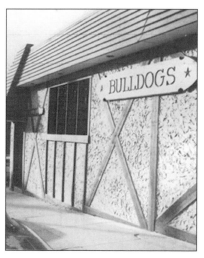

Bulldogs, where Spike had his final drinks, owned by Eddie Connors.

some memory that someone in the shooters' car had been unarmed during the assault. (Back at the garage on Marshall Street in Somerville, BULGER, the driver, berated himself for not carrying a weapon on the hit, and said he would never make that mistake again.)

100. FLEMMI stated that this war ended when Al ANGELI, the leader of the opposing faction, returned to the Boston area after hiding out on the West Coast with his family for more than a year. ANGELI came back in an attempt to make peace with ANGI-ULO. ANGIULO, WINTER and John MARTORANO met before the arrival of ANGELI, where the victim's fate was sealed. FLEMMI said that ANGELI had bought a new suit for the meeting and was carrying a Bible, but was shot in the head immediately after entering a car occupied by ███████ and MAR-

Charlie Raso, Medford bookie, worked for Winter Hill after demise of the Angeli gang.

TORANO (02/21/74). FLEMMI said that John MARTORANO was the actual individual who shot ANGELI. FLEMMI added that BULGER told him that as a result of the assistance the Winter Hill gang gave to ANGIULO, the members were paid some $50,000 in "expenses." FLEMMI noted that ANGELI had the $50,000 on his person when he was killed and this money was to be paid to ANGIULO by the victim. (Actually he had paid the money earlier to ANGIULO at a restaurant in the North End, with WINTER and MARTORANO sitting at the next table.) The Winter Hill gang also took over control of bookmaker Charlie RASO as a result of its elimination of the NOTARANGELIs. RASO subsequently became a very significant "earner" for Winter Hill.

4

Back in Boston

FLEMMI's return from "the lam," and the state of the Winter Hill Gang (05/06/74)

101. FLEMMI stated that he had nothing to do with SALEMME's arrest in New York (12/14/72). FLEMMI said that SALEMME had been living in an apartment in an upscale area on Park Avenue when the pair split up. FLEMMI speculated that Rhode Island LCN member Louis "Baby Shanks" MANOCCHIO had been the individual who gave up the information that led to SALEMME's arrest. MANOCCHIO had been staying with SALEMME at his New York apartment and is ██████ . FLEMMI recalled that in the early 1990's,

Rhode Island Mafia boss Louis "Baby Shanks" Manocchio.

MANOCCHIO would often tell SA-
LEMME that FLEMMI "was no good,"
and to stay away from him. FLEMMI
assumed MANOCCHIO had been
told by his ███████ that he was an
informant. FLEMMI asked his FBI
handler John CONNOLLY about his
arrest of SALEMME, and was told that
it was the result of an accidental meeting as reported in newspaper accounts
of the event. FLEMMI also added that
in around 1990 or 1991, he directly
asked CONNOLLY about ███████.
After speaking with FBI agent Nick

Disgraced ex-FBI agent John
"Zip" Connolly on his way to his
racketeering trial.

"Doc" GIANTURCO about the matter, CONNOLLY advised FLEMMI
to "stay away from MANOCCHIO." FLEMMI knew that this was a signal
from CONNOLLY that MANOCCHICO was ███████.

102. FLEMMI stated that soon after becoming a fugitive he made contact
with RICO. FLEMMI recalled one early conversation when he asked RICO
if anything was going on with the pending cases against him. RICO responded that "this will take some time to work out." FLEMMI added that at
least once a year he would leave a message for RICO at his Boston FBI office
and later in Miami. FLEMMI believes that on one occasion he may
have asked for Dennis CONDON, but never spoke directly with him.
FLEMMI added that he used the code phrase "Jack from South Boston called"
when attempting to contact RICO. FLEMMI stated that RICO didn't leave
return messages until April or May of 1974. FLEMMI added that during
this time period Howie WINTER and John MARTORANO were trying to
persuade Bob DADDIECO not to testify against him by giving DADDIECO
a truck and money. RICO, who was now stationed in Miami, told FLEMMI it
was now the time to return to Boston. FLEMMI said that RICO made a veiled
threat requiring his immediate compliance, saying, "I might not be here to
help you." FLEMMI also believed that RICO may also have had something
to do with DADDIECO recanting his testimony in the Fitzgerald bombing

case. FLEMMI speculated that RICO had to have assisted Winter Hill in the matter, because WINTER and MARTORANO would have had limited ability to successfully contact DADDIECO without some type of help.

103. FLEMMI stated that he did not really want to leave Montreal but decided that it was in his best interest to come home. WINTER and MAR-TORANO advised FLEMMI that Boston Police Detective Tom MITCH-ELL, a friend of RICO and Winter Hill, would take him into custody. FLEMMI contacted Attorney Bob Dinsmore and negotiated his surrender at Park Square in Boston. FLEMMI added that he made bail after spending four days in jail. FLEMMI immediately rejoined the Winter Hill gang and observed that the group was now heavily involved in sports betting, along with the other forms of gambling, shylocking and extortions. FLEMMI said that the gang controlled betting in the Lowell area through Charlie RASO (actually, through Jackie MCDERMOTT, another former Notarangeli bookie) and also had gaming offices with Tommy RYAN, Neddy RAIS,

Stevie Flemmi returns to Boston, 1974.

Lowell bookie Jackie McDermott, murdered by Billy Barnoski in 1988.

Nicky MONTALTO, Dick O'BRIEN, Bobby GALLINARO and some other South Shore bookmakers.

104. FLEMMI stated that these Winter Hill-controlled bookmakers either laid off bets to the gang or split a percentage of their business with the group. FLEMMI noted that according to MARTORANO, who controlled the gang's gambling activities, at the height of Winter Hill's gaming from 1975-1977, the group did approximately $2,000,000 of business a year. FLEMMI noted that due to MARTORANO's erratic betting of the gang's gambling profits, the members didn't always benefit from their labors. As the gang's new, sixth

Frankie "the Cat" Angiulo.

partner, FLEMMI was given a one-sixth share of all the gang's jointly produced proceeds, while also retaining for himself all of his own outside interests. FLEMMI added that to maintain Winter Hill's gaming operation, they often had to borrow money from Jerry ANGIULO, at one percent interest per week. The gang's debt to ANGIULO eventually rose to $250,000. FLEMMI said that Jimmy SIMS would then drop off Winter Hill's weekly one-percent payment of $2,500 to Frankie "the Cat" ANGIULO.

105. FLEMMI stated that the LCN tried to win him back from Winter Hill in early 1975, after the bombing and murder cases had been dismissed. FLEMMI recalled that Jerry ANGIULO gave him $50,000 to use as capital to rebuild his shylock business. FLEMMI also collected some of the old outstanding loans from his pre-fugitive days. WINTER asked FLEMMI to return the seed money to ANGIULO, and to take the same amount from Joe MCDONALD. FLEMMI agreed and was charged the usual one point a week for the MCDONALD monies. The shylock business quickly grew to the point where FLEMMI had approximately $100,000 out on the street. FLEMMI noted that ANGIULO was concerned about the Winter Hill gang's growing "strength," and often asked FLEMMI about the group's status. FLEMMI said he would give ANGIULO erroneous information about the gang. FLEMMI added that he also took back from ANGIULO his old South End/Roxbury/Dorchester numbers business with its 20-30 agents. FLEMMI also recalled attempting to take over the gaming organization run in Dorchester by ████████ and his ████████ sons. FLEMMI believed that this move on ████████ operation was dropped due to ████████ supportive relationship with Winter Hill during the 1960's gang war. FLEMMI noted that prior to the endeavor being dropped, ████████ son had actually pulled a gun on some Winter Hill members but no retaliation resulted from the incident.

106. FLEMMI stated that he, Jimmy MARTORANO and George KAUFMAN also opened Motorama Sales at WINTER's old garage on Marshall Street in Somerville. WINTER moved the old tenants of the garage into a larger building next door, and FLEMMI and his partners moved

in. FLEMMI said that the garage conducted a mixture of legal and illegal
businesses. KAUFMAN had corrupted
several insurance adjusters, who in-
flated claims and split the profits with
him. Cars were also often "stolen" with
the knowledge of the owners, for a share
of the insurance money. Additionally
the business would buy and fix for re-
sale wrecked cars using both legitimate
and stolen car parts. FLEMMI noted
that the garage was also used to store
and create "boilers" or untraceable stolen cars to be used in murders or other
serious violent crime. FLEMMI added
that Winter Hill maintained garages in
the Somerville area where these "boilers" were usually warehoused.

Jimmy Martorano, when he owned
Chandler's.

107. FLEMMI stated that each member of the Winter Hill gang had his
own side businesses that they did not
share with the others in the group.
John MARTORANO had a large
group of "boosters" who shoplifted expensive items, which MARTORANO
then sold at reduced rates. BULGER,
who had taken a low profile at first
with the Winter Hill gang, controlled
South Boston gaming and shylock activities. BULGER also had some business in Dorchester through BULGER's
underling ███████. BULGER's crew
included ███████, who ran the shylock business, Pat NEE the "muscle",

Jack Curran, one of Whitey's
Southie associates.

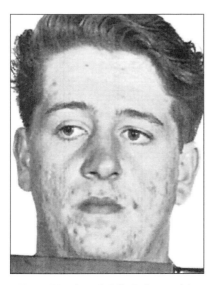 

| Kevin O'Neil, with Billy Bulger as his lawyer, beat a murder rap in 1968, later handled money for Whitey Bulger as weight ballooned to 400 pounds. | Whitey Bulger, his hair dyed black, under arrest in Revere for bank robbery in 1956. |

and Kevin O'NEIL, who was the business front, similar to George KAUFMAN's role with Winter Hill. FLEMMI noted that BULGER had dozens of other fringe personnel. FLEMMI does not recall BULGER participating in any bank robberies during the 1970's, but was aware that BULGER still had some of the money he had stolen during the 1950's bank holdups. BULGER claimed to have robbed some 17 banks and financial institutions during the 1950's. FLEMMI noted that BULGER maintained a tight control over all of South Boston, and spent a great deal of time gathering intelligence there.

108. FLEMMI stated that when he first arrived back in the Boston area, the Winter Hill gang threw a large party for him at the group's restaurant, CHANDLER's, located on Columbus Avenue in the South End of Boston. FLEMMI noticed that there were a large number of media people invited to the party along with organized-crime "wannabees" like John CALLAHAN and ██████. FLEMMI also later bumped into Dennis

1973 party at Chandler's. Back row, from left: Jimmy Martorano and Howie Winter, kissing actor "Alex Rocco," former Winter Hill associate then known as Bobo Petricone, and two unidentified men connected with the movie being shot, "The Friends of Eddie Coyle." Front row: Robert Mitchum, the star of "Eddie Coyle," and his driver, Winter Hill associate Fat Harry Johnson.

CONDON, who told FLEMMI that he had removed the federal fugitive warrants for his arrest on the BENNETT murder and the FITZGERALD bombing. FLEMMI said that he saw CONDON again in late 1974 or early 1975 at a meeting with John CONNOLLY which had been arranged by BULGER.

James SOUSA murder (10/06/74)

109. FLEMMI stated that the gold scam involving Jimmy SOUSA, Tony CIULLA and Billy BARNOSKI was already in progress by the time he arrived back in the Boston area after his

Bobo Petricone in less happy days, under arrest in 1961. He left Boston for Hollywood soon after.

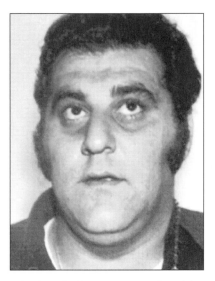

Fat Tony Ciulla, master race-fixer, his testimony brought down the original Winter Hill Gang.

Billy Barnoski, Ciulla's muscle, now serving a life sentence for murder.

years as a fugitive. FLEMMI said that he did not take part in any aspect of the scam, and did not bring back any gold from New York. FLEMMI said that after the gold scam imploded and threatened some senior gang members, SOUSA became a liability. (He had been arrested after a dentist the gang was trying to rip off by selling him fake gold bars suddenly pulled a gun in the supermarket parking lot across the street from the Winter Hill garage. CIULLA had then grabbed the dentist's young son—technically, a kidnapping. Joe MCDONALD, one of the gang's senior partners who was working as a backup gun, was now in danger of being arrested.) FLEMMI added that BARNOSKI and CIULLA were not eliminated because they were integral parts of the race-fixing scam that was continuing at the same time. FLEMMI recalled that he, ███████ , John MARTORANO, and BULGER met and decided that SOUSA had to be killed. FLEMMI remembered that Joe MCDONALD and Jimmy SIMS were fugitives at the time and were living in an apartment in Medford. On the morning of the murder, the garage was closed down and the help was sent away for a few hours. Thinking he was about to receive some money for legal fees, SOUSA had come to the garage and then been brought into the second interior office in the garage, where he was sitting with BARNOSKI and John MARTORANO. FLEMMI said that he was outside the office, and that ███████ was also in the garage, and had turned on the engine of a caterpillar bulldozer in order to muffle the planned gunfire. FLEMMI heard the shots and MARTORANO came out and asked for something to help catch the blood from SOUSA's head wound. FLEMMI stated that he picked up a paint can, walked into the office and caught the blood gushing from SOUSA's temple.

110. FLEMMI stated that Leo MC-DONALD went over to Lechmere Sales in East Cambridge and purchased a sleeping bag to put the body inside. FLEMMI and BARNOSKI tied SOUSA's body up with a rope, and then placed it in the sleeping bag. The body was then put into the trunk of a car that had been backed inside the garage and then driven to the apartment of SIMS and Joe MCDONALD in Medford. FLEMMI said that BULGER had come to the garage shortly after the murder and traveled out to the Medford apartment where the body had been taken. FLEMMI recalled that the LABELLA machine gun used during the NOTA-

Leo McDonald, Joe's brother, ran errands like buying sleeping bags in which to put bodies.

RANGELI war was at the Medford apartment, and that BULGER had commented on how foolish it was to have it hidden there. FLEMMI noted that the machine gun was disposed of a short time later. FLEMMI said that in the afternoon, MCDONALD and SIMS left the apartment with ███████ and pre-dug a grave in the Boxford, MA area. After ███████ return, ███████ and FLEMMI then drove the body up I-95 to a secondary road which had woods on both sides. FLEMMI speculated that the wooded area where the body was placed may have been a state park or a conservation area. The grave site was approximately 40 feet from the roadway, and SIMS and MCDONALD took the body out of the trunk and dragged it out to the hole, which was slightly uphill. FLEMMI estimated that the grave was four to five feet deep. FLEMMI and ███████ never got out of the car and left almost immediately. WINTER later returned to the burial spot and picked up the others. FLEMMI recalled that BARNOSKI, ███████ and John MARTORANO spread a rumor that SOUSA had left town and gone "on the lam."

Return to informant status (1974-1975)

111. FLEMMI stated that when he re-turned from "the lam," he observed that Jimmy BULGER had already estab-lished himself within the Winter Hill hi-erarchy. FLEMMI noted that BULGER had maintained a low profile until he was off parole. FLEMMI recalled that he had met BULGER once or twice in the 1960's, at his after-hours club on Dudley Street in Roxbury. FLEMMI's next encounter with BULGER was not until 1974, when he returned to Boston from "the lam." FLEMMI said that he and BULGER became friendly when Winter Hill began extorting indepen-dent bookmakers who took sports

In the 1970's, this was one of the few surveillance photos of Whitey Bulger.

and horse wagers. FLEMMI remembered one incident when the group ap-proached Bernie WEISMAN, and BULGER threatened WEISMAN with an axe. FLEMMI noted that WEISMAN collapsed a short time later.

112. FLEMMI stated that BULGER told him and the other Winter Hill partners that he was planning on meeting with S/A John CONNOLLY and was basically asking the gang's permission to do so. It was Winter Hill's un-derstanding that the relationship between BULGER and CONNOLLY was going to be strictly corrupt, and that no information was to be given to aid law-enforcement. FLEMMI said that the Winter Hill gang was comfortable

Senate President Billy Bulger at the St. Patrick's Day breakfast in 1996 with then-Sen. John F. Kerry and his wife Teresa Heinz Kerry.

that BULGER had CONNOLLY under control, and would not compromise the group. BULGER was soon referring to CONNOLLY by such derogatory nicknames as "Zip" and "Elvis." Sometime later BULGER confessed to FLEMMI that S/A CONNOLLY had met him "out of the blue" at Wollaston Beach in Quincy and approached him. CONNOLLY told BULGER that Jerry ANGIULO was giving information to the Boston Police which would eventually return him to prison. CONNOLLY wanted BULGER to give information to the FBI about the LCN in Boston. FLEMMI suspected that CONNOLLY had told BULGER that he too had been an informant for the FBI in the past. FLEMMI surmised that this knowledge regarding his informant status was the only reason why BULGER would have informed him of the FBI's request for information on the LCN. FLEMMI felt that CONNOLLY's compromising of his former informant status placed him in a very awkward position, and forced FLEMMI into cooperating again. FLEMMI added that he later heard from BULGER that he eventually agreed to cooperate with the FBI, but didn't want his brother Billy, who would soon become president of the MA State Senate, to know about his older brother's informant status.

113. FLEMMI stated that BULGER arranged a meeting for FLEMMI with S/A's John CONNOLLY and Dennis CONDON at an "obscure" Newton coffee shop. FLEMMI said that this meeting took place within one year from when he returned from Montreal, and that BULGER was not present for this meeting. FLEMMI said that after

Zip Connolly, already serving federal time, appears in a Florida court after being indicted for the 1982 murder of John Callahan.

introductions were made, the group primarily made small talk regarding H. Paul RICO. In later conversations with CONNOLLY and BULGER, it was acknowledged to FLEMMI that he had access to Larry BAIONE and Jerry ANGIULO, which BULGER did not have. BULGER advised FLEMMI that the FBI needed his contacts within the Boston LCN in order to successfully prosecute them. FLEMMI noted that CONDON's contact with him ended at this point, with the exception of one situation involving Alvin CAMPBELL. FLEMMI recalled that CAMPBELL's wife and/or baby were killed in a car accident after visiting CAMPBELL in prison. CAMPBELL then threatened the life of a federal court judge who had sentenced him to prison. FLEMMI thought that the judge involved was either David Mazzone or Andrew Caffery. CONDON then visited the Marshall Street garage looking for FLEMMI so that CAMPBELL could be warned not to follow through on the threats. FLEMMI passed the message on to CAMPBELL through MARTORANO, and the judge remained safe.

114. FLEMMI stated that he eventually agreed to become an informant again, with S/A CONNOLLY as the handler. FLEMMI as well as BULGER decided that supplying information to CONNOLLY was necessary to maintain the corrupt relationship and reap its benefits. FLEMMI also noted that to the best of his knowledge, no one in the Winter Hill gang, outside of BULGER, knew that he was also speaking with CONNOLLY. FLEMMI estimated that on average he would meet with S/A CONNOLLY twice a month, but noted that BULGER had much more contact with S/A CONNOLLY, who was both a friend and protégé of BULGER's brother Billy. (In 1968 CONNOLLY had been recommended to J. Edgar HOOVER for appointment to the FBI by then-U.S. House Speaker John McCormack of South Boston, with whom Billy BULGER had long been politically allied. McCormack had also closely monitored Whitey BULGER's treatment when he was incarcerated in federal prisons from 1956-65.)

Molesworth stamp case

115. FLEMMI stated that while he was still a fugitive, Jimmy SIMS and Joe MCDONALD were involved in the theft of a large amount of valuable stamps. FLEMMI was unfamiliar with the background on the case, but was aware that S/A John MORRIS from the Boston FBI office, was the case officer. (S/A Morris would later receive $7,000 in bribes from FLEMMI and BULGER.) FLEMMI stated that there was a Boston-area witness in the case, who had a shop on Bromfield Street. Upon his return to Boston, FLEMMI was asked to assist the Winter Hill group's efforts to kill this witness (Michael Kirzner 12/10/76). FLEMMI recalled that the witness lived in the Gloucester MA area, and the group decided to murder the witness while he was in transit. FLEMMI noted that ███████ and ███████ conducted surveillance on this witness prior to the shooting, and radioed ahead to FLEMMI and BULGER as the potential victim approached. FLEMMI said that BULGER pulled out and began traveling behind the witness' car. FLEMMI added that he and BULGER caught up with the witness' vehicle in the area of Route 1, the Newburyport Turnpike, and Route 128, near Gloucester.

116. FLEMMI stated that he fired one or two shots from an M1 rifle while approximately 20 to 30 feet away from the witness. The shot(s) were fired at

BS 87-15683

BRIEF PERSONAL HISTORY OF JAMES LOUIS SIMS

JAMES LOUIS SIMS, born March 5, 1935 at Boston, Massachusetts is a key member of the organized crime element in the Boston area referred to as the Howard T. Winter gang. This group has control of a large volume of the gambling, loansharking and other criminal activities in many areas of Greater Boston. He has a lengthy criminal record dating back to 1952 with conviction for crimes of violence. He has been a Bureau fugitive in the past for Unlawful Flight to Avoid Prosecution - Carrying an Unlawful Firearm. Subject has no known family ties having never lived with his mother stating he did not know his father and was designated a "state ward". It is reported that he was once married and may have a child, however, this has not been verified to date. Subject lived with a foster mother in Douglas, Massachusetts and graduated from Douglas High School. His Foster mother states she has not seen subject in over 26 years. Subject's only other known relative is a half-brother who claims not to have seen subject since childhood. Although SIMS has listed the employments of laborer, salesman and steeplejack, he has no verified record of employment. It is not believed he has been legitimately employed in the past 15 years. Through his organized crime associates, he has access to almost unlimited funds and contacts throughout the country. During the bloody gang wars in Boston during the late 1960's, SIMS, according to reliable informants, murdered several persons and gained the reputation as an assassin.

FBI history of Jimmy Sims.

BRIEF PERSONAL HISTORY OF JOSEPH MAURICE MC DONALD

JOSEPH MAURICE MC DONALD, born July 14, 1917 at Boston, Massachusetts, is also a key member of the organized crime element in the Boston area referred to as the Howard T. Winter gang. MC DONALD's primary role in this group was that of overseeing gambling and loansharking activities in certain areas of Boston. MC DONALD was the subject of cancelled IO Number 3856 issued October 20, 1964 following his escape from the Massachusetts Correctional Institution at Carver, Massachusetts. MC DONALD was a fugitive for almost three years before being apprehended. MC DONALD has a history of involvement in violent crimes. MC DONALD is separated from his wife and has not lived with her for approximately seven years. Subject has two living brothers, both of whom have criminal records and have been uncooperative in the past. MC DONALD has not been legitimately employed in over 16 years; however, when employed he worked as a truck driver and driver's helper. MC DONALD is known to be an extremely heavy drinker who of recent years goes off on drinking binges days at a time. MC DONALD is prone to violence especially when drunk. Subject through his organized crime associates has access to almost unlimited funds and contacts throughout the country.

FBI history of Joe McDonald.

an angle. FLEMMI noted that a round struck the door handle of the victim's vehicle, and that the bullet fragments from that shot then struck the witness on either side of the witness' back. FLEMMI said that the M1 jammed and he couldn't clear it before the victim's car swerved off the road. The witness was then taken to the hospital and survived his wounds. FLEMMI noted that although the group failed to kill the witness, the shooting was successful in convincing the victim not to cooperate further with the authorities. FLEMMI did not recall any assistance from corrupt law-enforcement in the Winter Hill gang's efforts to kill this particular witness.

117. FLEMMI stated that later in the 1970's, Joe MCDONALD and Jimmy SIMS were successful in their efforts to kill another witness, Raymond Alfred Lundgren (01/13/76), in the same Molesworth Stamp case. FLEMMI recalled that one day ▆▆▆▆▆▆▆ and John MARTORANO brought in a car that they wanted fixed up with new tires, and painted a neutral color. FLEMMI was told that the vehicle had to be "clean," without fingerprints or any other forensic clues, because it was going to be used by SIMS and MCDONALD on a "hit" out on the West Coast. FLEMMI said that MC-DONALD and SIMS traveled out to California and shot the witness on the front lawn of the witness' home in Sierra Madre CA. FLEMMI learned this information from John MARTORANO, who said that MCDONALD, wearing only a handkerchief in front of his face, walked up and shot the witness in front of the victim's wife. SIMS was appalled by MCDONALD's brazen methods during the murder, and announced that he would no longer participate in any more poorly planned crimes with MCDONALD. (According to FBI reports, hours after the Lundgren slaying, before it was reported on the news, the lawyer in San Francisco for one of the other witnesses received an anonymous telephone call from a male who said, "One down, two to go," and then hung up.)

Paul MCGONAGLE murder (11/18/74)

118. FLEMMI stated that BULGER had long thought about killing Paul MCGONAGLE, but that when the actual murder occurred it was basically a spontaneous act. MCGONAGLE had been a member of the old

Another unsolved murder in South Boston in 1973.

Mullens gang and BULGER still considered him a threat, not least because BULGER had murdered his brother by mistake years earlier. FLEMMI said that BULGER asked him to participate in the murder, but was unavailable when the opportune moment came. After MCGONAGLE disappeared, BULGER told FLEMMI that ████████ , ████████ and possibly MCGONA-GLE's friend Tommy KING were involved in the murder. It was FLEMMI's understanding that BULGER and ████████ had a suitcase of counterfeit money that they planned on showing MCGONAGLE. The group then met at the O Street clubhouse and with BULGER toting the suitcase, got into the back seat of a car with MCGONAGLE. BULGER opened the suitcase, took out a gun that was secreted inside and shot MCGONAGLE. ████████ and ████████ then dug a grave at Tenean Beach in South Boston, while BULGER conducted surveillance of the area. The group kept in contact via walkie-talkies. BULGER later pointed out MCGONAGLE's burial site to FLEMMI, which was at the end of the beach, near a chain-link fence.

Edward CONNORS murder (06/12/75)

119. FLEMMI stated that in his opinion the Eddie CONNORS murder occurred because the group was worried that CONNORS might cooper-ate with law-enforcement against them after a recent arrest. FLEMMI

did not recall any discussion about CONNORS bragging about his involvement with Winter Hill in the 1973 murder of Jimmy O'TOOLE. FLEMMI speculated that ▮▮▮▮▮ may have been more concerned that CONNORS could implicate ▮▮▮▮▮▮ in an armored-car robbery. It was not until a later date that FLEMMI learned that CONNORS had assisted the group in its efforts to kill O'TOOLE. FLEMMI also admitted that he had heard some type of rumors that CONNORS had assisted law-enforcement in the past.

Eddie Connors, owner of Bulldogs, murdered by Stevie Flemmi and Whitey Bulger in 1975.

120. FLEMMI stated that someone in the gang asked him to directly participate in the murder. FLEMMI was aware that WINTER was expecting to contact CONNORS at a pay telephone on the evening of the planned murder. FLEMMI added that the group also learned the location of the payphone. The booth was next to a gas station on Morrissey Boulevard in Dorchester. FLEMMI said that he and BULGER went to the scene in a stolen car driven by John MARTORANO, who parked on an adjoining side street, facing Morrissey Boulevard. FLEMMI was armed with a carbine and BULGER had a sawed-off shotgun and a .38 caliber revolver. FLEMMI and BULGER then exited the vehicle, and waited at the corner of the gas station. The pair then observed CONNORS inside the telephone booth with his car parked nearby. FLEMMI and BULGER then stepped out from the building and approached CONNORS. FLEMMI said that BULGER was somewhat closer to the victim, and BULGER opened fire with the shotgun. BULGER emptied both the shotgun and the handgun into CONNORS, and FLEMMI fired approximately seven rounds from the carbine to make sure the victim was dead. FLEMMI said that he shot from the hip and was about 10 to 12 feet away from CONNORS when he opened fire.

121. FLEMMI stated that he and BULGER returned to MARTORANO in the waiting car and drove off. At a nearby traffic light BULGER switched positions with MARTORANO, and drove directly to Somerville. The stolen car was then parked in a six-bay garage that Winter Hill controlled, and the weapons were later disposed of. FLEMMI recalled that he may have worn a hat and glasses during the murder to disguise his appearance. FLEMMI stated that all of the gang's law-enforcement contacts were queried for any information as to the status of the murder investigation. However, the group apparently was not suspected in this rubout.

Thomas KING and Buddy LEONARD murders (11/05/75)

122. FLEMMI stated that Tommy KING and Buddy LEONARD were killed to "settle old scores" they had with BULGER. FLEMMI said that KING was a big physical guy who had been a friend of his brother, Jimmy the Bear FLEMMI. FLEMMI added that BULGER was looking for a reason to kill King, and told the other Winter Hill members that KING had said something inappropriate to a little girl, and that the child's father had taken exception to the remark. KING then threatened the father who came to complain to BULGER. BULGER told the others that KING's conduct made him look bad. After KING allegedly threatened to kill Boston Police Detective Eddie WALSH,

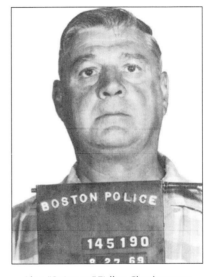

Alan "Suitcase" Fidler, Charlestown gangster and Connors partner, mentioned briefly in Billy Bulger's memoir, *While the Music Lasts*.

FLEMMI, ▮▮▮▮▮ and MARTORANO finally agreed with BULGER that KING had to be eliminated. A plot to murder him was then hatched. KING was told that the gang was going to kill another individual, Alan "Suitcase" FIDLER, a partner of Eddie CONNORS, and that KING's assistance was needed. FLEMMI said that KING met the group at the Columbia Road Nursing Home meeting site in South Boston, wearing a bullet proof vest. KING then got into the front seat of a stolen car driven by BULGER. MARTORANO was seated in the rear of the same car. FLEMMI said that BULGER brought several handguns and walkie-talkies to the meeting spot, and distributed them to everyone sitting in the "ruse hit team's" vehicle. As was planned by BULGER, KING was given a weapon that contained blank rounds.

123. FLEMMI stated that he followed the BULGER-driven "boiler" out of the parking lot, reportedly to make the "ruse hit" on FIDLER. FLEMMI said that MARTORANO shot KING in the head shortly after leaving the meeting spot and before the cars reached Preble Circle in South Boston. FLEMMI added that ███████ and ███████ had already pre-dug a burial spot for KING near Quincy Shore Drive. FLEMMI further stated that right after the murder, while the body was still in the front passenger seat of the car and blood was smeared all through the vehicle's interior, MAR-

TORANO asked BULGER to pull over so he could check on the status of a horse race. (MARTORANO denies this.) After MARTORANO made his telephone call, the two vehicles cara-vanned to Quincy, where the body was dropped off with ███████ and ███████. FLEMMI, ███████, and MARTORANO then left the area. FLEMMI stated that hours later on that same evening, BULGER, ███████ and ███████ killed LEONARD, but that this aspect of the plot was mostly unknown to the remaining Winter Hill members. FLEMMI noted that LEON-ARD was not well liked by most of the Winter Hill gang, and that BULGER had a particular distaste for the victim.

Buddy Leonard, smalltime Southie criminal, murdered by Whitey in 1975.

Buddy Leonard under arrest. Note the cigarette in his left hand.

Patsy FABIANO murder (03/30/76)

124. FLEMMI stated that after Joe BARBOZA was murdered in San Francisco (02/11/76) by J.R. RUSSO, he was told by Jackie SALEMME that the LCN had been responsible for the slaying. FLEMMI recalled that FABIANO had been in hiding for a long time after his old underworld boss BARBOZA had cooperated in a series of cases against the LCN in the late 1960's. With BARBOZA dead, FLEMMI knew that it was just a matter of time before the LCN would tie up other loose ends and kill FABIANO. FLEMMI stated

Patsy Fabiano, Barboza associate, murdered by Mafia in North End in 1976.

that one day FABIANO walked into the Marshall Street garage to socialize. As part of the conversation, FLEMMI asked FABIANO what type of
activities he was involved in. FABIANO responded that he was currently
"running with" LCN associate ██████. FABIANO further added that he
was meeting ██████ for dinner and that he had to pick up linguine for
the meal. FLEMMI stated that he immediately knew that the LCN was setting FABIANO up for execution. FLEMMI added that he did not reveal
to FABIANO his thoughts on the LCN's plans for him. FLEMMI further
stated that a few days later FABIANO's body was found in the backseat of a
car in the North End. Although FLEMMI had no substantive information
on who actually murdered FABIANO, he is sure that the LCN was involved.

125. FLEMMI stated that the Boston LCN were not "hunters" of their potential murder victims, unlike Winter Hill, and would bide their time for
years to deal with a situation. FLEMMI added that the LCN would wait until
their victims were totally helpless or completely surrounded before taking
action. FABIANO's murder would be an example of how the LCN took its
time to settle an old score. FLEMMI cited the murders of Boston hoodlums
Joey NAPOLITIANO and Joey JAMMONI in New York as another example of typical LCN slayings (08/07/78). FLEMMI said that NAPOLITANO
was killed because NAPOLITANO had been bragging to people that he was
connected to the Boston Mafia, and had also been disrespectful to made
member Joe RUSSO. FLEMMI learned from Frank SALEMME that New
York LCN members lured NAPOLITANO and JAMMONI into a garage,
and killed them for the Boston Mafia. JAMMONI was killed solely because
he happened to be with NAPOLITANO.

George HAMILTON murder (04/25/76)

126. FLEMMI stated that George HAMILTON was murdered as a favor by
Bill STUART for ██████. FLEMMI noted that ██████ had some type
of problem with HAMILTON and that ██████ asked STUART to assist
him with the situation. FLEMMI added that ██████ did not ask STUART
to kill HAMILTON, but that this was the solution to the problem that the
former Boston Police detective chose. STUART had assisted the Roxbury

gang on many occasions in the past, and had even attempted to set up Jimmy O'TOOLE to be murdered by the group. FLEMMI noted that STUART planned to have Earl SMITH assist him with the murder. FLEMMI added that SMITH was known to be a law-enforcement informant, who had begun cooperating with the authorities back in the early 1960's after ███████ was arrested for rape while ███████ .

127. FLEMMI stated that STUART was holding some firearms for Frank SALEMME while SALEMME was in state prison for the FITZGERALD bombing. FLEMMI said that in spite of his warnings, he speculated that Frank SALEMME allowed STUART to use one of his stored handguns to kill HAMILTON. FLEMMI stated that STUART admitted to him that he was responsible for HAMILTON's death. STUART told FLEMMI that he shot HAMILTON through the doorway of the victim's house. FLEMMI added that SMITH drove the get-away car. FLEMMI further noted that he advised John CONNOLLY about his knowledge on this murder.

Richard CARIGNAN's murder and disappearance

128. FLEMMI stated he is unsure who killed and then buried the body of convicted bank robber Dick CARIGNAN after his release from prison (11/02/76). FLEMMI and particularly his brother Jimmy the Bear had been friendly with CARIGNAN and his brother Roger during the 1960's. FLEMMI noted that the CARIGNAN brothers often robbed banks together, and that Dick in particular was very dangerous and had murdered several people. FLEMMI also recalled driving CARIGNAN out to Los Angeles while he was a fugitive, and also holding some $65,000 of the bank robber's money. FLEMMI acknowledged that the Bear wanted to steal the money from CARIGNAN, but stated that the money was eventually returned to him.

129. FLEMMI said that after CARIGNAN got out of prison he began "shaking down" well-known local fence George TAYLOR, who owned a jewelry store in Brookline Village. TAYLOR, who was a friend of the

Winter Hill gang, contacted FLEMMI, who along with BULGER and WINTER had a sit-down with CARIGNAN to resolve the problem. CARIGNAN was told to leave TAYLOR alone but initially resisted the order. CARIGNAN's refusal angered WINTER and BULGER but eventually they calmed down and TAYLOR was left alone by CARIGNAN. FLEMMI stated that he never saw CARIGNAN again. FLEMMI believes that someone told him that CARIGNAN had attached himself to some forgotten group, and that this group killed CARIGNAN with a shotgun and buried the body in Dracut. FLEMMI did not recall telling anyone that CARIGNAN had been killed by ██████████ and buried on Joe MURRAY's property in Maine.

Other Winter Hill criminal ventures in the 1970's

130. FLEMMI stated that Winter Hill was involved in several thefts of art and jewelry. FLEMMI recalled that Howie WINTER, Joe MCDONALD and Jimmy SIMS had approximately a half dozen "hot" paintings that had been purchased for $6,000 from the thieves that had stolen the artwork. The paintings were stored in an attic belonging to a brother of MCDONALD. FLEMMI noted that WINTER attempted to locate these paintings after MCDONALD's arrest in the late 1970's. FLEMMI said that MCDONALD and SIMS would not release the stolen paintings, saying that the *objets d'art* couldn't be found. FLEMMI also recalled that the group regularly purchased large amounts of stolen jewelry. The jewelry was usually divided up and sold by the gang members.

Richard CASTUCCI murder (12/29/76)

131. FLEMMI stated that John MARTORANO had been making "layoff" bets with a Colombo family connected bookmaker from New York, named "Jack" LNU (last name unknown). MARTORANO met "Jack" through Richard CASTUCCI. (Castucci was a Revere businessman and high-roller with connections to both LCN and Winter Hill. In the 1960's he had owned the Ebb Tide Lounge on Revere Beach, a well-known organized-crime hangout where many crimes were planned, including the Teddy DEEGAN hit.) MARTORANO traveled to New York on occasion

to "settle up" with "Jack" and on one or two occasions FLEMMI traveled with him. During this time period, Joe MCDONALD and Jimmy SIMS were still fugitives from the stamp case, and MARTORANO wanted to get an apartment for them. MARTORANO also wanted the apartment to socialize in while visiting New York. "Jack" told MARTORANO that he had a friend who had an apartment available near Washington Square in Greenwich Village. MARTORANO took the apartment and planned to move the two fugitives in. At some point BULGER

Richie Castucci, left, at Sammy Davis Jr.'s wedding in Las Vegas in 1960. At right, Rodney Dangerfield.

advised FLEMMI that "the Feds are watching the apartment, because there are two fugitives from Boston staying there." FLEMMI noted that this information had to have come from CONNOLLY. The gang determined that the fugitives had to be warned, and an unknown member, possibly Leo MCDONALD, contacted his brother Joe. Joe MCDONALD was told not to go back to the apartment, and arrangements were made for the two fugitives to meet BULGER and FLEMMI at the New York Port Authority bus terminal.

132. FLEMMI stated that MCDONALD and SIMS wanted to know the source of the information, and he and BULGER felt it was important to impress upon the two fugitives the fact that the intelligence had come from CONNOLLY. BULGER also wanted SIMS and MCDONALD to be careful not to reveal the source of this information to anyone. FLEMMI added that BULGER had insisted on being present when the information was discussed with SIMS and MCDONALD to emphasize the need to protect the source of the information, i.e. CONNOLLY. FLEMMI said that he and BULGER traveled to New York, but that SIMS and MCDONALD never showed up to the meeting to discuss the situation. FLEMMI added that at some later point, BULGER advised CONNOLLY that MCDONALD and SIMS had been warned about not returning to the apartment. BULGER

also learned from CONNOLLY that the information regarding the apartment had come first from a New York source to the New York FBI office, including the fact that two Boston area fugitives were staying there. This information from the New York source was then passed to the Boston FBI office.

133. FLEMMI stated that he had been the gang member who had picked up the apartment key from "Jack", and had advised "Jack" that the residence was going to be used by two guys from Boston. FLEMMI said that the group believed that CASTUCCI was responsible for the leak of the information to the New York source, which was assumed to be "Jack." The group felt that CASTUCCI would have known that both MCDONALD and SIMS were fugitives, and must have passed this on to "Jack." FLEMMI noted that CONNOLLY may have even mentioned CASTUCCI's name to BULGER when the warning about the apartment was

Richie Castucci at age 28.

first given. At a meeting with ▆▆▆▆▆, BULGER, FLEMMI and John MARTORANO, it was decided that CASTUCCI had to be killed for this violation. According to FLEMMI, the driving force behind the decision came from MARTORANO.

134. FLEMMI stated that another important reason why CASTUCCI's murder took place when it did was because of the large amount of money that was owed by the gang to "Jack," through CASTUCCI. FLEMMI said that the decision to kill CASTUCCI came a couple of weeks after MCDONALD and SIMS were warned, and at a time when the group owed "Jack" through CASTUCCI approximately $130,000. FLEMMI added that Winter

Richie Castucci in the trunk of his Cadillac, wrapped in one of Leo McDonald's sleeping bags.

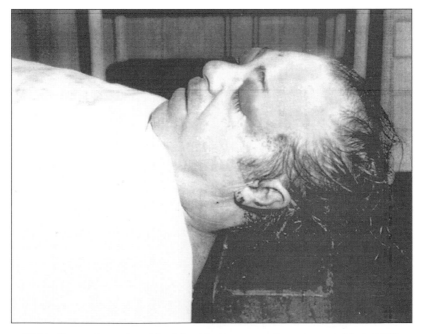

Richie Castucci, murdered by John Martorano, on the autopsy table in 1976.

Hill was also responsible to CASTUCCI for an additional $100,000. On the day of the murder, CASTUCCI was supposed to collect a down payment on the debt from the gang. He arrived at the garage on Marshall Street and parked outside. MARTORANO and BULGER went with CASTUCCI to a nearby apartment on Marshall Street to count the money the gang had delivered to CASTUCCI. FLEMMI remained at the garage, and at some point BULGER came back and said that MARTORANO needed him at the apartment. FLEMMI walked over to the apartment and found CASTUCCI already dead with a bullet wound in the head. It was FLEMMI's understanding that MARTORANO had shot CASTUCCI at he sat at a small table across from BULGER. BULGER flinched when MARTORANO fired the one shot from his .38 caliber revolver. FLEMMI noted that he as well as ▆▆▆▆▆ were well aware that CASTUCCI was going to be murdered that day.

135. FLEMMI stated that Leo MCDONALD was again dispatched to Lechmere to purchase a sleeping bag to hold the body. (When he returned, he told MARTORANO, "You owe me $6.") FLEMMI and BULGER then trussed the body by folding up the legs at the knees and binding the shoulders together as closely as possible. The sleeping bag was then tied up and the body taken out the cellar door of the apartment. The corpse was then placed in the trunk of CASTUCCI's Cadillac and driven by ▆▆▆▆▆ and BULGER out to the parking lot of an apartment complex in Revere. FLEMMI and Leo MCDONALD followed CASTUCCI's car and picked up ▆▆▆▆▆ and BULGER after CASTUCCI's car was parked. In a conversation after the murder, FLEMMI learned that when CASTUCCI was attempting to purchase the Squire Lounge, he had gone to Winter Hill for a loan. WINTER, Joe MCDONALD and Jimmy SIMS at the time scratched together $25,000 and legitimately invested in the Squire through CASTUCCI.

136. FLEMMI stated that he never heard, nor was aware that anyone from Winter Hill spoke to Sandra CASTUCCI after the murder regarding the gang's ownership stake in the Squire Lounge. FLEMMI noted that Mrs. CASTUCCI was ▆▆▆▆▆, during this time period. FLEMMI also does not remember any conversation with Raymond PATRIARCA Sr. over

Undated surveillance photo of Peter Fiumara, left, one of the owners of the
Squire Lounge in Revere, with Henry Tameleo, out on a weekend furlough.

the Squire's ownership, but did recall that PATRIARCA put in his own claim
on money owed by CASTUCCI. FLEMMI does have a memory of going
to the Squire Lounge and talking with Peter FIUMARA, and FIUMARA's
girlfriend, the club manager. At this meeting FIUMARA and his girlfriend
were pressed for Winter Hill's share of the Squire. FLEMMI stated that
eventually Winter Hill turned over to the LCN its share of the Squire as partial payment on other monies owed. FLEMMI also had no knowledge on
the murder of Chris D'AMELIO (02/10/79) a close friend of CASTUCCI's.

137. FLEMMI stated that some time after CASTUCCI's murder, "Jack"
put in a claim over the gaming debts still owed by Winter Hill. ████████ , a
Colombo Family member, came to Boston with "Jack" to pressure Winter
Hill for the money. (Actually, "Jack" did not come to Boston, but a couple
of other New York LCN members did accompany ████████ .) FLEMMI
noted that BULGER had done prison time with ████████ . FLEMMI said

that MARTORANO suggested that the gang put a "show on" for the visiting guests, and had some 40 to 50 of the Hill's gangland associates hanging around at the garage in a show of force when the New Yorkers arrived. ▬▬▬▬ arrived at the garage with New England LCN member Angelo "Sonny" MERCURIO, the liaison between Winter Hill and ANGIULO. ▬▬▬▬ pressed "Jack's" claim for the gambling debts. MARTORANO or BULGER told the visitors that "Jack" was an FBI informant, and that Winter Hill wasn't going to pay the money. FLEMMI added that ▬▬▬▬ appeared not to believe Winter Hill's information on "Jack" but finally agreed that the gang did not have to pay the debt.

Sonny Mercurio, liaison between Mafia underboss Jerry Angiulo and the Winter Hill Gang.

138. FLEMMI stated that Jerry ANGIULO was as pleased as Winter Hill by the outcome of the meeting, because the Hill's strength and connections with the Boston LCN reflected well on him as the local Mafia boss. FLEMMI added that he and BULGER informed John CONNOLLY about the meeting with ▬▬▬▬ over "Jack's" money. CONNOLLY was well aware of the "beef" and that "Jack" was the New York FBI informant who had gotten the intelligence on MCDONALD and SIMS being at the apartment. FLEMMI also recalled that BULGER discussed with CONNOLLY the false story they had decided to plant that certain unnamed bookmakers had murdered CASTUCCI because he had been cheating them by past-posting on horse races. This fabricated story was concocted to divert suspicion away from the Winter Hill organization. (At a meeting of federal law-enforcement agencies in Boston after

CASTUCCI's murder, S/A CONNOLLY flatly asserted that, "Winter Hill doesn't kill that way.")

139. FLEMMI stated that he and to the best of his knowledge, BULGER were never confronted by CONNOLLY as to whether the information that he had given to Winter Hill led to CASTUCCI's murder. FLEMMI was present for several post-homicide meetings with CONNOLLY where CASTUCCI's status as the source of the fugitive information was discussed. FLEMMI said that he had a vague memory that BULGER had questioned CONNOLLY as to who the suspects were in the CASTUCCI murder. CONNOLLY told BULGER that he and FLEMMI were suspects in this homicide. FLEMMI added that CONNOLLY acted normally during these post-homicide conversations and never asked at any time if they had been involved in the CASTUCCI murder. FLEMMI further stated that at no time during their entire relationship did CONNOLLY ever ask him not to injure any individual about whom he had leaked information. FLEMMI also added that BULGER never claimed that CONNOLLY made any such request to him either.

Barney BLAINE (BLOOM) murder (12/22/77)

140. FLEMMI stated that it is his opinion that Jewish bookmaker Barney BLAINE, a/k/a Barney BLOOM, was killed over a personal "beef," not because of any issue with the betting line. FLEMMI added that BLOOM did nothing that justified his murder, and that it only occurred because BULGER and ANGIULO hated BLOOM. FLEMMI stated that one day BLOOM was up at the garage

William "Skinny" Kazonis, Mafia associate, Angiulo once told Skinny he was "sweating like a faggot."

visiting George KAUFMAN and was overheard making a derogatory comment about ANGIULO. FLEMMI noted that LCN associate William "Skinny" KAZONIS was visiting the garage at the same time. BULGER then blew the comment out of proportion, and blasted BLOOM for what he had said. FLEMMI said that word of BLOOM's derogatory comment got back to ANGIULO and ANGIULO at some point later had BLOOM killed.

Francis GREEN extortion (10/13/77)

141. FLEMMI stated that Howie WINTER had asked BULGER and FLEMMI to help out a female friend of WINTER's, named FNU (first name unknown) Tobin, who operated a credit union and was having a problem with a customer. FLEMMI learned that the customer's name was Francis GREEN and that he had failed to pay back a loan. FLEMMI, BULGER and John MARTORANO agreed to help WINTER's friend and traveled down to Dedham to Green's business, the Backside Restaurant. The group met with GREEN and BULGER controlled the conversation. BULGER told

St. Agatha's School, Milton, Class of 1955. Top left, future Congressman William Delahunt. Top row middle, Johnny Martorano.

GREEN he had to pay back the money that was owed, and that if he did not, they would cut off GREEN's ears and stuff them in his mouth. FLEMMI noted that the discussion was brief. FLEMMI said that as the group was leaving MARTORANO saw his grade-school classmate, William Delahunt, then the District Attorney of Norfolk County (and later a Congressman). MARTORANO greeted Delahunt and introduced BULGER and FLEMMI to Delahunt. FLEMMI said that MARTORANO and Delahunt reminisced about their schoolyard football exploits while he and BULGER waited. After a few minutes the discussion broke up and the group departed the restaurant.

142. FLEMMI stated that a short time after this meeting BULGER told S/A CONNOLLY the entire story regarding the GREEN extortion. FLEMMI noted that he was present when BULGER related the story to CONNOLLY. FLEMMI added that CONNOLLY agreed to keep the gang up to date on any information concerning this extortion. FLEMMI said that there was some type of desultory investigation by the FBI, but that GREEN would not testify against them, and nothing came of the matter. FLEMMI did recall that GREEN later testified on some other type of case for the FBI. FLEMMI did not recall U.S. Attorney (and future U.S. District Court judge) Ted Harrington having anything to do with the GREEN investigation. FLEMMI did remember that neither he nor BULGER received any money for their intervention, and that it was done strictly as a favor to WINTER.

Sal Sperlinga under arrest in the pinball-machine case.

Middlesex County extortion case (02/01/78)

143. FLEMMI stated that Howie WINTER was the force behind Winter Hill's efforts to control vending and amusement machines in Somerville. WINTER wanted to put the group's pinball machines into as many clubs

and taverns in the city as possible. FLEMMI noted that Winter Hill's competition in the vending and amusement machine business was an established company owned by a man named FNU (first name unknown) ROBINSON. FLEMMI stated that WINTER wanted to put Winter Hill's machines in clubs and taverns where ROBINSON's equipment was already situated. WINTER told ROBINSON to remove his machines, ROBINSON refused and threats were made to ROBINSON by WINTER.

144. FLEMMI stated that S/A CONNOLLY learned that a state extortion case with some FBI involvement was being built against WINTER after ROBINSON and others complained to the Middlesex County district attorney. (The case was being handled by the first assistant district attorney, John F. Kerry, the future U.S. Senator and Secretary of State.) CONNOLLY suggested to BULGER that WINTER should speak with ROBINSON and work out an amicable settlement to the situation. FLEMMI said that WINTER did not take the advice, and instead invested his time and efforts in getting a hair transplant. FLEMMI and

Howie Winter with the hair plugs that had become his preoccupation.

BULGER then spoke with WINTER's friend and associate in the vending machine venture, Sal SPERLINGA. SPERLINGA was also advised to speak with ROBINSON. SPERLINGA told BULGER and FLEMMI that he wasn't concerned, that the investigation was a political witch-hunt and wouldn't affect them. SPERLINGA apparently did not warn WINTER and both were soon indicted. WINTER received a substantial state prison sentence and SPERLINGA was murdered in Magoun Square while out on work release. FLEMMI stated that with the group's undisputed boss in prison, Winter Hill was suddenly a very different organization. FLEMMI added that he now looked at WINTER in a different light, realizing that his actions had been stupid, and had needlessly imperiled both himself and the gang.

Howie Winter under arrest, with a scally cap covering the hair plugs.

BS 92-1950

Informant advised that a new procedure has been set up on Winter Hill whereby hardly anyone is allowed to talk with HOWIE WINTERS, particularly those people with a hard luck story. Informant stated that WINTERS has a big heart and has been a soft touch for people who are unable to keep up their obligations to the Hill. Accordingly, all these people now go through WHITEY BULGER who informant described as a vicious animal who will not take "no" for an answer.

Castucci reports to FBI on Whitey's growing influence in the gang in 1976.

Blackfriars murders (06/28/78)

145. FLEMMI stated that he occasionally patronized the Blackfriars restaurant on Summer Street, as did many others from all walks of life including former television reporter Jack KELLY. FLEMMI noted that

KELLY was gathering background for a book, which explained why KELLY was so often there. FLEMMI also indicated that the Blackfriars had become a haven for drug users and dealers, and that it was a drug rip-off that was behind the murders that occurred there. FLEMMI stated that he believes that it was Billy IERARDI, Bobby ITALIANO and Nick FEMIA who did the killings and that the murders were committed to cover up the theft of two kilograms of cocaine. (IERARDI and ITALIANO were tried and acquitted of the five murders; FEMIA

Jack Kelly, former TV reporter, one of five murder victims at Blackfriars in 1978.

The Blackfriars massacre was the biggest story in the city.

was never charged.) FLEMMI added that he and girlfriend Marilyn DIS-ILVA, a Blackfriars waitress, were in the restaurant the night the murders took place, and that DISILVA wanted to stay at the club after closing. FLEMMI had seen BARBOZA associate Nick FEMIA in the club, and had gotten a sense that something was amiss. FLEMMI convinced DISILVA to leave the club with him, probably saving her life. After the bodies were discovered, FLEMMI advised S/A CONNOLLY about his suspicions about FEMIA and FEMIA's East Boston associates, IERARDI and ITALIANO. FLEMMI noted that Winter Hill members had once tracked ITALIANO down in East Boston and gave him a severe beating because ITALIANO had robbed $12,000 from a Winter Hill-connected bookmaker named ███████ .

Bobby Italiano, accused Blackfriars shooter, celebrates his acquittal.

William Ierardi, likewise acquitted, soon ended up back at MCI Walpole.

146. FLEMMI stated that according to BULGER, John CONNOLLY obtained copies of the Boston Police photos taken at the crime scene in the Blackfriars. FLEMMI indicated that BULGER wanted the photos both for his own curiosity, and to be used on a scam to be perpetrated on ███████ . FLEMMI said that ███████ had owed $60,000 to one of the murder victims, Vinnie SOLMONTE, the owner of Blackfriars. Armed with the crime-scene photos from the BPD, BULGER went to ███████ office that afternoon and showed ███████ the gruesome pictures, claiming that he

had taken them himself after murdering SOLMONTE and the four others. Thus, BULGER claimed, ▇▇▇▇▇▇ now owed him the $60,000 he had owed SOLIMONTE. Terrified, ▇▇▇▇▇▇ promptly paid the money which was split by FLEMMI, BULGER and ▇▇▇▇▇▇ . FLEMMI noted that the idea for the scam on ▇▇▇▇▇▇ came from BULGER.

147. FLEMMI stated that he learned much later that IERARDI had said in an interview that he and BULGER had committed the murders at the Blackfriars. FLEMMI learned this information from CONNOLLY who indicated that IERARDI had become an informant for the FBI. CONNOLLY had also learned from S/A Mike BUCKLEY that IERARDI had failed a polygraph regarding these murders. CONNOLLY subsequently passed that information onto FLEMMI and BULGER. FLEMMI noted that FEMIA never admitted to him that he was involved in the Blackfriars massacre. FLEMMI added that he liked FEMIA and even tried to help FEMIA overcome his severe drug habit, but Winter Hill cut him loose after some cocaine fell out of his pocket one day at the Lancaster Street Garage. (When FEMIA went to work for BULGER, CONNOLLY filed a report saying that FEMIA had nothing to do with the Blackfriars murders. After BULGER fired FEMIA, Connolly filed a new report claiming that FEMIA had in fact committed the murders.) FLEMMI noted that Jerry ANGIULO had always wanted to kill FEMIA because FEMIA was the last remaining associate of Joe BARBOZA. FEMIA was shot to death during a botched robbery attempt in East Boston (12/19/83), during which he was apparently under the influence of drugs, looking away from his victims and talking to people who weren't there.

In the (Drug) Money

LEPERE and ■■■■■■ *Drug trafficking (1978-1984)*

148. FLEMMI stated that Frank LEPERE had a relationship with BULGER prior to his meeting LEPERE. FLEMMI indicated that LEPERE was involved in bookmaking and FLEMMI believed that BULGER controlled the bookmaker that LEPERE dealt with. According to FLEMMI, LEPERE was involved in the kidnapping of a Michael ROMANELLI (circa November 1978) who had used LEPERE's fish dock in Plymouth to offload a shipment of marijuana. At the time, LEPERE owned and operated the company, Mid Cape Fish, and was also involved in illegal swordfish smuggling. According to FLEMMI, ROMANELLI subsequently went to Winter Hill and offered them $600,000 to help settle "the beef" that he had with LEPERE. Winter Hill passed on ROMANELLI's offer because at the time Howie WINTER did not want to get involved in anything to do with drug trafficking. Sometime shortly thereafter, LEPERE and his partner ■■■■■■ kidnapped ROMANELLI. Subsequent to the kidnapping, LEPERE called for a meeting with BULGER.

149. FLEMMI stated that he attended this meeting and that this was the first meeting that he was involved in with BULGER and LEPERE. This first meeting occurred in the late 1970's, and took place near the Gillette Company in South Boston, which was located behind the gang's TRIPLE O's tavern. At the meeting LEPERE told BULGER and FLEMMI that he had been doing very well lately and wanted to give them something. LEPERE subsequently handed BULGER a bag containing $25,000 in cash. FLEMMI indicated that he and BULGER split the money from LEPERE and that a portion of this $25,000 went into the "Ex" fund (expense fund). It was at this point that FLEMMI became aware that LEPERE was involved in drug trafficking and that LEPERE wanted to secure BULGER and FLEMMI's muscle in case he ever had a problem.

FRANK LePERE
Was living it up

Frank LePere—Stevie claimed he didn't realize at first that he was a drug dealer.

150. FLEMMI stated that he and BULGER continued to have a relationship with LEPERE up to the time of LEPERE's arrest in November 1984. FLEMMI stated that throughout the early 1980's, LEPERE was involved in numerous marijuana importations, and as a result he and BULGER received a share of the profits. FLEMMI said that during the time that LEPERE was a fugitive (circa Nov. 1983 to Nov. 1984) he continued to import large shipments of marijuana into the United States, often utilizing the Hudson River in New York as an offload point. FLEMMI visited LEPERE several times in 1983-84 while LEPERE was "on the lam" and living in a high-rise in New York. Later LEPERE built a mountain-top retreat near Lake George in New York.

151. FLEMMI stated that on one occasion LEPERE gave him $1,000,000 in cash which he transported back to Massachusetts. FLEMMI stated that he and BULGER split $500,000 of this money, and the remainder of the cash was given to LEPERE's partner, ▇▇▇▇▇▇. On another occasion FLEMMI and BULGER received an additional $500,000 in cash from LEPERE in New York. FLEMMI also recalled receiving between $400,000 and $500,000 in cash from LEPERE's other partner ▇▇▇▇▇▇, who coordinated and managed LEPERE's drug organization in Massachusetts while LEPERE was a fugitive in New York. FLEMMI estimates that he and BULGER received over $2,000,000 from LEPERE's marijuana business over the years. FLEMMI indicated that some of the LEPERE's drug proceeds were funneled to Winter Hill associate John MARTORANO, who was a fugitive during this time frame. Furthermore, FLEMMI stated that the "Ex" fund received a share of the LEPERE monies, as well as the gang's corrupt law-enforcement contacts.

152. SHORTLY after LEPERE's arrest, FLEMMI met with ▇▇▇▇▇ on New Market St. in Boston, MA to discuss LEPERE and ▇▇▇▇▇ source of information in the United States Attorney's office in Boston. Both FLEMMI and BULGER were aware that LEPERE had cultivated a law-enforcement source, David TWOMEY, who had been a prosecutor in the Boston office of the U.S. Attorney. FLEMMI was aware that TWOMEY provided significant high-level information, which was comparable to his own law-enforcement source, Richard SCHNEIEDERHAN of the Mass. State Police. FLEMMI recalled LEPERE asking him to check with his

David Twomey, corrupt federal prosecutor.

law-enforcement source about radio frequencies that LEPERE's group was using, and whether certain offload sites were under surveillance. FLEMMI

stated that SCHNEIEDERHAN provided him with information relating
to the fact that law-enforcement was
using some type of electronic beacons
which through triangulation could locate LEPERE's boats. FLEMMI added
that LEPERE's group did change some
offload sites and routes of travel during
this period.

Mass. State Trooper Richard
Schneiderhan, the gang's best source
in the MSP.

153. FLEMMI reported that he became aware that LEPERE received additional confidential law-enforcement
information from David TWOMEY
that caused LEPERE to be concerned
that there was an informant within
his group. In response to TWOMEY's
information, LEPERE administered
polygraph examinations to several individuals within his crew. FLEMMI
said that during the meeting on New Market Street, he convinced ███████
that TWOMEY would eventually cooperate with law-enforcement and
give testimony against both LEPERE and ███████ . FLEMMI advocated
that the two drug dealers should "beat TWOMEY to the punch," and
cooperate with law-enforcement against TWOMEY. ███████ then convinced LEPERE of the merits of cooperating against TWOMEY, and soon
thereafter the pair agreed to assist in an investigation targeting TWOMEY.
FLEMMI noted that there was an understanding between the Winter
Hill group that LEPERE and ███████ would refrain from giving up any
incriminating information on either FLEMMI or BULGER.

154. FLEMMI stated that prior to TWOMEY's criminal trial, he and
BULGER traveled to ███████ office near Massachusetts General
Hospital, and met with LEPERE, who was accompanied by his wife. The

purpose of this meeting centered around BULGER and FLEMMI's request for a "severance payment" to FLEMMI's law-enforcement source who had provided confidential information regarding LEPERE over the years. FLEMMI stated that LEPERE paid $50,000 in cash as the result of this request. FLEMMI additionally reported that the "severance payment" story was just a ruse, and that he and BULGER split the money.

155. FLEMMI stated that in approximately 1980 at LEPERE's request, FLEMMI and BULGER assisted LEPERE with a problem that had arisen within LEPERE's ongoing drug-distribution business. This request for intervention related to LEPERE's problem with ███████. Additionally, not long after the ███████ situation was resolved, LEPERE had another problem which required FLEMMI and BULGER's assistance. On this occasion LEPERE was having problems with his long time associate Salvatore "Mike" CARUANA. LEPERE and CARUANA had been mutual business partners for several

Salvatore "Mike" Caruana, another of Stevie and Whitey's drug dealers, eventually murdered by the Mafia in CT.

years in the marijuana business and had made a great deal of money together before going their separate ways. In the early 1980's Arnold KATZ, a well-documented drug distributor, was working for LEPERE. Prior to this KATZ had worked with both LEPERE and CARUANA on joint importations. FLEMMI said that a problem had ensued when a CARUANA distributor from Cape Cod ███████ utilized a LEPERE and KATZ source of supply from Colombia, South America without the authorization of LEPERE and KATZ. KATZ complained to LEPERE who in turn went to BULGER and FLEMMI. LEPERE claimed that the Cape Cod distributor who worked for CARUANA owed them $600,000. FLEMMI subsequently talked via telephone with Mike CARUANA about the situation and during the conversation CARUANA became very loud and angry. FLEMMI then told CARUANA to be very careful not to push him.

156. FLEMMI stated that a meeting regarding the situation was eventually held at CARUANA's Peabody home. According to FLEMMI, ex-cop Joseph MONGIELLO drove him to the meeting. FLEMMI said that he was armed with a handgun in case the meeting turned violent. FLEMMI added that at CARUANA's request, Raymond PATRIARCA Jr. attended the meeting as the mediator. As the meeting progressed the issue of who owed what monies to whom was discussed. PATRIARCA Jr. claimed that LEPERE

Joe Mongiello, former cop, Winter Hill associate.

owed him money for operating his drug business, at which time FLEMMI responded by indicating that LEPERE had paid CARUANA $9,000,000 from drug proceeds over the years. FLEMMI said that PATRIARCA Jr. appeared taken aback at this comment. Although CARUANA denied receiving the $9,000,000, FLEMMI surmised that CARUANA had not informed and/or paid PATRIARCA Jr. his rightful share of the drug money. As a result of this sit-down, the Cape Cod drug trafficker was forced to pay LEPERE $600,000. FLEMMI said that ▆▆▆▆▆ collected the money from the Cape Cod trafficker ▆▆▆▆▆ and LEPERE paid Winter Hill (i.e., BULGER and FLEMMI) $200,000 out of the cash for their assistance with "the beef." FLEMMI added that LEPERE and ▆▆▆▆▆ split the remaining cash.

157. FLEMMI stated that he recalled meeting with CARUANA during the fall of 1980, shortly after the Lancaster Street electronic surveillance was conducted by the Mass. State Police. FLEMMI said that he and BULGER met with CARUANA at the Howard Johnson restaurant located near Andrew

Square on the Expressway. The meeting had to do with CARUANA's gold business. BULGER and FLEMMI subsequently traveled with CARUANA to meet with a gold dealer in Rhode Island, whom CARUANA intended to extort. After observing CARUANA's demeanor with the gold dealer, both BULGER and FLEMMI decided to back away from CARUANA. In approximately 1987, FLEMMI heard that Billy GRASSO's LCN crew from Connecticut had "clipped" CARUANA and buried him in a garage in Connecticut. FLEMMI is not sure where he heard the information, but indicated that CARUANA was killed because of a number of problems he had with the Mafia and that ████████ authorized the murder. According to FLEMMI, ANGIULO had been "knocking" CARUANA for some time, and the LCN was concerned about CARUANA "rolling" if he were apprehended on the outstanding DEA drug indictment/warrant.

FBI Race Fix case and the aftermath 1976-1979

158. FLEMMI stated that the race fix scam started even before he had returned from "the lam" in 1974. FLEMMI said that Fat Tony CIULLA and Billy BARNOSKI were heavily involved in the scam which entailed the holding back of a number of horses during a race and betting on the other horses with as many bookmakers as possible. FLEMMI noted that Jerry ANGIULO had advised Howie WINTER and John MARTORANO not to involve themselves in anything CIULLA was part of. FLEMMI was further told that CIULLA's own brother-in-law Ed ARDOLINO also

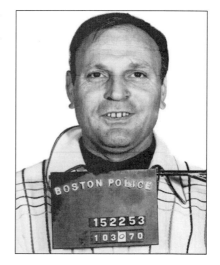

Ed Ardolino, Fat Tony's brother-in-law, warned the Hill not to trust Ciulla.

warned Winter Hill to maintain a hands-off approach to any scam involving CIULLA. FLEMMI stated that he thought that the scam was a bad idea, and had no role in it, except in locating bookmakers that Winter Hill could place bets through. As one of the six Winter Hill "partners," FLEMMI also received a one-sixth share of the proceeds. FLEMMI noted that he only made a small amount of money from the scam.

159. FLEMMI stated that CIULLA began cooperating after getting arrested, and it became well-known that an investigation into the race fix scam was in progress. The magazine *Sports Illustrated* even ran a cover story about the scheme. S/A CONNOLLY advised BULGER that the investigation of the scam was taking place, and that he and FLEMMI were being looked at as possible targets for indictment. CONNOLLY later told BULGER that he would try and keep him and FLEMMI from being indicted. CONNOLLY told BULGER that he was going to speak with his C-3 supervisor, SS/A John MORRIS, and Organized-Crime Strike Force Chief Jeremiah O'Sullivan about BULGER and FLEMMI's jeopardy. FLEMMI learned that MORRIS had joined forces with CONNOLLY in shielding BULGER and FLEMMI from honest law-enforcement. FLEMMI also learned from BULGER that

Jeremiah O'Sullivan, federal prosecutor Whitey claims he received immunity from, with Diane Kottmyer, future state judge who would joke with Zip Connolly at his farewell dinner about the South Boston Liquor Mart.

CONNOLLY and MORRIS then spoke with O'Sullivan. O'Sullivan was told that the FBI's mandate was the Mafia, and that BULGER and FLEMMI were too valuable as informants on the LCN to lose simply because of their allegedly slight involvement in the race-fixing case. FLEMMI acknowledged that he clearly was of much greater value to the FBI against the Mafia than BULGER.

160. FLEMMI stated that O'Sullivan responded by saying that the FBI case officer on the investigation would have to be consulted as to whether or not to prosecute FLEMMI and BULGER. FLEMMI speculated that S/A Daly, the race-fix case officer, had to be advised of their informant status. FLEMMI also noted that he and BULGER were going to meet directly with O'Sullivan to discuss the situation, but that this gathering was cancelled for some unknown reason. FLEMMI said that BULGER actually met O'Sullivan at a later date in a hotel, and although FLEMMI was supposed to go, he did not. Shortly before the indictments were unsealed, BULGER was told by CONNOLLY that he and FLEMMI would not be prosecuted. FLEMMI also told CONNOLLY to thank O'Sullivan for his intercession. FLEMMI added that there is no question in his mind that the sole reason he and BULGER were not indicted and convicted on the race fix case was because of their informant status. FLEMMI reported that in the mid-to-late 1980's, he warned CONNOLLY that Jerry ANGIULO had advised him that the LCN wanted to kill O'Sullivan. FLEMMI also recalled a previous warning to the FBI that the LCN had also wanted to kill United States Attorney Paul Markham, a cousin of Ted Kennedy's, in the late 1960's.

161. FLEMMI stated that everyone in the Winter Hill gang appeared to be pleased with the news that he and Bulger were not going to be indicted in the race fixing case. John MARTORANO and Howie WINTER had been far more involved in the daily operations of the scam and had coordinated the wagering with the bookmakers on the races. The other soon-to-be-indicted members of Winter Hill knew that there was more direct evidence against them and were glad that someone from the group would be out on the street to protect the mob's interests. FLEMMI added that at the time,

WINTER was already in custody on the Middlesex extortion case, and that MARTORANO was going to jail for several months because of a 1975 gaming wire in Plymouth County.

162. FLEMMI stated that the remaining Winter Hill gang members met at a local restaurant to discuss the status of the gang after the indictments on the race fix case came down. The meeting was attended by John MARTORANO, FLEMMI and BULGER. MARTORANO outlined for the group how the bookmaking operation was going to be split up. MARTORANO would take the sports betting operation, and Joe MCDONALD, Howie WINTER and Jimmy SIMS would keep the numbers and shylock operations. MARTORANO offered to BULGER and FLEMMI a share in his gaming operations, but both declined the offer. FLEMMI noted that while MARTORANO assumed all of the balances with the sports gaming agents, he had really taken the "cream" of the gang's gambling business. MARTORANO also suggested that the group charge "rent" to the remaining bookmakers, similar to the way things operated in New York.

163. FLEMMI stated that he, BULGER and MARTORANO then created the system of "rent collection" from bookmakers and others involved in illegal activities within the metropolitan Boston area. The three partners also shared equally in the proceeds from the "rent" scheme. FLEMMI said that the trio spoke with Charlie RASO, Dick O'BRIEN, John MAQUARDO, Chico KRANTZ, Jimmy KATZ, Howie LEVENSON, Eddie LEWIS, Tommy RYAN, Bernie WEISMAN and others to notify them of the change to "rent". The bookmakers were advised that

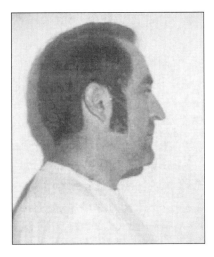

Bobby Gallinaro, Somerville bookie, excused from paying "rent."

paying "rent" did not entitle them to having Winter Hill act as their collection agency, but rather it would protect them from the extortionate demands of other violent criminals, specifically the LCN. FLEMMI noted that the group received "rent" from Bobby GALLINARO for a short time, but that GALLINARO complained to MARTORANO, who asked BULGER and FLEMMI to pass on that particular shakedown.

164. FLEMMI stated that during the restaurant "breakup" meeting, he and BULGER agreed to assume all of the gang's remaining debts. These debts included approximately $250,000 on shylock loans from Jerry ANGIULO, as well as another $60,000 owed to ▮▮▮▮▮ and others. FLEMMI said that there was some strain between MCDONALD and WINTER over the mismanagement of money they and SIMS had invested in various schemes. MCDONALD took advantage of WINTER's absence and began taking control of WINTER's assets. One such asset that MCDONALD took custody of was WINTER's share of ▮▮▮▮▮ in Everett.

165. FLEMMI stated that MARTORANO also notified the group during the "breakup" meeting, that he was going "on the lam" because of his pending indictment in the race-fixing case. FLEMMI later advised WINTER about the breakup of the group's financial assets and other news at a meeting at MCI Shirley. WINTER at some point also sent word to BULGER and FLEMMI to have the gang move out of the Marshall Street Somerville garage, so that he could rent the building to some new, paying tenants. George KAUFMAN then located a suitable new garage for the gang on Lancaster Street in the West End of Boston.

Operation Lobster

166. FLEMMI stated that Billy DAGGETT came to him to check if the "fence" that DAGGETT's group was dealing with was connected to any organized-crime group. DAGGETT's gang was considering robbing the "fence" and did not want to cause a problem with the LCN or Winter Hill if the "fence" was aligned with either of the major gangs. FLEMMI checked

with BULGER who in turn spoke with CONNOLLY. CONNOLLY confirmed to BULGER that the "fence" was actually an FBI Special Agent, Nick "Doc" Gianturco, a native of Chelsea. BULGER advised FLEMMI of the situation who then advised DAGGETT that the fence was "connected." FLEMMI added that BULGER separately developed information that a Charlestown gang was also contemplating robbing this same "fence."

FBI agent Nick "Doc" Gianturco, the M.C. of Zip's retirement dinner who later followed him to Boston Edison.

FLEMMI's parents assaulted and robbed (06/11/79)

167. FLEMMI stated that his parents were assaulted and robbed by five black youths after a car accident on Blue Hill Avenue in Mattapan.

Mary Flemmi after her assault by a gang of blacks on Blue Hill Avenue in Mattapan; Stevie would soon move her to South Boston.

FLEMMI recalled that after his parents' car crashed into a telephone pole, some of the juveniles climbed in a window of the vehicle, and stole his parents' jewelry. FLEMMI was asked about reported boasts he was alleged to have made regarding murdering the five teens involved in the robbery. FLEMMI denied taking any action against these individuals, but noted that he was aware that one of the teens was later shot and killed by a retired police officer. FLEMMI stated that he had no knowledge of any one of the juveniles being killed in a drive-by shooting. Shortly after the attack, FLEMMI moved his parents to the then all-white neighborhood of South Boston, buying them a small house at 832 East Third Street across a courtyard from the home of BULGER's younger brother, State Senate President William M. Bulger.

Jimmy FLEMMI's overdose and death (10/16/79)

168. FLEMMI stated that his brother was addicted to illegal drugs ever since being shot by Jimmy O'TOOLE in 1965. FLEMMI added that his brother's hatred for Larry BAIONE and "Skinny" Peter LIMONE was well known. FLEMMI noted that O'TOOLE had been a friend of BAIONE's. FLEMMI had escaped during a weekend furlough in 1976, and after wrecking his ex-wife's home in Hyde Park and killing her cat, fled Massachusetts. He spent three years "on the lam" before being recaptured in MD in 1979 and returned to MCI Norfolk. FLEMMI said that he blames the LCN for the "hot shot" of heroin that killed his brother Jimmy at MCI Walpole. FLEMMI has no specific in-

Jimmy the Bear's final mugshot; four months later he would die of a drug overdose.

formation on the LCN's involvement in the death, but clearly believes that there was some type of Mafia participation in his brother's demise.

Louie LITIF murder (04/13/80) and related slayings

169. FLEMMI stated that he was familiar with Louie LITIF from the South End. Later FLEMMI had more contact with LITIF when they both became associated with BULGER. FLEMMI said that LITIF was conducting book-making activities in South Boston under BULGER's authorization, but was not liked by BULGER. LITIF was loud and a flashy dresser, even to the point of color coordinating his underwear. According to BULGER, despite deny-ing it, LITIF was also involved in drug trafficking which clearly angered the South Boston crime boss. LITIF also owned a South Boston bar with well-known shylock Jimmy "the Juice" MATERA. MATERA and LITIF often clashed as both had large egos. FLEMMI said that eventually LITIF killed MATTERA. Immediately prior to his murder, MATERA told the bartender (Robert CONRAD) at the pair's tavern that if "something happens to me, Louie's involved." FLEMMI said that LITIF killed MATERA in the bar's cel-lar, shooting him four times in the head. LITIF later murdered and buried CONRAD the bartender in Canada while "on the lam." FLEMMI noted that the bartender is buried outside the property lines of LITIF's home in Nova Scotia. (Despite searches, CONRAD's body has never been found there.)

Louie Litif in his days as a typical Boston hood.

Jimmy "the Juice" Matera, murdered by his partner, Louie Litif.

170. FLEMMI stated that he does not know exactly who physically murdered LITIF but is sure that at a minimum, BULGER at least had him killed by proxy. FLEMMI suspects that LITIF's murder was committed by someone close to him. FLEMMI also noted that BULGER appeared happy to hear the news that LITIF was dead, and that because of this, he didn't ask any questions about the death. FLEMMI surmised that since LITIF was a significant underling, BULGER would have gone all out to find who murdered LITIF if he had not been involved. FLEMMI also is of the opinion that LITIF could have significantly hurt BULGER, should he have chosen to cooperate with law-enforcement after his arrest on the MATERA murder. FLEMMI also learned from BULGER after the murder that LITIF had been an FBI informant for S/A John CONNOLLY. FLEMMI stated that he does not recall telling MARTORANO in the Plymouth House of Correction that "they killed Louie," but indicated that it was possible that he did. (According to most accounts, LITIF was murdered by BULGER upstairs at Triple O's, after which his body was then put in the trunk of his wife's car, which was then driven to the South End by Brian HALLORAN, another reason for BULGER to later want HALLORAN dead.)

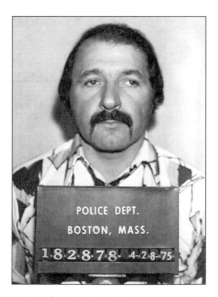

As a drug dealer, Litif now dressed
differently.

Brian Halloran—Whitey ordered him
to dispose of Litif's body.

Robert LAMONICA murder (05/31/80)

171. FLEMMI stated that he was aware from general street talk that LA-MONICA had a problem with Freddie WEICHEL and possibly another individual named ▮▮▮▮▮. FLEMMI indicated that he believes WEICHEL was involved in the shooting death of LAMONICA in Quincy or Braintree. FLEMMI added that no one, including WEICHEL, ever admitted to him to having been involved the crime. FLEMMI noted that he was friendly with WEICHEL, as were Jimmy BULGER and Kevin WEEKS. FLEMMI further stated that he doesn't recall any discussion about WEEKS or S/A John CONNOLLY seeing WEICHEL on the

Fred Weichel, still in prison, claims he was framed by the Bulger gang for murder.

Eddie MacKenzie, Southie drug dealer and author, revealed the existence of the "Dog Room," where Whitey and others allegedly raped underage girls.

night of the murder. FLEMMI also does not remember BULGER ever saying in his presence that he wanted to frame WEICHEL for the LAMONICA murder.

172. FLEMMI stated that WEICHEL once wrote a letter to FLEMMI while he was incarcerated in Plymouth, offering to have South Boston

Tulsa PD wanted poster, with mentions of Whitey's "extreme bad breath" and his likely presence in "homosexual. . .nudist facilities."

After his rivals were disposed of, Whitey began dressing somewhat more flamboyantly, favoring leather and Village People attire.

drug dealer and later author Eddie MACKENZIE testify on his behalf. FLEMMI was aware that BULGER hated MACKENZIE and never wanted anything to do with MACKENZIE. FLEMMI added that on one occasion MACKENZIE was seen with FLEMMI's son Stephen HUSSEY in a car, and BULGER warned FLEMMI to get his son away from MACKENZIE. FLEMMI further added that he had never personally met MACKENZIE, and that the tales about BULGER being down at the "Dog Room" raping underage girls is a fabrication. FLEMMI did acknowledge that BULGER at one time had a 15-year-old girlfriend whose name was "Tammy." FLEMMI had no information on the persistent rumors that BULGER is bisexual. (On a wanted poster issued by the Tulsa OK police during BULGER's flight, it was speculated that BULGER might be hiding out in "gay nudist camps." The Tulsa PD also alerted the public to BULGER's "extreme bad breath.")

"Sonny" COLANTONIO and Robert PERRONE murders (12/02/80)

173. FLEMMI stated that he and BULGER played significant roles in the 1980 murders of Dominic "Sonny" COLANTONIO and Robert PER-RONE. FLEMMI added that these murders were instigated by ███████ and ████████. FLEMMI said that he had been friendly with Sonny COL-ANTONIO for many years, and actually owned a Dorchester tavern with him in the 1960's called Lombardi's. FLEMMI noted that the barroom, which was located at Devan Street and Columbia Road, was quite profit-able for a time and featured a room with illegal card games. The bar also had after-hours liquor service. FLEMMI said that the Boston police were aware of the violations occurring within the establishment but only required that the barroom's outside lights be turned off at the end of the licensed business hours. After a few years, the partners sold the tavern, but they maintained contact as COLANTONIO came by with stolen property, which FLEMMI would fence. Later FLEMMI became aware that COLANTONIO was employed by the ████████ organization, off-loading marijuana. FLEMMI also knew that COLANTONIO was hanging around with violent South Boston-based criminals, Jimmy KEARNS, Billy KELLEY and Tommy NEE. FLEMMI said that this group was busy shaking down local drug traffickers and bookmakers.

174. FLEMMI stated that one day ████████ came to him at the Lan-caster Street garage, and told him that COLANTONIO was "shaking him down" over his ████████ and ████████ drug operation. ████████ then asked FLEMMI to get COLANTONIO "off his back", and didn't care how FLEMMI did it. ████████ added that he was concerned that COLANTO-NIO would harm his family. FLEMMI advised BULGER and then con-tacted KEARNS and told him to kill COLANTONIO. FLEMMI reminded KEARNS that KEARNS owed him a favor for the assistance that was rendered when Larry BAIONE wanted him killed, after the Chico AMICO murder in 1966. Following the murder of COLANTONIO and PERRONE, FLEMMI learned from KEARNS that they (KEARNS, ████████ and NEE) had in fact accomplished the assigned task. FLEMMI estimated that it was a few weeks in between the time that he asked KEARNS to kill COLANTONIO,

and when the murders took place. FLEMMI added that BULGER was well aware of the plan to kill COLANTONIO and approved of the scheme, but it was FLEMMI who met alone with KEARNS and asked KEARNS to do the murder. FLEMMI noted that this meeting also took place at the Lancaster Street garage.

175. FLEMMI stated that he learned from ████████ that COLANTONIO and PERRONE were in a car when the murders took place, and that the victims had been told that the group was going to "take down a couple of drug dealers." Once the two were in a car, thinking that they were going to participate in a shakedown, they were murdered. FLEMMI was of the understanding that NEE was the actual shooter. FLEMMI said that neither ████████ nor KEARNS ever explained why the bodies of COLANTONIO and PERRONE were dumped in different spots. FLEMMI added that ████████, NEE and KEARNS were never paid for the murders. However in 1981, after ████████ had been indicted for drug trafficking charges and later arrested in 1984, FLEMMI received $50,000 in cash. The payment from ████████ to FLEMMI was made in part because of the COLANTONIO and PERRONE murders. FLEMMI also recalled that BULGER discussed the murder of COLANTONIO with S/A John CONNOLLY. FLEMMI did not recall telling S/A CONNOLLY that the actual killers of COLANTONIO and PERRONE were KEARNS, ████████ and NEE.

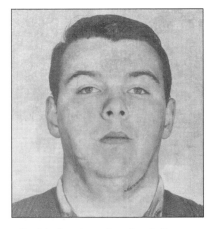

176. FLEMMI stated that he was aware that ████████ had also killed several other individuals. ████████ told BULGER that he had a personal problem with flyweight boxer Joey "Runt" INGEMI, and killed the victim alone one night while riding home with him (12/13/82). ████████ told BULGER that he shot INGEMI in the victim's car and dumped the

Pat Linskey, longtime South Boston associate of Whitey Bulger.

body in a Dorchester field. FLEMMI added that ▆▆▆▆▆ had also killed Vito IVASKA (01/14/82). FLEMMI said that ▆▆▆▆▆ bragged to him and BULGER that he had committed the homicide after being asked by BULGER what had happened to the victim. FLEMMI noted that Tommy NEE was himself murdered a short time later in that alcove of the Pen tavern in South Boston. ▆▆▆▆▆ admitted to both FLEMMI and BULGER that he had done the shooting. FLEMMI said that after killing NEE, ▆▆▆▆▆ ran to his apartment which was around the corner from the Pen. FLEMMI said that the shooting was over a personal "beef" the pair had. FLEMMI further noted that BULGER was gladdened by NEE's murder, and that BULGER made a point of learning about any homicides that occurred in South Boston. BULGER always wanted to know who in his immediate neighborhood was "capable," i.e., able to plan and commit a murder and escape arrest. Such persons might someday represent a threat to BULGER himself, and thus he felt compelled to keep close tabs on their activities.

Roger WHEELER murder (05/27/81)

177. FLEMMI stated that after John MARTORANO had gone "on the lam" from the race fixing case in 1978, the two partners would contact each other through George KAUFMAN. FLEMMI added that neither he FLEMMI nor MARTORANO had each other's pager numbers. KAUFMAN would notify each partner when contact was desired, and calls were arranged with each party using pay telephones. FLEMMI said that during this time period, he often used a pay telephone located at a barroom at Copeland and Garnett Streets in Quincy. FLEMMI and KAUFMAN also spoke to MARTORANO via two office telephones located at a carpet store near the gang's garage. FLEMMI

Marked for death: millionaire Tulsa businessman Roger Wheeler.

recalled that the telephone number at the carpet store had several number 2's in it. FLEMMI noted that BULGER only spoke on the phone with MARTORANO one or two times in all the years that MARTORANO was a fugitive, once when MARTORANO's father died.

178. FLEMMI stated that on one of these pay telephone calls, he was advised by MARTORANO that John CALLAHAN had a proposition for the remaining Winter Hill partners— FLEMMI, MARTORANO, Joe MC-DONALD and BULGER. FLEMMI learned that CALLAHAN was attempting to purchase World Jai Alai, and was concerned about the LCN or other organized-crime groups' efforts to extort protection money from him. CALLAHAN wanted the Winter Hill partners to provide the "muscle" to keep these other underworld groups

John Callahan, always described as a "wannabe."

at bay. In return for this assistance, CALLAHAN was willing to pay BULGER, MARTORANO and FLEMMI $10,000 a week skimmed from the parking concessions, and an as-yet-to-be-determined percentage of the overall business. The Winter Hill partners would also not be required to invest any money up front, which was another attractive selling point for the group. MARTORANO then advised FLEMMI to speak with BULGER about the idea and if interested to talk directly to CALLAHAN about the deal.

179. FLEMMI stated that he had not had a lot of previous contact with CALLAHAN, but was aware that CALLAHAN had donated money to the Irish Republican Army in the past and had some type of business connection with Howie WINTER. FLEMMI was also aware that CALLAHAN had been employed by World Jai Alai when he returned to Boston in 1974.

CALLAHAN was also a friend of Jimmy MARTORANO and appeared to enjoy the company of underworld figures. FLEMMI added that because of these friendships with gangland characters, CALLAHAN lost his Connecticut gambling license, which meant he could no longer operate the World Jai Alai fronton there. FLEMMI said that he often saw CALLAHAN at John and Jimmy MARTORANO's South End restaurant, CHANDLER's, where he was frequently in the company of Howie WINTER and Joe MCDONALD. FLEMMI noted that CALLAHAN had a lot of college girls around him and would use cocaine with many of the other members and associates of the Winter Hill gang. FLEMMI recalled that CALLAHAN had once come up to him in Pal Joey's bar and tried to get him to encourage John MARTORANO to kill South Boston drug trafficker ███████. It was FLEMMI's understanding that ███████ had previously threatened to kill CALLAHAN. FLEMMI's belief was that the dispute between ███████ and

Whitey in white, 1980's.

CALLAHAN was over ███████. To incite FLEMMI, CALLAHAN told him that ███████ had been "badmouthing" MARTORANO. However, CALLAHAN was not successful in gaining his FLEMMI's cooperation in eliminating ███████.

180. FLEMMI was aware that since the time that MARTORANO went "on the lam" in Florida, he had become friendlier with CALLAHAN than

he had been in Boston. FLEMMI knew that CALLAHAN had helped MARTORANO obtain an apartment, a car, and at times held money for MARTORANO. FLEMMI said that he and BULGER were not very close to CALLAHAN when he was first introduced into the Winter Hill inner circle. FLEMMI added that their attitudes changed toward CALLAHAN, and contact increased, after he mentioned his interest in opening a Jai Alai fronton on an Indian reservation. FLEMMI noted that this conversation about the fronton and the Indian reservation was the reason that he and BULGER were not surprised by CALLAHAN's proposal for Winter Hill to be involved in the pending World Jai Alai sale. FLEMMI also thought that some time in the past that CALLAHAN may have done business with Raymond PATRIARCA Sr.

181. FLEMMI stated that he and BULGER went to a meeting at CALLA-HAN's apartment/office on Commercial Street in Boston. FLEMMI said that Brian HALLORAN arrived shortly after he and BULGER had shown up at CALLAHAN's apartment. FLEMMI noted that HALLORAN was not well liked by any of the remaining Winter Hill gang members, which

was probably why he abruptly left the apartment without any conversation between any of the parties. In the meeting with CALLAHAN, all of the details of the deal as laid out in MARTORANO's previous telephone call were confirmed. FLEMMI and BULGER also learned that former FBI S/A H. Paul RICO, and CALLA-HAN's former partner ███████ were part of the proposed ownership team. RICO, now retired from the FBI and living in the Miami area, had become vice president for security of World Jai Alai, and had hired several other ex-FBI agents to work for the company. ███████ was going to be ███████

Brian Halloran, as the drugs and booze began to take their toll.

business because CALLAHAN would not be able to obtain the necessary gambling license(s) for the organization. CALLAHAN would then control the business ███████ . CALLAHAN invited FLEMMI to contact RICO if the Winter Hill partners had any further questions about the proposal. FLEMMI added that he never met ███████ at any point in time.

182. FLEMMI stated that he contacted RICO at the Miami World Jai Alai fronton by leaving messages in the same fashion as he had done when he was a fugitive in the late 1960's and early 1970's. FLEMMI said that he would initiate the contact with RICO by first speaking with RICO's secretary, using the code phrase "Jack from South Boston" was calling. During a second call to RICO's office, FLEMMI would be given a call-back number for RICO. FLEMMI would then speak to RICO at

H. Paul Rico aged badly, despite his new home in the Sunshine State.

the directed telephone number. FLEMMI stated that when he first spoke to RICO, the retired special agent confirmed that the purchase of World Jai Alai by CALLAHAN was strictly a legitimate business deal. RICO also verified that he, and CALLAHAN wanted Winter Hill assistance in keeping the LCN at bay. RICO also reiterated the terms of the proposition to the Winter Hill partners, including the weekly $10,000 parking lot concession skim, and a potential future percentage of the overall World Jai Alai business.

183. FLEMMI stated that he was aware that RICO and Dennis CONDON were still friendly and occasional golf partners. FLEMMI added that he was very comfortable talking with RICO about the proposal because of their past relationship, and in particular because of the assistance the former FBI Special Agent had previously given him. BULGER was advised of the details of the telephone call with Paul RICO, and indicated that he wanted to be part of the deal.

184. FLEMMI stated that some time later he was again contacted by John MARTORANO through KAUFMAN. MARTORANO said that CALLA-HAN's proposed deal to purchase World Jai Alai had fallen through. MAR-TORANO added that the current owner of World Jai Alai, Roger WHEELER was being exceptionally difficult to deal with, and that CALLAHAN, RICO and ████████ were all very angry about the situation. MARTORANO fur-ther said that CALLAHAN wanted to kill WHEELER. FLEMMI inferred from the conversation with MARTORANO, that RICO and ████████ also agreed that WHEELER should be eliminated. MARTORANO then indi-cated that BULGER and FLEMMI should again speak directly to CALLA-HAN. FLEMMI advised BULGER of his conversation with MARTORANO, and BULGER questioned the wisdom of killing a legitimate businessman like WHEELER. FLEMMI was also against the idea at this point in time.

185. FLEMMI stated that a day or so later, he and BULGER met CALLA-HAN at the Black Rose Tavern in Boston. CALLAHAN confirmed that the proposed deal was dead because of WHEELER's unreasonableness and that he and the other partners, RICO and ████████ , wanted WHEELER eliminated. During the course of this half-hour meeting, CALLAHAN said that MARTORANO and Joe MCDONALD would handle the mur-der. BULGER and FLEMMI did not volunteer to assist with the murder. CALLAHAN also said that ████████ would supply the necessary personal information on WHEELER to allow the murder to be carried out. The personal information was going to be passed from ████████ to RICO, who in turn would give it to CALLAHAN. CALLAHAN was then going to pass the data on to MARTORANO. FLEMMI noted that MARTORANO and MCDONALD later verified this information on WHEELER's back-ground, which included WHEELER's daily schedule. The group was as-sured that if WHEELER's murder took place, the purchase of World Jai Alai by CALLAHAN would be certain, and Winter Hill would be in for a financial "windfall." CALLAHAN felt that WHEELER's widow would be much more willing to negotiate a sale of the business.

186. FLEMMI stated that CALLAHAN again suggested that FLEMMI speak directly with RICO if there were any questions about the plan. FLEMMI

stated that he contacted RICO once again as "Jack from South Boston," and that RICO confirmed that he, ███████ and CALLAHAN wanted WHEELER killed. FLEMMI stated that if RICO had said that he wanted no part in the murder of WHEELER, then he and BULGER would most probably not have become involved. FLEMMI also stated that he discussed the situation regarding the dissemination of the WHEELER's personal information with RICO, and that RICO clearly knew that MARTORANO was going to use the data in stalking the intended victim.

187. FLEMMI stated that he again spoke with MARTORANO via pay telephone and was asked to send some equipment out to Wheeler's hometown of Tulsa OK that would be used in the murder. MARTORANO asked for a sub-machine gun with a silencer, a .38 caliber long-barrel handgun, a slim jim for opening car doors, and a dent puller. MARTORANO wanted these items sent via Greyhound bus, and indicated that after waiving identification, the partners were to send the items addressed to "Joe Russo." FLEMMI

Phil Costa, Stevie's underling, brought the lime to the burials to speed decomposition.

J.R. Russo, Mafia hitman and amateur fashion designer.

agreed to send the package out as soon as possible. FLEMMI stated that the requested equipment was located in a hide, in the basement of ████████ residence in South Boston. FLEMMI added that he had built the hide in ████████ house. FLEMMI and BULGER called ████████, who asked if the group had a problem. BULGER told ████████ that MARTORANO had to "clip" someone out in Oklahoma, and needed the firepower. BULGER and FLEMMI removed the weapons and some ammunition and everything was wrapped in a blanket, along with the slim jim and dent puller, and placed in a zippered duffle bag. FLEMMI then took the items to his Marconi Club in Roxbury and packed them in a suitcase, and had Phil COSTA take the bag to George KAUFMAN. COSTA and KAUFMAN together shipped the suitcase out to Oklahoma.

188. FLEMMI stated that the next thing he heard about the situation was a news report on television reporting WHEELER's murder in the parking lot of a private golf club in Tulsa. FLEMMI estimated that WHEELER's

Roger Wheeler shot an 88 in his final round of golf, just before Johnny
Martorano shot him in the head.

murder took place approximately 10 days after the equipment was shipped to Oklahoma. FLEMMI then contacted BULGER, who said that he had just spoken to John CONNOLLY, and was told by CONNOLLY that "no one can say you did the shooting, I'd be your alibi."

189. FLEMMI stated that the weapons and equipment were returned to Boston, with the exception of the .38 caliber handgun, which MARTORANO and MCDONALD disposed of in a swampy area of Tulsa. The remaining items were shipped back via Greyhound bus in the same fashion as before. FLEMMI noted that at a subsequent meeting in New York, MARTORANO may have mentioned that the .38 caliber handgun used in the murder had blown up or that the ammunition caused some type of a problem. FLEMMI also said that BULGER may have discussed the problem MARTORANO had with the handgun during the WHEELER murder with ▮▮▮▮▮▮.

190. FLEMMI stated that he has no knowledge if CALLAHAN had ever asked Brian HALLORAN to participate in the WHEELER murder plot. FLEMMI also did not recall talking to MARTORANO out in Oklahoma, but acknowledged that it was possible. FLEMMI believes that CALLAHAN gave MARTORANO $50,000 to the group either before or after the WHEELER murder. FLEMMI recalled that he and BULGER each received $8,000 out of the money paid by CALLAHAN. FLEMMI added that they were paid out of the share MARTORANO had from Winter Hill "scores" that were made while MARTORANO was a fugitive. FLEMMI acknowledged that he held these monies for MARTORANO. FLEMMI said that MARTORANO usually received his money via FedEx or in swaps similar to the way the CALLAHAN money was handled.

Leaked information regarding John MARTORANO while he was a fugitive

191. SHORTLY after John MARTORANO became a fugitive in 1979, FLEMMI was told by S/A CONNOLLY that MARTORANO was staying in Miami. FLEMMI noted that CONNOLLY first gave this information to

BULGER, but that he got the news directly from CONNOLLY a short time later. FLEMMI said that CONNOLLY did not tell FLEMMI the source of the information on MARTORANO's whereabouts. FLEMMI then advised George KAUFMAN to warn MARTORANO and this message was relayed. FLEMMI then reported to CONNOLLY that MARTORANO had been advised of the tip. FLEMMI said that he and BULGER discussed the benefits of MARTORANO's fugitive status with CONNOLLY. FLEMMI said that it was CONNOLLY's idea not to bring MARTORANO back to Boston, and to leave him permanently "on the lam." FLEMMI said that MARTORANO represented "the bogeyman" to any of their potential assas-

Sonny Mercurio: "I advocate everybody run away."

sins, particularly from the LCN. FLEMMI added that these potential assassins knew that MARTORANO would try to avenge his (and BULGER's) murders, and therefore afforded the pair a degree of protection. FLEMMI added that MARTORANO only planned on staying away from Boston for a short period of time, until he got the plea bargain on the race-fixing case that best suited him. (The theory was that law-enforcement, wanting to close the books on a case, would always be willing to agree to give any fugitive the shortest sentence imposed on any of the other defendants who had actually gone to trial. The theory was once succinctly summed up by LCN member Angelo "Sonny" MERCURIO in federal court: "Power of the lam means lesser sentence. I advocate everybody run away.") FLEMMI noted that CONNOLLY also revealed that the FBI wasn't really trying very hard to find MARTORANO.

192. FLEMMI stated that CONNOLLY again warned Winter Hill a second time about MARTORANO's whereabouts prior to the Jai Alai murders in approximately 1981. Again the initial warning went to BULGER, but was repeated to FLEMMI a short while later, directly from CONNOLLY. FLEMMI recalled that CONNOLLY said that MARTORANO was staying in Fort Lauderdale and that the FBI was looking for MARTORANO there. FLEMMI spoke to MARTORANO directly regarding this warning. But MARTORANO was reluctant to move because he had just gotten in some new

Johnny Martorano on his boat off Fort Lauderdale.

furniture. FLEMMI insisted, and MARTORANO eventually moved from the apartment. FLEMMI noted that MARTORANO was not always careful while a fugitive. FLEMMI added that friends told him and BULGER that MARTORANO was hanging around with unreliable characters, like ██████ , and ██████ . FLEMMI recalled that ██████ had bumped into MARTORANO at a restaurant named ██████ . FLEMMI added that once MARTORANO moved to Boca Raton there were far fewer problems with him bumping into the wrong people. FLEMMI noted that he did not recall any information from CONNOLLY regarding Joe MCDONALD's whereabouts.

Robert "Mustard" MCCARTHY

193. FLEMMI stated that he has been friends with Robert "Mustard" MCCARTHY since childhood. FLEMMI said that he and MCCARTHY were partners in a shylock business prior to when he went "on the lam" in 1969. The two partners also purchased a tavern together, and called the place "MCCARTHY's." FLEMMI admitted that he really owned and controlled the barroom, but on paper the owner was MCCARTHY. FLEMMI and MCCARTHY continued to conduct shylock operations at the bar until it was sold. MCCARTHY then took over the shylock business, and paid FLEMMI $200 to $300 a month for his share of the business. MCCARTHY continued to pay FLEMMI the monthly fee up until the time

FLEMMI went to jail in Plymouth in 1995. FLEMMI said that Phil COSTA picked up the monthly payment from MCCARTHY after FLEMMI was incarcerated. MCCARTHY also sent money orders to FLEMMI's residence during his time at Plymouth. FLEMMI noted that Frank SALEMME got a portion of MCCARTHY's payment, and that MCCARTHY was aware of this arrangement. FLEMMI said that SALEMME received his money up until his arrest as a fugitive in August 1995 in West Palm Beach FL. FLEMMI also noted that while SALEMME was incarcerated in state prison for the FITZGERALD bombing, he gave SALEMME's wife Alice $200 a month. This money also originated from Mustard MCCARTHY.

Bobby "Mustard" McCarthy, a childhood friend of Stevie Flemmi's.

194. FLEMMI stated that he assisted MCCARTHY in recouping loans on only a few occasions. FLEMMI said that he usually would identify himself to the debtor, and attempt to work out a payment plan. FLEMMI would never threaten the person in arrears, and was only interested in recouping as much money as possible. FLEMMI remembered having to collect $5,000 from ███████ , and another similar amount from ███████ . FLEMMI further added that MCCARTHY used a pizza shop in the Lower Mills section of Dorchester as a location for envelopes to be dropped off by shylock clients. FLEMMI and COSTA on occasion picked up the monthly payment at the pizza shop. MCCARTHY was also involved in a card game with Dick O'BRIEN in Allston, and later in Quincy. FLEMMI said that he did not receive a piece of the profits made from the card game. FLEMMI added that there was a time period when MCCARTHY was involved in ███████ , but that FLEMMI put an end to that partnership.

195. FLEMMI stated that when MCCARTHY's tavern was sold, he only received $20,000 from the sale. BULGER was angered by the small payment FLEMMI was given, and called MCCARTHY down to the South Boston Liquor Mart. FLEMMI said that BULGER chastised MCCARTHY and got an additional $20,000 out of MCCARTHY. FLEMMI gave BULGER $10,000 of this money. FLEMMI recalled that in 1974, MCCARTHY was a big loser to ███████ in a card game. MCCARTHY quickly arranged to have ███████ robbed of the $20,000 he had lost. FLEMMI said that Jerry ANGIULO wanted to kill MCCARTHY over the incident, suspecting that MCCARTHY was behind the robbery. FLEMMI met with ANGIULO and assured the LCN underboss that MCCARTHY would never be involved in such an act. ANGIULO accepted FLEMMI's explanation and the problem passed without further incident or payments of money by MCCARTHY. MCCARTHY later admitted to FLEMMI that he was in fact involved in the robbery. FLEMMI said that he used this situation as a reason to get MC-CARTHY to stop drinking.

███████

196. FLEMMI stated that ███████ was another long-time friend, and noted that he ███████ owned an ███████. FLEMMI admitted that ███████ used to cut pay checks for him so that he could appear to have legitimate income. These checks were then cashed at ███████, which was owed by another of FLEMMI's friends, ███████. FLEMMI said that ███████ was then given back the cash from these checks. ███████ also registered a car in the ███████ name that FLEMMI had actually purchased himself. FLEMMI admitted that this was done in an effort to hide his ownership of the vehicle. FLEMMI also acknowledged assisting ███████ with the collection of a $110,000 debt from an individual in Revere. FLEMMI had told the debtor that he and ███████ were partners in the ███████, and that the debtor was actually stealing from him. FLEMMI put this individual on a payment plan and the debt was eventually paid off. FLEMMI noted that he was also instrumental in convincing ███████ bookkeeper to take a pay cut.

Debra Davis murder (09/17/81)

197. FLEMMI stated that he first met Debra DAVIS when she was working at convicted fence George TAYLOR's jewelry shop in Brookline. FLEMMI said that Ms. DAVIS was 17 or 18 years old when they first met, soon after his return from "the lam." FLEMMI said that Ms. DAVIS was married when he first met her, and that he paid for her divorce. FLEMMI added that her ex-husband was incarcerated at the time and was bothering her, so he sent a threatening message into the jail, and she never heard from him again. FLEMMI and Ms. DAVIS began dating and eventually moved in together. FLEMMI denied having any involvement in the death of Daniel JASSIE (03/08/77), a friend of Ms. DAVIS. FLEMMI did recall that one of the DAVIS brothers had mentioned that JASSIE had been killed with a shotgun and that the death had something to do with a problematic marijuana deal.

Stevie met Debbie Davis when she was 18—and already married.

198. FLEMMI stated that in approximately 1981, he traveled to Haiti with ▬▬▬▬, in order to get a divorce from his first wife, Jeanette. FLEMMI added that Attorney Richard Egbert had arranged for this Haitian divorce. FLEMMI obtained this divorce to help

Richie Egbert, Mob lawyer.

improve his relationship with Ms. DAVIS, which was troubled at that time. FLEMMI said that Ms. DAVIS had met a new wealthy suitor, named Gustav LNU (last name unknown) while on vacation with her mother in Mexico. FLEMMI said that both Ms. DAVIS and her mother told him about the Mexican boyfriend. Ms. DAVIS was also unhappy that FLEMMI was spending too much time away from her, and suspected that he was seeing other women. Ms. DAVIS often complained when FLEMMI was summoned away from her, after being paged by BULGER or S/A CONNOLLY. FLEMMI noted that this was a time period when there was a great deal of activity going on in his life, and therefore he was under a great deal of stress.

199. FLEMMI stated that on one occasion he and Ms. DAVIS were to-gether at the Bay Tower Room at 60 State Street and he was called away. Ms. DAVIS demanded to know where FLEMMI was going, and he admitted out of frustration that he was going to see an FBI agent, who was a friend of BULGER's. BULGER was very angry when he learned from FLEMMI that Ms. DAVIS was now aware of their relationship with S/A CONNOLLY. FLEMMI recalled that Ms. DAVIS' brother Ronald was stabbed to death in MCI Walpole that year (03/17/81). Ms. DAVIS demanded in front of one of the surviving DAVIS brothers that FLEMMI "use your FBI friends and find out who killed my brother." FLEMMI noted that Ronnie DAVIS had made offensive remarks to Larry BAIONE at a wedding. FLEMMI even-tually learned from Phil WAGGENHEIM that another inmate ███████ had killed Ronald DAVIS. FLEMMI stated that the former inmate was later killed in Revere, but that he was not involved in this murder.

200. FLEMMI stated that the problems with Ms. DAVIS were also affect-ing his relationship with BULGER. FLEMMI said that BULGER didn't like Ms. DAVIS, and wasn't very skilled in his relationships with women. As FLEMMI's romance with Ms. DAVIS cooled, BULGER insisted that Ms. DAVIS had to be eliminated because of her knowledge of BULGER's and FLEMMI's association with law-enforcement. FLEMMI said that he finally assented to BULGER's demands and allowed BULGER to plan the murder.

Deb Davis always had more than her share of suitors.

At one point she wanted to become a model.

201. FLEMMI stated that during this time period, he was in the process of purchasing his parents their new home in South Boston. FLEMMI noted that Bulger had urged him to buy the home, which was directly across from the residence of Bulger's younger brother, the president of the State Senate and now one of the most powerful politicians in the state. FLEMMI said that Ms. DAVIS agreed to meet FLEMMI at the new house to look around. Ms. DAVIS arrived at the residence just ahead of FLEMMI and BULGER. FLEMMI said that BULGER had visited the O Street clubhouse, and seen ████████ and ████████ there but that he was unsure if BULGER had already advised ████████ and ████████ of the plot to kill Ms. DAVIS. FLEMMI noted that the Winter Hill gang members really didn't have much of a choice which crimes they would be asked to be involved in. (At one trial, Kevin WEEKS was asked what would have happened if he had refused to a dig a grave in which to bury the latest murder victim. WEEKS' response: "Then I would have been going into the hole too.")

202. FLEMMI stated that he and BULGER then drove down the street to the empty house where Ms. DAVIS was waiting outside. BULGER

unlocked the door and began strangling Ms. DAVIS as soon as the trio
entered the home. BULGER then carried Ms. DAVIS' body down the stairs
to the basement, while continuing to
strangle her. FLEMMI said that he was
upset by the events and quickly went
back upstairs after Ms. DAVIS' body
was brought to the cellar. BULGER
then prepared the corpse for burial by
removing her clothes, then trussing
the body with rope and wrapping her
face and/or entire remains with plastic
bags. FLEMMI did not recall any duct
tape being applied, nor did he kiss his
longtime paramour goodbye or tell her
that she was "going to a better place"
(as has been suggested elsewhere).
FLEMMI said the murder happened
very quickly and that he became emotionally distraught. FLEMMI added
that he contemplated killing BULGER
right after Ms. DAVIS' murder.

Billy Bulger marching in the St.
Patrick's Day parade.

203. FLEMMI stated that the murder
took place in the afternoon and they
waited until about 6 p.m. that night to
put Ms. DAVIS' body into the trunk
of ▮▮▮▮▮▮ car. The car with the
body was then driven to ▮▮▮▮▮▮
home in Quincy and parked in the
garage. BULGER then picked out a
burial spot under the Neponset River
bridge, and he and FLEMMI dug the
grave. FLEMMI said that ▮▮▮▮▮▮
and ▮▮▮▮▮ then drove the car

Kevin Weeks' least favorite mugshot.

containing the corpse out to the burial spot, and dropped off the body. Neither ███████ nor ████████ appeared satisfied with the location of the grave, but FLEMMI noted that they didn't have any choice in the matter. FLEMMI said that he then drove Ms. DAVIS' car to the parking lot of their residence in Randolph.

204. FLEMMI stated that he was told by Olga DAVIS that she was going to the Randolph Police to report her daughter's disappearance. FLEMMI advised Olga DAVIS that he was going to send some people to track Ms. DAVIS' supposed movements in Texas. FLEMMI also mentioned to BULGER that he had told Mrs. DAVIS a fabricated story regarding Debbie DAVIS' alleged appearance in Texas. FLEMMI stated that he never discussed Debbie DAVIS' disappearance with S/A CONNOLLY, but suspects that BULGER did. FLEMMI added that no one in law-enforcement ever approached him to discuss Ms. DAVIS' disappearance. FLEMMI further

Olga Davis, right, Deb's mother; Stevie wept with her after Deb "disappeared."

stated that he has no memory of telling John MARTORANO that he had "accidentally" strangled Ms. DAVIS. FLEMMI did recall that BULGER told MARTORANO that "Debbie's gone" during a later meeting at LaGuardia airport. FLEMMI also said that months, possibly years later, he directed George KAUFMAN to obtain Ms. DAVIS' dental records from Brookline dentist ▮▮▮▮▮▮▮ in order to prevent their use in identifying her remains if they were ever found. FLEMMI admitted that he destroyed the dental records after receiving them from Kaufman.

205. FLEMMI stated that he and BULGER attempted to extort drug trafficker ▮▮▮▮▮▮▮ at MCCARTHY's tavern, shortly before the bar was sold. FLEMMI said that he and BULGER had received information from an unknown source that ▮▮▮▮▮▮ had been smuggling in marijuana in sail boats and was storing it in South Boston. ▮▮▮▮▮▮ was in business with ▮▮▮▮▮▮, as well as ▮▮▮▮▮▮. ▮▮▮▮▮▮ told BULGER and FLEMMI that he was not operating in South Boston, and the pair accepted that explanation for the moment. FLEMMI recalled that he and BULGER searched for a local warehouse in which ▮▮▮▮▮▮ was allegedly storing his marijuana. FLEMMI also recalled that at about the same time period, BULGER may have also attempted to extort ▮▮▮▮▮▮ as part of the same shakedown involving ▮▮▮▮▮▮. FLEMMI reiterated that he and BULGER never obtained any money from this group.

Brian HALLORAN and Michael DONAHUE murders (05/11/82)

206. FLEMMI stated that one night in 1981 Brian HALLORAN walked into a restaurant in Chinatown and shot drug dealer George PAPPAS in the head (10/13/81). FLEMMI learned from street talk that the reason for the shooting was a drug dispute. FLEMMI also said that Jackie SALEMME was not actually involved. FLEMMI noted that Jackie SALEMME had been sitting with PAPPAS at the time of the shooting. FLEMMI also heard from some forgotten source that Michael DONAHUE was the driver of the waiting car that HALLORAN escaped in after the PAPPAS murder. (According to other accounts of the PAPPAS murder, when he fled the restaurant HALLORAN left behind both his car keys and his trademark scally cap.)

FLEMMI said that he had no memory of anyone within the LCN advising him that the organization wanted to kill HALLORAN in order to protect Jackie SALEMME from having to testify under oath. FLEMMI also does not recall any discussion with S/A CONNOLLY concerning anyone planning to kill HALLORAN. FLEMMI did remember at some point talking with BULGER about concocting stories about other groups wanting to murder HALLORAN. FLEMMI assumes that BULGER then passed this idea on to CONNOLLY, who eventually filed reports alleging that several crews, including Charlestown and Somerville gangsters, wanted HALLORAN dead. FLEMMI said he later heard another street rumor that HALLORAN was cooperating with law-enforcement, possibly the MA State Police, while out on bail for the PAPPAS murder. (This false report was also written up by CONNOLLY.) FLEMMI said that everyone on the street was avoiding any contact with HALLORAN because of these rumors.

Michael Donahue, innocent bystander, murdered by Whitey Bulger in 1982.

207. FLEMMI stated that he had learned that there had been a couple of attempts on HALLORAN's life by former Mullens gang member, Jimmy "the Weasel" MANTVILLE and ███████. A second attempt on

Weasel Mantville, one of the Mullens.

HALLORAN's life was made by Charlestown's ███████. FLEMMI recalled being told by BULGER that HALLORAN was wearing an FBI body wire and was attempting to instigate an incriminating conversation with John CALLAHAN regarding the WHEELER murder. FLEMMI said that BULGER received this information concerning HALLORAN's decision to wear a wire in an urgent message from John CONNOLLY. FLEMMI also remembered being advised at some point by BULGER that John CONNOLLY had told him that HALLORAN had implicated BULGER and FLEMMI in the WHEELER homicide case. FLEMMI said that at this point BULGER's only focus was on eliminating HALLORAN as a potential witness against him.

208. FLEMMI stated that he and BULGER met CALLAHAN at the Wharf restaurant in Boston's North End to discuss the situation regarding HALLORAN. FLEMMI recalled that the owner of the restaurant came over to the table and was introduced to him and BULGER by CALLAHAN. CALLAHAN was advised that HALLORAN was cooperating with law-enforcement and wearing a body wire to record anyone who would speak with him. FLEMMI said that CALLAHAN was told not to let HALLORAN know that he was aware that HALLORAN was cooperating. CALLAHAN advised that HALLORAN had been trying to reach out for him, but that he had been successful in avoiding HALLORAN.

209. FLEMMI stated that he and BULGER knew that due to HALLORAN's friendship with CALLAHAN, it was possible that HALLORAN had information regarding their involvement in the WHEELER murder. FLEMMI said that it was also possible that CALLAHAN had actually offered the murder contract to HALLORAN. FLEMMI, WEEKS and BULGER began searching the area for HALLORAN, but found it difficult to locate him. FLEMMI recalled that he and BULGER located HALLORAN one night at Dapper Dan's in Somerville, but didn't take any action because the intended victim was accompanied by longtime Winter Hill associate Joseph MONGIELLO. FLEMMI further noted that it took about a month from the time that the group first started hunting HALLORAN before they were able to kill him.

210. FLEMMI stated that he learned the details of HALLORAN's murder after the fact from BULGER and WEEKS at a meeting conducted the same night as the homicide. FLEMMI noted that the meeting took place at his mother's South Boston residence. FLEMMI said that BULGER recounted the details of the shooting as WEEKS was sitting in the front parlor. The events began when Winter Hill associate John HURLEY observed HALLORAN on Northern Avenue at a low bar known as The Pier. He then went directly to BULGER and Kevin WEEKS at the group's South Boston appliance store. BULGER instantly swung into action, and contacted ███████. BULGER attempted to reach FLEMMI, but was unable to find him. FLEMMI noted that he may have been attending or en route to a meeting with corrupt MA State Police trooper Dick SCHNEI-DERHAN out in the Blue Hills in Milton. FLEMMI had a voice pager and recalled BULGER's message that day, "The Balloon has burst." HALLOR-AN's code name was "Balloonhead."

John Hurley tipped Whitey as to where Halloran was drinking.

211. FLEMMI stated that the group had a "souped-up" high performance car that had been modified at the cost of approximately $25,000. FLEMMI said that ███████ had done the modifications on the car. The vehicle had

Jimmy Flynn—named by Brian Halloran with his last breath as his killer, because Whitey had worn an Afro wig for the hit.

been purchased by ███████ and was known by the group as the "tow truck." FLEMMI admitted that he had registered the "tow truck" and filled out the paperwork while wearing gloves so that there would be no finger-prints. FLEMMI said that just prior to HALLORAN's murder, BULGER picked up the "tow truck" and changed his appearance by donning a Afro wig which made him look like Jimmy FLYNN, a Winter Hill associate who was known to dislike HALLORAN. ███████ was also wearing some type of disguise during the murder, and later admitted to FLEMMI during a walk on a South Boston beach that he ███████ was in the back seat dur-ing the "tow truck" shooting, but that his weapon jammed. FLEMMI was also advised that WEEKS acted as the lookout and was equipped with a walkie-talkie.

212. FLEMMI stated that when the group waited in the "tow truck" until they saw HALLORAN leaving the bar with Michael DONAHUE. DONA-HUE and HALLORAN got into DONAHUE's car, with HALLORAN in the passenger seat. At this point BULGER, the driver of the "tow truck," began shooting with a carbine. BULGER fired at the front passenger seat, where HALLORAN was sitting. From the back seat of the "tow truck," ███████ was also firing at HALLORAN. FLEMMI said that according to BULGER, DONAHUE was killed soon after the gunfire erupted. Already wounded, HALLORAN jumped out of DONAHUE's vehicle in an attempt to escape, but was quickly gunned down in the street. FLEMMI related that the BULGER-driven "tow truck" made a U-turn during the shoot-ing and eventually fled the area, losing a hubcap on the viaduct ramp in the process. A short time after the murders, CONNOLLY told BULGER that "you guys are going to get a lot of heat" because of these homicides. FLEMMI recalled being present when BULGER told CONNOLLY that Jimmy FLYNN, the original suspect in the murders, had not been in-volved in HALLORAN and DONAHUE's death. (As he lay dying in the street, responding Boston police had asked HALLORAN who had shot him. With his dying breath, HALLORAN responded, "Jimmy FLYNN." FLYNN would later be tried, and acquitted, of the murders. His attorney was Richard EGBERT.)

213. FLEMMI stated that it was clear in his mind that CONNOLLY knew that BULGER and the others had murdered HALLORAN and DONAHUE. FLEMMI noted that CONNOLLY regularly advised BULGER and FLEMMI of the status of the HALLORAN/DONAHUE murder investigation. FLEMMI also added that he believed that it was an agent named Dennis O'CALLAGHAN who that evening directly leaked to BULGER the fact that the police had the license plate of the shooter's car in these murders.

(HOWEVER, IN a 2005 deposition, FLEMMI said that he no longer believed O'CALLAGHAN was the agent who leaked the information about the license plate. O'CALLAGHAN would later deliver a flowery tribute to CONNOLLY at Zip's retirement dinner at Joe Tecce's in 1990, and in 1994 would tip off CONNOLLY that BULGER and FLEMMI were about to be indicted, enabling BULGER to flee and avoid capture for 16 years. When he died in 2004, the headline of O'CALLAGHAN's obituary in the Boston *Globe* would say that he had "fought mob.")

FLEMMI NOTED that BULGER said that CONNOLLY had been present when this information was leaked, which took place during the infamous "Beck's beer" meeting at BULGER's apartment. BULGER had served the imported German beer to the FBI agents who were taking a break from investigating the murders. After several beers, the agents informed BULGER of several important details of the investigation that enabled him to avoid arrest. When the agents left, BULGER told his associates, "Thank God for Beck's beer." FLEMMI acknowledged that in the Wolf hearings he had testified that John MORRIS had leaked the details about the "tow truck's" license plate, but admitted that he had perjured himself. FLEMMI said that this critical information had resulted in the "tow truck" being chopped up at ▉▉▉▉ garage. FLEMMI also noted that after ▉▉▉▉▉ was arrested in the 1990 DEA drug case, BULGER contemplated killing ▉▉▉▉ because of his ▉▉▉▉ connection to the "tow truck."

John CALLAHAN murder (07/31/82)

214. FLEMMI stated that BULGER began to be concerned about CALLA-HAN folding under the heat of law-enforcement scrutiny. BULGER learned from CONNOLLY that after HALLORAN's murder, CALLAHAN was one of the focal points in the WHEELER investigation. CONNOLLY also advised BULGER that the FBI wanted to talk to CALLAHAN and that the FBI might be able to put a lot of pressure on CALLAHAN. FLEMMI added that he was present at a subsequent meeting with CONNOLLY and BULGER where the information concerning CALLAHAN's vulnerability to law-enforcement pressure was recapped. FLEMMI noted that this second meeting with CONNOLLY occurred within a day or two from the time BULGER first brought the information to his attention. FLEMMI said that CONNOLLY had learned this information from general conversation about the case within the Boston FBI office. FLEMMI was aware from CONNOLLY that he regularly gathered information about FLEMMI and BULGER from the general office conversation, as well as reading it off the group's informant-information "rotar," which was accessible to all agents. BULGER felt that CALLAHAN was untested and had no reliability with the group because he had gone to an Ivy League college, had never been arrested nor done any time in prison. FLEMMI admitted that he too became concerned about CALLAHAN's trustworthiness.

215. FLEMMI stated that contact was made through KAUFMAN to MARTORANO to arrange a face-to-face meeting in New York. BULGER, FLEMMI and MARTORANO met in a reduced-rate room at a hotel at New York's LaGuardia Airport. FLEMMI noted that MARTORANO had a connection at the hotel with someone in the reception area. MARTORANO was updated by BULGER and FLEMMI on the HALLORAN/DONAHUE murder investigation and the CALLAHAN situation. MARTORANO was told that HALLORAN had advised the FBI that MARTORANO had been involved in the WHEELER homicide. FLEMMI noted that he and BULGER deliberately failed to mention to MARTORANO that they too had been named as co-conspirators in the WHEELER murder plot by HALLORAN.

216. FLEMMI stated that BULGER told MARTORANO that CALLAHAN was not going to stand up and suggested that MARTORANO eliminate CALLAHAN in Florida. FLEMMI said that MARTORANO was advised that the Boston FBI office considered CALLAHAN the focus of its ongoing homicide probes. FLEMMI noted that this piece of information concerning law-enforcement's targeting of CALLAHAN was attributed generally to "the Feds." But he admitted that BULGER could have actually used John CONNOLLY's name. FLEMMI further clarified that whichever reference BULGER used regarding the source of the CALLAHAN information, "the Feds" or John CONNOLLY, he is sure that the information was supplied by John CONNOLLY. FLEMMI added that notwithstanding the "Beck's beer meeting," CONNOLLY was the only source within the FBI that he and BULGER regularly spoke with at that time, and that all information from the FBI was filtered through CONNOLLY.

MARTORANO WAS initially resistant to the idea of killing his good friend CALLAHAN, but eventually agreed. FLEMMI recalled that MAR-TORANO was asked whether CALLAHAN "could do 20 years," at which point MARTORANO acknowledged that he could not and therefore had to be murdered. FLEMMI further indicated that upon returning to Massachusetts, he and BULGER again met with CONNOLLY and recapped their conversation in New York with MARTORANO, in which MARTORANO agreed to murder CALLAHAN. FLEMMI stated that this meeting occurred several weeks before CALLAHAN was murdered. MARTORANO then consented to commit the murder himself with Joe MCDONALD down in Florida. FLEMMI was also of the understanding that MARTORANO was supposed to bury CALLAHAN after the murder. FLEMMI stated that BULGER did most of the talking for both of them during the meeting.

217. FLEMMI stated that MARTORANO had some initial difficultly locating CALLAHAN, and that he called MARTORANO asking about the delay and offering his assistance. MARTORANO declined the offer and indicated that Joe MCDONALD would assist him. FLEMMI initially said that he was not notified of CALLAHAN's murder by MARTORANO, but

first read about it in the newspaper. At a later date FLEMMI reconsidered and recalled that in fact MARTORANO had directly advised him of CALLAHAN's slaying. After the murder, FLEMMI said that BULGER told him he was angry MARTORANO hadn't buried CALLAHAN's body. BULGER said of MARTORANO: "He should of (sic) gotten off his fat ass, there's a lot of sand down there, it would have been easy to bury him." FLEMMI noted that the gun used in CALLAHAN's murder was not sent down from Boston, and that the weapon must have been acquired in Florida by Joe MCDONALD. FLEMMI also remembered that MARTORANO had told him that MCDONALD had planted a watch taken off CALLAHAN's corpse in some long-since forgotten location. (It was actually left in the men's room of a Cuban bar in Little Havana—to make it appear that "bad Cubans" had murdered CALLAHAN.)

218. FLEMMI said that a few weeks after CALLAHAN's murder, MARTORANO called FLEMMI through KAUFMAN requesting an update for MCDONALD on the status of the World Jai Alai purchase. FLEMMI noted that MCDONALD and RICO had a long history together dating back to the "Irish" gang war. (MCDONALD had agreed to take part in both the WHEELER and CALLAHAN murders to return the favor RICO had done for MCDONALD's late partner Buddy MCLEAN in 1964 by setting up Ronald DERMODY to be murdered, and then allowing MCLEAN to hide out in his own home in Belmont after the slaying.)

A MEETING WAS set up with RICO, after the usual messages were exchanged, and FLEMMI flew to Florida accompanied by a girlfriend, ███████ . FLEMMI noted that he and ███████ stayed at the Thunderbird Hotel while in Miami. Ms. ███████ remained at the hotel, while FLEMMI traveled to the Dania Jai Alai fronton and met MARTORANO outside the building. FLEMMI added that it was extremely hot that day, 105 degrees outside according to the weather reports. MARTORANO went inside the fronton and waited in the lounge. FLEMMI then met RICO in another part of the lounge, and was told that there was no deal to be made, and for FLEMMI to pass the information on to the others involved. FLEMMI advised RICO that MARTORANO was currently in the lounge, and pointed MARTORANO out. MARTORANO then walked over and was introduced to RICO, and said that Joe MCDONALD had asked him to speak directly to RICO about the deal. RICO reiterated the fact that the sale appeared dead. FLEMMI further noted that there was no discussion about the four murders, and that after a short time MARTORANO left the lounge.

219. FLEMMI stated that he and RICO continued their conversation in the fronton for a few more minutes. RICO warned FLEMMI that there was a lot of law-enforcement interest in the World Jail Alai case. FLEMMI left the fronton and never spoke with RICO again until the FBI informant hearings in front of U.S. District Court Judge Mark Wolf in 1998. Initially FLEMMI stated that he did not recall giving S/A CONNOLLY information about CALLAHAN having any involvement with "bad Cubans" prior to his murder. FLEMMI speculated that BULGER had passed this false story on to CONNOLLY. At a later meeting FLEMMI acknowledged that he did remember giving CONNOLLY this information himself. FLEMMI said that this information was concocted by himself and BULGER and then passed on to CONNOLLY. The pair assumed that CONNOLLY would pass this information on to law-enforcement officials after the homicide. FLEMMI may have also mentioned to MARTORANO similar information that would have thrown suspicion on other groups, such as the concocted "bad Cubans." FLEMMI also noted that he does not believe that CONNOLLY ever met with CALLAHAN before his murder to take a statement from him.

220. FLEMMI stated that CONNOLLY continually kept him and BULGER informed about the progress of the investigation by S/A's Montanari and Brunnick of the four Jai Alai murders. FLEMMI recalled CONNOLLY stating that Montanari and Brunnick had "files on the case that reached the ceiling". CONNOLLY sarcastically commented that "Montanari is trying to make a career out of the Jai Alai case." FLEMMI noted that Joe MCDONALD was arrested on a train in New York a short time after the meeting with RICO. FLEMMI added that he visited MCDONALD in jail in New York after the arrest.

"Bucky" BARRETT murder (07/26/83)

221. FLEMMI stated that Arthur "Bucky" BARRETT was a leading figure in the infamous Medford Depositors Trust robbery that took place on Memorial Day weekend 1980. (Hundreds of safe-deposit boxes were looted by robbers who had drilled into the bank from the building next door after cutting the alarm systems.) FLEMMI and BULGER learned that ████████ was involved in the robbery and kidnapped ████████ out of a Charlestown barroom using a replica machine gun. BULGER and FLEMMI were able to convince ████████ to reveal the details of the robbery to them. ████████ was then instructed to approach another figure in the robbery, Metropolitan Police Captain Gerald CLEMENTE, and to ask for tribute money for FLEMMI and BULGER. FLEMMI has some memory that CLEMENTE may have been told that some of the money looted from the bank's safe-deposit boxes had belonged to Winter Hill. ████████ did as he was told, but CLEMENTE refused to pay. Jerry ANGIULO then approached BULGER and FLEMMI through Phil WAGGENHEIM about assisting him in collecting on a claim that he had some $250,000 taken in the robbery. BARRETT

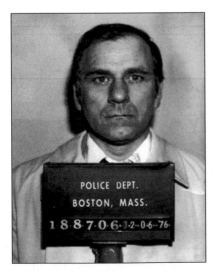

Arthur "Bucky" Barrett, accomplished thief, murdered by Whitey in 1983.

Corrupt MDC Police Capt. Gerry Clemente, who took part in the Depositors Trust burglary with Barrett in 1981.

Bucky Barrett's last driver's license.

was then summoned to the Lancaster Street garage and asked about ANGIULO's claim. BARRETT said that he had not been aware of anything taken that belonged to ANGIULO. FLEMMI further indicated that he and BULGER also claimed that Winter Hill money had been stolen during the Medford Depositors Trust robbery. BARRETT advised FLEMMI and BULGER that he was aligned with Frank SALEMME and was going to see SALEMME in state prison regarding the claims of ANGIULO and Winter Hill.

222. FLEMMI stated that he learned that when BARRETT went to MCI Norfolk to discuss the matter with the imprisoned SALEMME, SALEMME called FLEMMI and BULGER "jackals." FLEMMI noted that SALEMME contacted him and BULGER, and they dropped their demands, but were angered by BARRETT's response. FLEMMI noted that BARRETT was eventually extorted directly by ANGIULO. FLEMMI learned through BAIONE that BARRETT paid ANGIULO the entire $250,000 that he had demanded. ANGIULO offered BULGER and FLEMMI $50,000 out of the BARRETT money, but the pair refused the cash out of respect to SALEMME. FLEMMI

heard from an unknown source that BARRETT paid ANGIULO up to $600,000. While in custody in 1995 SALEMME claimed to FLEMMI that he never received any of BARRETT's money. FLEMMI noted that BULGER passed on the details of the Depositors Trust robbery to CONNOLLY.

Frank Salemme under arrest in New York City in 1972.

223. FLEMMI stated that on 04/06/83, a warehouse containing marijuana, located on D Street in South Boston, was raided by DEA and FBI agents. As a result of this seizure, BARRETT was subsequently arrested along with others. BARRETT's involvement in a South Boston-based drug trafficking operation that was not BULGER-controlled further angered the Winter Hill bosses. FLEMMI said that he and BULGER decided that because of all the trouble that BARRETT had generated, BARRETT was going to be extorted as soon as the opportunity presented itself. FLEMMI said that he and BULGER were able to convince ████████ to help them shake down BARRETT. ████████ told BARRETT that he had a friend who had some stolen diamonds for sale. BULGER supplied ████████ with some sample diamonds and BARRETT expressed interest in making a purchase. FLEMMI said that a more extensive viewing of the diamonds was arranged, and ████████ brought BARRETT to ████████ home at ████████ in South Boston. ████████ and BARRETT entered the home and were immediately seized. FLEMMI noted that he, BULGER, ████████, and Kevin WEEKS were present when BARRETT was grabbed. FLEMMI added that ████████ was told to leave the residence soon after arriving.

224. FLEMMI stated that BARRETT was questioned in the kitchen area of the residence about money he had made from various crimes, including the

Medford Depositors Trust bank robbery. FLEMMI noted that BARRETT was secured with chains once he was brought into the kitchen. BARRETT confessed that he once had $500,000 in gold but had lost it to ANGIULO. BARRETT also said that he had some $60,000 in cash hidden under the washing machine at his home. BARRETT arranged to have his wife leave the home after turning off the burglar alarm, so that the cash could be retrieved by BULGER and FLEMMI. FLEMMI stated that BARRETT also had money waiting for him at ██████ . FLEMMI said that ██████ , WEEKS and ██████ picked up approximately $10,000 from the bar. FLEMMI said that the money was eventually split up among the group, with some going into the Ex fund. BARRETT was also interrogated about ██████ drug trafficking organization, and at some point called both brothers in an attempt to extort more money. FLEMMI noted that both of the ██████ refused to come up with any cash.

225. FLEMMI stated that originally the intent had only been to extort BARRETT, but that BULGER did not want to let BARRETT go. FLEMMI added that BULGER talked him into eliminating BARRETT. FLEMMI noted that one of the concerns was that BARRETT would again go to SALEMME and complain about being extorted. FLEMMI said that at some point everyone involved had to realize that BARRETT was going to be murdered. BULGER subsequently decided to take BARRETT into the basement of the residence and began walking BARRETT down the stairs. FLEMMI said that he was in the kitchen and ██████ and WEEKS were in the living room, as BARRETT began descending the cellar stairway in front of BULGER. FLEMMI observed BULGER put a Mac 10 machine gun with a silencer up to BARRETT's head at the top of the stairs. BULGER then took out his glasses and flipped off the weapon's safety and shot BARRETT. FLEMMI noted that BARRETT had walked down a few stairs when BULGER fired the weapon at him.

226. FLEMMI said that he saw BARRETT's body fall down the stairs, and noted that blood quickly pooled on the bottom step. FLEMMI recalled dragging the body, possibly with WEEKS, to the back of the cellar. The

body was stripped naked and then FLEMMI removed BARRETT's teeth using pliers. FLEMMI said that BULGER had discussed with him during an earlier conversation the absolute importance of removing a murder victim's teeth in order to make identification of the body more difficult. FLEMMI said that he could see a single gunshot wound to the back of BARRETT's head but did not recall observing an exit wound. FLEMMI noted that in either this shooting or with the later MCINTYRE murder, Kevin WEEKS appeared shocked that the victim had been killed. FLEMMI believes that ██████████ and WEEKS dug a grave for the body in the rear basement's dirt floor. FLEMMI noted that it had been BULGER's idea to use the dirt floor cellar as a burial spot for BARRETT and that it was done against his advice. FLEMMI called Phil COSTA, who delivered lime, which was placed below and on top of the body after it was placed in the grave. FLEMMI crushed the victim's teeth using a hammer, and then flushed the remnants down the toilet. FLEMMI added that the house was cleaned up and the group then left the home.

227. FLEMMI stated that prior to the murder, he had asked BARRETT if he had any contacts within law-enforcement. BARRETT answered in the negative, but BULGER indicated that he believed that BARRETT did have connections. FLEMMI later heard from BULGER that BARRETT had given information to law-enforcement in the past, but never was personally given any confirmation on the matter. FLEMMI said that ██████████ was told what had transpired with BARRETT the next day, but did not have advance knowledge that the group was going to kill BARRETT. FLEMMI added that ██████████ should have surmised that BARRETT was likely to be killed, given the circumstances under which the extortion was going to take place. FLEMMI also did not recall ██████████ being given any of the money that was taken from BARRETT's residence.

██████████ extortion and World Jai Alai grand jury appearance (11/08/83)

228. FLEMMI stated that ██████████ had told him that John CALLAHAN had bank accounts in Switzerland. FLEMMI also learned that ██████████

and ▮▮▮▮ had access to the account or the money that had been in the Switzerland. FLEMMI said that ▮▮▮▮ arranged to have ▮▮▮▮ go to Triple O's for a meeting. FLEMMI added that he, BULGER and possibly Kevin WEEKS spoke with ▮▮▮▮. This meeting was conducted on the second floor of the bar, and the gang demanded money that they claimed Winter Hill had invested with CALLAHAN. FLEMMI said that ▮▮▮▮ was threatened with a replica Thompson machine gun and was clearly frightened. ▮▮▮▮ admitted that there was a Swiss bank account and he would attempt to retrieve the owed money. FLEMMI said that ▮▮▮▮ made one or two trips to Switzerland and withdrew the money from CAL-LAHAN's account.

229. FLEMMI stated that the Winter Hill/South Boston group was paid approximately $500,000 to $600,000 of CALLAHAN's money. FLEMMI said that the money came in increments, and was dropped off with George KAUFMAN. FLEMMI said that he split up the money, and that he, ▮▮▮▮, BULGER, WEEKS and George KAUFMAN each received approximately $60,000 apiece, with the Ex fund getting an equal share. FLEMMI added that shortly after the extortion, ▮▮▮▮ was subpoenaed by the grand jury investigating the World Jai Alai murders and related crimes. FLEMMI does not recall much direct conversation with CONNOLLY about the grand jury, but knew that the gang received some information through BULGER.

230. FLEMMI stated that ▮▮▮▮ was instructed to tell the grand jury that Bucky BARRETT had been the one who had gotten money from CALLAHAN's bank accounts. FLEMMI said that he was the one who came up with the idea to blame the extortion on the missing BARRETT. FLEMMI added that ▮▮▮▮ had been the one who passed the story on to ▮▮▮▮. FLEMMI also confirmed that ▮▮▮▮ was shown a picture of BARRETT so that he could intelligently describe BARRETT. FLEMMI could not recall for sure where the photo of BARRETT was

obtained, but believed that the picture came from BULGER. FLEMMI further added that he recalled discussions about some property on High Street in Boston, and its involvement in the extortion. FLEMMI did not recall attorney ██████ having any involvement in the grand jury questioning of ██████ . FLEMMI speculated that CONNOLLY would have had to have known about the extortion, but did not recall any specific conversation about it with CONNOLLY.

231. FLEMMI stated that he occasionally saw ██████ around town after the extortion and had been told by a long-forgotten source that he ██████ and his partner ██████ skimmed $50,000 a week out of their ██████ . FLEMMI added that Winter Hill associate ██████ had robbed ██████ of a large amount of cash, but that there had been little or no police investigation about it. FLEMMI also said that he was aware that ██████ was a thief because ██████ had embezzled money from a Swiss bank account belonging to ██████ .

232. FLEMMI stated that he and BULGER were summoned to the Boston FBI office for photos, as part of the same grand jury investigation that had ensnared ██████ . At first FLEMMI said that he directly discussed with CONNOLLY this aspect of the grand jury investigation. At a later discussion, FLEMMI felt that CONNOLLY had only spoken directly with BULGER, and that this information was then passed on to him. CONNOLLY advised BULGER that he and FLEMMI were both suspects in the Jai Alai murders, and told them to dress in business attire so that they did not look like criminals. CONNOLLY also arranged an interview with BULGER and FLEMMI for S/A Montanari, which was conducted at the gang's O Street clubhouse (11/02/83). FLEMMI noted that both CONNOLLY and BULGER had to convince him to do the interview. FLEMMI stated that CONNOLLY was not present during the interrogation. FLEMMI noted that he and BULGER were questioned together and that neither he nor BULGER was asked any difficult questions.

Stevie Flemmi mugshot 1982; Zip Connolly told him and Whitey to wear business attire.	Whitey didn't want to look like the hitman who murdered Roger Wheeler.

"STIPPO" RAKES/SOUTH BOSTON LIQUOR MART Extortion (03/24/84)

233. FLEMMI stated that as far as he knew, the event that began the Stephen "Stippo" RAKES extortion was a request to BULGER for assistance on some telephone bomb threats RAKES had received soon after opening his new package store, the South Boston Liquor Mart. According to BULGER, the request for help was made by ▮▮▮▮▮▮▮. FLEMMI said the problem regarding the threats were addressed, and that these attempts at intimidation had come from some other South Boston area liquor store owners. The other package-store owners had been concerned that the new package store, with its convenient parking and location between two large public-housing projects, was cutting into their businesses. FLEMMI next learned that RAKES was interested in selling the business, and that this offer to BULGER also came from ▮▮▮▮▮▮. FLEMMI noted that he had heard, again from BULGER, that RAKES had financial problems from the start and had opened

the store "on a shoestring." FLEMMI noted that RAKES was not well liked in the South Boston community because RAKES was a ■■■■■ .

234. FLEMMI stated that he was present when Stephen "Stippo" RAKES was first negotiating the price on the liquor store with James BULGER. This initial meeting took place at RAKES' apartment in South Boston. FLEMMI believes that a price for the business was mentioned and had a feeling that it was for approximately $60,000. FLEMMI was unsure whether Kevin WEEKS was present for this discussion. Initially FLEMMI indicated that he was present for the meeting at which the sale was actually consummated. At later discussions on this topic, FLEMMI said that he was not present at the final meeting when the money was exchanged, but had learned the details of the meeting from BULGER and WEEKS.

Stippo Rakes, who owned the South Boston Liquor Mart—very briefly.

235. FLEMMI stated that the purchase of the liquor store was initially a completely legitimate transaction, but that at the last second RAKES demanded more money. It was FLEMMI's understanding that at some point in the discussion, after the additional money was demanded by RAKES, Kevin WEEKS pulled out a handgun and placed it on the table. FLEMMI noted that WEEKS had a deep hatred for RAKES even before the dispute over the sales price developed. FLEMMI said that BULGER was playing with RAKES' young daughter, and that the child reached for the weapon that had been placed on the table. BULGER quickly grabbed the firearm, and put the weapon away. FLEMMI was unsure if he heard about the incident with the gun immediately after it happened or at another later

time. (RAKES' recollection is that it was FLEMMI who had the gun, and that when RAKES' daughter attempted to pick it up, FLEMMI said, "It would be a shame if she had to grow up without a father.") FLEMMI also added that he believes that RAKES reneged on the deal with BULGER and WEEKS because he had come to realize that the situation with the bomb threats had been completely resolved.

236. FLEMMI stated that RAKES behaved normally after the sale of the store, and that relations with the gang were not strained, as they would have been if the store had actually been extorted in the fashion that RAKES now claims. FLEMMI also noted that he was very friendly with ████████, and that she never complained nor spoke negatively about the circumstances surrounding the sale of the store. FLEMMI did recall that BULGER was concerned about rumors circulating in South Boston that the store had been extorted from RAKES, and that RAKES had been subsequently murdered. FLEMMI said that BULGER arranged for RAKES to return from vacation at Disneyworld in FL, so that RAKES could be seen standing out with BULGER on a South Boston street corner in an effort to show that he was alive and well. FLEMMI noted that he was again not present for this public spectacle of RAKES and BULGER together waving at passersby as if they were at a late-campaign political standout. FLEMMI was then asked about RAKES' subsequent position with the MBTA. FLEMMI said that at first he thought that William BULGER must have assisted RAKES in obtaining the job with the MBTA. In a later conversation, after further consideration, FLEMMI said that he strongly doubted that RAKES had any assistance from either James or William BULGER in obtaining this position. FLEMMI noted that William BULGER saved those types of public payroll jobs for his very closest political associates, and jealously doled these positions out. (RAKES never claimed to have gotten his later T job through William BULGER, even though the joke at the time was that MBTA stood for "Mr. Bulger's Transportation Authority." RAKES said he obtained his T job after paying $3,000 cash to the driver of another South Boston politician.)

237. FLEMMI stated that BULGER put up $5,000 in his mother's name as his share of the money used to purchase the building which housed the liquor store. FLEMMI noted that this money eventually was repaid to BULGER out of the Mary Irene Trust account. FLEMMI also recalled

South Boston Liquor Mart. During election season, politicians vied to have their signs in the front windows, as the seal of approval from Whitey Bulger.

investing and losing $25,000 in a sporting-goods store that was located in the building that contained the Rotary Variety Store. FLEMMI did not own an interest in the South Boston Liquor Mart business, but was paid $500 a week as an employee in what amounted to basically a "no-show" job. FLEMMI noted that he did work a few hours a week, mostly taking orders over the telephone. FLEMMI also received $800 a month in rent money from the liquor store. FLEMMI said that he cashed the $500 payroll check, and claimed the salary and rent money on his income taxes as legitimate income, but in fact returned the $500 cash to the liquor store.

238. FLEMMI stated that even after the gang took over the liquor store, it was not particularly lucrative, and that a lot of money had to be invested into it in order to build up the business. FLEMMI said that because the profit margin was so small, the gang tried to sell in volume. FLEMMI noted that they did recruit area barrooms for liquor purchases, although they understood this was a violation of state law. FLEMMI also noted that RAKES could not have made these same illegal sales during the brief time he owned the business. FLEMMI said that the gang tried to keep the operation as legitimate as possible, and to the best of his knowledge did not launder any

of the proceeds from any of the group's illegal activities through this "cash" business, with the exception of minor maintenance. (Given the store's central location, local politicians soon began asking if they could put their campaign signs in the mart's front windows. The fact that the store was owned by well-known organized-crime figures did not deter the South Boston elected officials; competition was keen for the front-window space.)

239. FLEMMI stated that at some point, BULGER had advised him that Julie RAKES' uncle, Boston Police Detective Joe LUNDBOHM had approached FBI S/A John CONNOLLY regarding the sale of the liquor store to the gang. FLEMMI noted that he was aware that in the 1960's, his shylock associate Peter POULOS had paid bribe money to LUNDBOHM. CONNOLLY advised BULGER that RAKES was told that he would have to wear a body wire and record some incriminating conversations which would back up the claim that the store had been taken from him through extortion. FLEMMI noted that RAKES refused to wear the body wire for the FBI. FLEMMI said that the gang took this as a clear warning that they should be particularly careful if RAKES came around the store.

Det. Joe Lundbohm, Julie Rakes' uncle, interceded with the wrong FBI agent—Zip Connolly. Lundbohm later went to federal prison for aiding gambling enterprises.

240. FLEMMI stated that he has no knowledge of ▮▮▮▮ going to the MA state Attorney General's office. FLEMMI added that it was not until the post-1995 trial discovery that he learned that Julie Rakes did not want to sell the business. FLEMMI said that during the federal grand jury probe of the early 1990's, Stephen RAKES came to BULGER and advised him that he had been questioned about the sale of the store. RAKES informed BULGER that he had told the grand jury that the sale was a legitimate transaction. FLEMMI noted that to the best of his memory, RAKES was the only

source of information to the gang about this particular line of inquiry by the grand jury.

241. FLEMMI stated that later when the liquor store was bought by Kevin O'NEIL and ███████, he sold his share of the building to BULGER for $100,000. FLEMMI said that he was paid in cash by BULGER, but on his taxes only claimed that he made $40,000 from the deal. FLEMMI recalled that ███████ charged $17,000 for legal work on the sale of the building. FLEMMI said that ███████ bill was paid from money from the "Ex Fund". FLEMMI also noted that he sold his share of a check-cashing business, housed at the Rotary Variety Store, to Pat LINSKEY for $10,000. LINSKEY also became a silent partner with O'NEIL in the South Boston

Corrupt FBI agent John Morris took at least $7,000 from Stevie and Whitey.

Liquor Mart for $25,000. FLEMMI was aware of LINSKEY's investment in the liquor store through direct conversation with LINSKEY and O'NEIL. FLEMMI also remembered that the gang had a guardrail installed in the parking lot of the Liquor Mart by a City of Boston work crew through a connection that O'NEIL had within the Boston Parks Department. FLEMMI further added that CONNOLLY learned about a complaint that the FBI had received regarding the installation of the guardrail and subsequently CONNOLLY warned BULGER. The gang then had the guardrail removed immediately. (The city crew had been observed by a Boston *Globe* photographer who had surreptitiously taken pictures of the installation from nearby Preble Street. When the photographer with some excitement presented the pictures to the editors of the *Globe*, they expressed no interest in printing them. The photographer later testified in federal court that after being rebuffed by the *Globe* editors, he then turned the photos over to an

FBI agent he knew. That agent innocently took the photos to CONNOLLY and MORRIS, who immediately told BULGER to remove the guardrails.)

John MCINTYRE murder (11/30/84)

242. FLEMMI stated that S/A John CONNOLLY had advised FLEMMI and BULGER that one of the two individuals on their IRA gun-smuggling ship VAL-HALLA was an informant. The ship had been boarded by Irish law-enforcement and its contraband cargo seized. CON-NOLLY did not know which of the two individuals was the actual informant. FLEMMI also noted that these two individuals had been photographed by a newspaper at the time the boat was boarded again when it returned to Boston. FLEMMI remembered see-ing a photo of these two individuals on the ship. FLEMMI added that CON-

John McIntyre, police informer whose identity was leaked to Whitey, who then murdered him in 1984.

NOLLY had first advised BULGER of the existence of an informant on the VALHALLA, but later at a subsequent meeting confirmed the details of this data directly to FLEMMI. FLEMMI recalled that one of the two individuals on the VALHALLA at the specified time was John MCINTYRE. FLEMMI said that BULGER figured out that MCINTYRE had to have been the infor-mant. The plan was then to confront MCINTYRE at ■■■■■■. FLEMMI said that MCINTYRE was brought to ■■■■■■ South Boston by ■■■■■■. MCINTYRE was asked to carry in some beer that was in the vehicle that MCINTYRE and ■■■■■■ had arrived in. ■■■■■■ had told MCINTYRE that the beer had been purchased for ■■■■■■ walked into the home first, followed by MCINTYRE.

243. FLEMMI stated that MCINTYRE was immediately confronted by BULGER, who was armed with a .22 caliber pistol with a silencer.

MCINTYRE was questioned in the kitchen and admitted that he was working with DEA or Customs and the Quincy Police. MCINTYRE also talked about the $20,000 he had invested with the group for a proposed drug smuggle after the marijuana-smuggling ship RAMSLAND was seized. MC-INTYRE said that $20,000 came from the law-enforcement organization that he was cooperating with. FLEMMI noted that BULGER had concocted this proposed post-RAMSLAND smuggle and had instructed ██████████ to invite MCINTYRE to invest in the concocted scheme. FLEMMI added that he, WEEKS and ██████████ were present when MCINTYRE was confronted about the VAHALLA by BULGER.

244. FLEMMI said that MCINTYRE swore he had not been the informant on the VALHALLA, but apologized to ██████████ for working with law-enforcement after the gun smuggle. (MCINTYRE had never mentioned FLEMMI and BULGER by name to law-enforcement, referring to them only as "the two guys who ride around together.") FLEMMI noted that BULGER initially thought MCINTYRE had been the informant that had actually given up the VALHALLA. FLEMMI added that he did not recall whether there was any further conversation about the RAMSLAND smuggle. At some point later, BULGER admitted to FLEMMI that there had to have been another informant on the VALHALLA. MCINTYRE was also questioned about the ██████████ and their net worth. BULGER then told MCINTYRE to calm down, that they were going to give him some money so he could go "on the lam." FLEMMI and BULGER took MCINTYRE downstairs, telling MCINTYRE that they were going to talk some more. FLEMMI noted that there had been no discussion about murdering MC-INTYRE prior to MCINTYRE's arrival at the house, but that MCINTYRE's fate was sealed once he confessed to cooperating with law-enforcement. FLEMMI said that when the group got to the basement, BULGER began strangling MCINTYRE with a rope, but wasn't successful. FLEMMI noted that MCINTYRE wasn't resisting, and appeared to just give up. FLEMMI added that BULGER then shot MCINTYRE in the back of the head to make the situation more humane for the victim. (According to some accounts, BULGER asked MCINTYRE if he wanted to be shot, and MCINTYRE replied, "Yes please.")

245. FLEMMI stated that he caught MCINTYRE's body as he fell, but couldn't determine if MCINTYRE was dead, even after checking for a pulse. FLEMMI told BULGER to shoot MCINTYRE again, and as FLEMMI held up MCINTYRE's lifeless head by the hair, BULGER subsequently fired additional rounds into the side of his head. FLEMMI then went about removing the victim's teeth and recalled that MCINTYRE may have had some type of a partial dental plate. The body was then stripped naked and placed in a grave that was dug in the basement by ▇▇▇▇▇ and WEEKS. FLEMMI said that the cellar was picked up, and he noted that there had not been very much blood after the shooting. FLEMMI said that the victim's teeth were crushed and disposed of, and the area of the grave sprayed with water to help pack the soil down. FLEMMI did not recall applying lime to MCINTYRE's body, but may have.

Debra HUSSEY Murder (January-February 1985)

246. FLEMMI stated that Debra HUSSEY's murder, like Debra DAVIS', was very difficult and emotionally draining for him. Initially FLEMMI

Deb Hussey: Stevie and Whitey "had had enough," murdered 1985.

Michelle Davis, Deb's younger sister, another underage girl raped by Stevie; died of a drug overdose at age 38.

denied having a sexual relationship with his stepdaughter Debra HUSSEY, as well as ▮▮▮▮▮ , and Michelle DAVIS, Debra DAVIS' younger sister. After discussing the subject of potential sexual abuse for a second time, FLEMMI admitted that he received fellatio from Ms. HUSSEY and Michelle DAVIS, but only after the young women were of age. (Michelle Davis died of a drug overdose in 2006 on the day she was released from the South Bay House of Correction. She was 38 years old and had black hair.) FLEMMI maintained that he never had any sexual relations with ▮▮▮▮▮ . FLEMMI added that he initially denied having sexual relations with Ms. HUSSEY because he was embarrassed by his behavior. FLEMMI also admitted that one of the reasons Ms. HUSSEY was killed was because of the sexual-relations issue. FLEMMI also added that another reason for her murder was her erratic and troubling behavior. FLEMMI said that Ms. HUSSEY had often embarrassed his policeman brother Mike, because she was often arrested for prostitution in Boston's Combat Zone. Ms. HUSSEY also stole money from a local bookmaker known as Mickey X as well as from her own family. FLEMMI recalled that Ms. HUSSEY even stole jewelry from her half-sister Stephanie.

247. FLEMMI stated that on one occasion at four in the morning, Ms. HUSSEY was being held against her will in a residence in Dorchester. Ms. HUSSEY contacted FLEMMI, who won her release. Ms. HUSSEY also disliked BULGER, and was often disrespectful to BULGER. FLEMMI added that Ms. HUSSEY would use drugs while staying with her mother, and sometimes even brought home black male prostitution clients to the family's residence, which caused FLEMMI additional embarrassment. FLEMMI acknowledged that most of this problematic behavior was the result of her drug use, which included heroin. FLEMMI further added that Ms. HUSSEY was also dropping his name as well as BULGER's when she got into trouble or needed something from someone. FLEMMI stated that he tried to help her by giving her money and getting her an apartment in Mansfield, MA. FLEMMI noted that he also sent Ms. HUSSEY to several drug rehabilitation programs. FLEMMI said that eventually he and BULGER had had enough of her behavior and decided to kill her.

248. BULGER knew that because of the emotional ties, FLEMMI would not be able to kill Ms. HUSSEY by himself. FLEMMI said that he and Ms. HUSSEY drove to ████████ home at ████████ in South Boston under the pretense that they were looking for an apartment for her. FLEMMI stated that Ms. HUSSEY was immediately throttled by BULGER in the front room of the residence. FLEMMI indicated that although no conversation with WEEKS or ████████ had occurred prior to Ms. HUSSEY's murder, the fact that BULGER told WEEKS and ████████ to meet him at ████████ should have caused WEEKS and ████████ to assume that Debra HUSSEY was to be murdered. FLEMMI noted that he never had any conversation regarding Ms. HUSSEY's homicide with WEEKS or ████████ either before or after the murder. FLEMMI said that the body was brought to the cellar, where FLEMMI stripped it and pulled out the teeth. FLEMMI does not recall strangling Ms. HUSSEY in the basement with a rope, after BULGER had first strangled the victim on the first floor. FLEMMI admitted that he may have twisted her light beige sweater around her neck, while stripping the body. FLEMMI does not remember twisting the sweater around her neck using a stick in a fashion similar to the way a tourniquet is utilized.

249. FLEMMI stated that he wanted to move the bodies buried in the home at ████████ , even before ████████ wanted to sell the house. FLEMMI was also adamant that ████████ not know the new location that the bodies were going to be buried. FLEMMI said that BULGER chose the location on Hallett Street in Dorchester, across the street from Florian Hall. FLEMMI said that the grave was pre-dug, and refilled with duffle bags full of dirt. FLEMMI noted that he was not happy with the location that BULGER had chosen. FLEMMI added that BULGER placed a $20 bill on top of the refilled hole as a test to see if the potential grave site had been stumbled upon by anyone. FLEMMI also built a blind so that one of the group could conduct a surveillance of the area while the digging of the grave, and later burial, took place.

250. FLEMMI stated that he ████████ , and Kevin WEEKS dug up the bodies of John MCINTYRE, Arthur "Bucky" BARRETT and Debra HUSSEY

from in the cellar at the ▓▓▓▓▓ South Boston location. The remains were then placed in body bags that FLEMMI had gotten a week before, from a friend in the funeral-home business named ▓▓▓▓▓ FLEMMI added that Ms. HUSSEY's corpse had some flesh clinging to the bones after it was exhumed. FLEMMI also said that during the reburial, one of the group (FLEMMI, BULGER, WEEKS) remained on surveillance and was heavily armed should a problem arise. FLEMMI recalled that a male individual stopped at the burial site to urinate while the group was there, but that no action was taken to harm this individual. FLEMMI also remembered that he had left one of the now-empty body bags in the grave with the remains, and that this mistake made BULGER very angry. FLEMMI noted that after ▓▓▓▓▓ was arrested and later sent to prison on the armored-truck robbery, ▓▓▓▓▓ asked BULGER where MCINTYRE's body was buried.

BULGER's South Boston based drug trafficking and extortions (1980-1990)

251. FLEMMI stated that BULGER first became involved in drug trafficking through ▓▓▓▓▓ of South Boston. According to FLEMMI, BULGER personally liked ▓▓▓▓▓, and respected how carefully ▓▓▓▓▓ was in handling his ▓▓▓▓▓ illegal activities. FLEMMI indicated that ▓▓▓▓▓ had been incarcerated at MCI Walpole prior to hooking up with BULGER, and that due to his ▓▓▓▓▓ time in prison he ▓▓▓▓▓ was very suspicious of people and exceptionally paranoid. FLEMMI indicated that on several occasions in the early 1980's, he and WEEKS would wait outside ▓▓▓▓▓ residence for hours while BULGER met with ▓▓▓▓▓ inside. According to FLEMMI, ▓▓▓▓▓ put together the drug part of the organization during the early 1980's, utilizing such individuals as ▓▓▓▓▓ and Paul "Polecat" MOORE. Initially, FLEMMI did not receive any money from the drug aspect of the organization. However, as time passed and the group started making significant amounts of money, he received a share of the profits. FLEMMI estimated that he pocketed approximately $1,000 to $1,500 per week from this South Boston-based drug trafficking organization.

252. FLEMMI stated that during the mid-1980's, ▓▓▓▓▓ tried to break away from the group. According to FLEMMI, BULGER forced ▓▓▓▓▓

to continue managing the business for a short time. Eventually, ██████████ was successful in convincing BULGER that the business could continue without him, and shortly thereafter was allowed to return to Florida where he was residing. FLEMMI indicated that after ██████████ left, ██████████ assumed control of the day-to-day business of the drug-distribution ring, with the assistance of ██████████ and John "Red" SHEA. In addition, FLEMMI stated that several years prior to ██████████ leaving South Boston, he and BULGER brought Hobart WILLIS under the umbrella of the organization.

Red Shea, ran one of Whitey's cocaine rings.

253. FLEMMI stated that the opportunity presented itself to bring WILLIS into the "fold" when WILLIS ran into trouble with the LCN. FLEMMI said that WILLIS made disparaging remarks about the "Italians," and the information got back to the LCN. As a result of WILLIS' remarks, the LCN discussed "clipping" (i.e., murdering) WILLIS. FLEMMI and BULGER ultimately interceded with Larry BAIONE, and the LCN dropped its plan. WILLIS was subsequently fined $200,000, which was split up between FLEMMI/BULGER and BAIONE. Thereafter, Hobart WILLIS came under the South Boston umbrella and paid "rent" to FLEMMI and BULGER for the next three to four years. WILLIS paid approximately $1,500 a month in "rent" to operate his drug business. FLEMMI further noted that WILLIS' group also included ██████████. FLEMMI was also aware that ██████████, who owned and operated ██████████ in Roxbury, was involved with the South Boston group in cocaine trafficking.

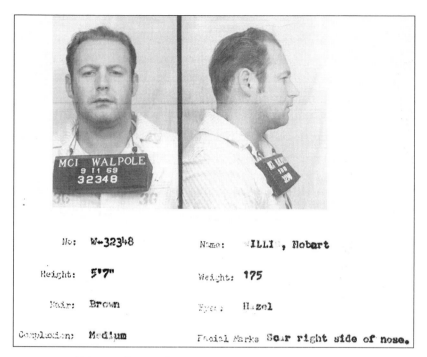

No: W-32348   Name: ⁀ILLI⁀, Hobart

Height: 5'7"   Weight: 175

Hair: Brown   Eyes: Hazel

Complexion: Medium   Facial Marks Scar right side of nose.

Hobart Willis, another "rent-paying" Southie drug dealer.

254. FLEMMI stated that he met Attorney Richard Egbert in the early 1970's at CHANDLER's Restaurant in the South End. FLEMMI indicated that at the time Attorney Egbert was very friendly with Jimmy MARTORANO and Howie WINTER, and as a result became friendly with the rest of the Winter Hill gang. FLEMMI stated that in 1990, after the DEA investigation in which 51 individuals from the BULGER gang were arrested, he arranged for Attorney Egbert to take over the representation of John "Red" SHEA from Attorney Anthony Cardinale. As noted above, "Red" SHEA ran one of the drug-distribution groups in South Boston, and also had the connection to the group's Florida source of supply.

255. FLEMMI stated that he took this action on behalf of "Red" SHEA with Attorney Egbert in order to have more control over SHEA so that SHEA would never seriously consider cooperating with the government. (SHEA never did cooperate, serving his entire 12-year sentence.) FLEMMI

said that Attorney Egbert would control the witness and for this service, FLEMMI paid Egbert's fee of $70,000. FLEMMI added that Attorney Egbert's fee came out of the "Ex" (expense) fund. FLEMMI later had a "falling out" with Attorney Egbert over the representation of FLEMMI's son, Stephen HUSSEY. This problem occurred after the 1995 indictment in United States v. Stephen J. FLEMMI et al., and related to a perjury case against HUSSEY. FLEMMI indicated that during the case Attorney Egbert ████████ . HUSSEY was subsequently found guilty, and FLEMMI blamed Egbert for not representing his son at trial.

256. FLEMMI stated that he did recall participating with BULGER and WEEKS in "shaking down" another South Boston drug trafficker, ████████ for approximately $60,000, relative to a shooting incident ████████ brother had with Charlestown-based hoodlums. FLEMMI believes that he received approximately $10,000 from ████████ extortion. On another occasion BULGER and WEEKS approached ████████ for the purpose of extorting him for dealing drugs in South Boston. FLEMMI believes Sonny BAIONA, an LCN associate who operated out of a tavern in the South End, may have interceded on ████████ behalf. FLEMMI does not recall how much if any monies were received.

257. FLEMMI stated that he was not aware of the organization being involved in the distribution of any so-called "gangster grass." However, FLEMMI had heard that Jimmy KEARNS, Billy KELLEY and Tommy NEE grabbed an unidentified large-scale drug trafficker in Texas, and that this drug dealer was killed during an attempted drug rip-off of $10,000,000 worth of marijuana. FLEMMI stated that ████████ was also part of the group that participated in the drug "rip-off." FLEMMI further reported that he was with BULGER and WEEKS when they paid a visit to ████████ at his apartment. FLEMMI stated that on this occasion BULGER, FLEMMI and WEEKS used a ruse to extort ████████ . BULGER told ████████ that he had sold drugs to a kid whose father was attempting to take out a "contract" on his life. FLEMMI believes that this extortion was successful, but does not recall how much money was obtained. FLEMMI noted that

during this same meeting it was decided that ██████ would now work with ██████ Paul "Polecat" MOORE in the drug organization managed by ██████. ██████ were also told to pay an additional sum of money to operate their shylock business in South Boston.

Joe MURRAY drug trafficking activities with the BULGER/FLEMMI gang

258. FLEMMI stated that during the early 1980's, BULGER and FLEMMI had been hearing street rumors that Joseph MURRAY of Charlestown was making substantial amounts of money in the drug business. In April 1983, Joseph MURRAY's organization surfaced directly on BULGER and FLEMMI's radar when law-enforcement raided a warehouse on D Street in South Boston and seized several tons of marijuana. As a result of the above raid, BULGER and FLEMMI had ██████ set up a meeting with MURRAY which occurred at the park near the Bunker Hill monument in Charlestown. At this meeting BULGER told MURRAY that the above seizure had adversely affected his criminal activities, and as a result MURRAY was being fined. FLEMMI indicates that MURRAY paid a "fine" of approximately $60,000.

259. FLEMMI reported that a short time after this, he met with MURRAY's associate ██████ at MURRAY's bar across from ██████ in Charlestown. FLEMMI stated that this meeting had been set up by John HURLEY and related to a fund-raising effort for the Northern Aid Society. At about this time FLEMMI and BULGER became aware of MURRAY's efforts to ship arms to the IRA in Ireland. According to FLEMMI, MURRAY was an IRA sympathizer who in 1983 organized a shipment of arms to be sent from Boston to Ireland via the vessel VALHALLA. BULGER and FLEMMI provided some of the weapons that were sent on the VALHALLA. FLEMMI's younger brother Michael, a Boston Police officer also provided some bullet-proof vests that were part of the shipment. As is documented, the VALHALLA was intercepted off the coast of Ireland transferring weapons to the vessel the MARITA ANN. FLEMMI noted that he believes that MURRAY's group had successfully sent weapons over to the IRA approximately

one year prior to the VALHALLA shipment. The MARITA ANN was subsequently seized by Irish authorities (circa 10/29/84). The VALHALLA returned to Boston Harbor and was subsequently seized by USCG/DEA on October 16, 1984.

Stevie's brother, crooked BPD cop Michael Flemmi.

260. FLEMMI stated that in addition to their involvement in MURRAY's arms shipment to Ireland, FLEMMI and BULGER were involved in other criminal ventures with MURRAY. FLEMMI said that he and BULGER were due to receive an equal share of the proceeds from a marijuana importation that Joseph MURRAY was planning to bring in on the ship RAMSLAND during this same time period in the fall of 1984. FLEMMI indicated that this shipment of marijuana was seized by DEA/USCG (11/16/84). FLEMMI reported that he and BULGER were extremely upset when the RAMSLAND, with 36 tons of marijuana, was seized in Boston harbor. FLEMMI said that he and BULGER were to receive approximately $2,000,000 apiece as their share of the profits if the smuggle had been successful.

261. FLEMMI stated that he also recalled a meeting which began the integration of the MURRAY organization into a source of supply for BULGER's South Boston-based drug distribution group. This meeting occurred in approximately 1983 and is referred to as "the M Street Park meeting." According to FLEMMI, a meeting was to be held at ████████ home in South Boston, which was located adjacent to the M Street park. FLEMMI indicated that he was upstairs in ████████ residence when the meeting occurred. FLEMMI noted that he was advised of the purpose of the meeting beforehand by BULGER. The rationale for the meeting was to put ████████ together with Joseph MURRAY. FLEMMI recalled utilizing night-vision binoculars

while looking out of the window of ███████ house at BULGER, MUR-RAY and ███████ meeting in the street below. FLEMMI stated that the night-vision binoculars that he utilized were destined ultimately to be part of the shipment of arms to Ireland aboard the VALHALLA. FLEMMI also recalls a tool-box full of cocaine left at ███████ home by MURRAY either later that night or at a subsequent meeting. FLEMMI is unsure whether or not WEEKS was present when this cocaine was delivered to South Boston.

262. FLEMMI stated that sometime after the M Street park meeting he recalled being picked up by BULGER and WEEKS in South Boston and driven to the vicinity of the D Street housing projects. During the ride FLEMMI came to understand that WEEKS had a kilogram of cocaine in his possession, and that the group was en route to deliver it to someone in the projects. FLEMMI indicated that he was very upset with both BULGER and WEEKS and voiced his strong opinion that this was very risky due to the fact that the "DEA was all over South Boston." FLEMMI was aware that the DEA was specifically targeting BULGER et al. FLEMMI stated that the kilogram was delivered over his objections. FLEMMI said that BULGER felt exceptionally comfortable in his native South Boston, and therefore

Kevin Weeks, before he got fat.

Kevin Weeks, after he got fat.

often threw caution to the wind when he was engaged in criminal activity there. This arrangement between BULGER's gang and MURRAY's organization from Charlestown went on for several years. FLEMMI said that during the late 1980's (circa 1988-1989) MURRAY began distancing himself from BULGER's South Boston outfit. BULGER eventually agreed to let MURRAY go his separate way. But he insisted that MURRAY make a "severance payment" prior to ending the relationship. According to FLEMMI the gang received $500,000 from MURRAY for this "severance payment." FLEMMI claimed he pocketed approximately $90,000.

263. FLEMMI stated that sometime in the early 1990's, he acquired a small vial of poison from Joseph MURRAY. FLEMMI stated that MURRAY told him that the poison allegedly came from a chemist employed by the CIA, and that it was made from some form of marine life which was undetectable during an autopsy. MURRAY explained to FLEMMI that the slightest contact on a person's skin would result in death. MURRAY advised FLEMMI that he had tried the poison out on a dog, and that it had worked very well. Sometime in approximately 1992, FLEMMI gave Frank SALEMME a small portion of this poison. FLEMMI maintained this poison in a vial contained within an oil can located in the basement of his mother's home in South Boston. After his indictment in January 1995, FLEMMI instructed his son Stephen HUSSEY to get rid of the poison. (MURRAY was convicted of federal crimes in the late 1980's and ended up at the Danbury CT prison. He began writing anonymous letters to then Assistant U.S. Attorney General William Weld exposing in detail the crimes of the BULGER/FLEMMI organization. Among other things, he correctly named the murderers of Brian HALLORAN and Michael DONAHUE. Eventually two Boston FBI agents were sent to Danbury to interview MURRAY. The two S/A's from Boston then reported that Murray had no credible information. MURRAY was later released from prison and was shot to death by his wife in Maine in the early 1990's.)

▬▬▬▬ *assisted drug extortion (mid 1980's)*

264. FLEMMI stated that at various times when the occasion presented itself, he and BULGER would take advantage of extortion opportunities.

These situations were commonly referred to as "targets of opportunity." FLEMMI indicated that on one such occasion during the mid-1980's, ██████████, a South Boston associate, identified a marijuana dealer who was ripe for extortion. A meeting was arranged for the extortion victim to meet FLEMMI, BULGER and WEEKS at JC Hillary's restaurant in Dedham MA. Prior to the meeting a background investigation was conducted on the dealer, and photographs of the individual's home were obtained. FLEMMI said that during the meeting, WEEKS displayed a gun to the victim as well as the photos of the victim's residence. The victim was subsequently extorted for $100,000 which was split four ways between FLEMMI, BULGER, WEEKS and ██████████. Some time shortly after this incident Attorney Richard Egbert spoke with FLEMMI and asked that the group leave the individual alone in the future, due to the fact that the victim was a client and friend of Attorney Egbert's.

██████████ extortion (mid 1980's)

265. FLEMMI stated that in the early to mid 1980's, he and BULGER were involved in the extortion of a large-scale marijuana trafficker named

Joe Yerardi, Newton bookie
and loan shark.

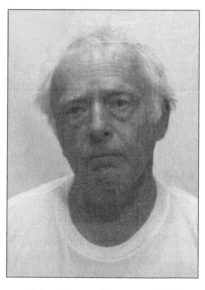

Myles Connor, the master thief,
fallen on hard times.

██████. FLEMMI stated that ████████ also had a penchant for gambling. ████████ was betting with Joey YERARDI at the time, and owed YERARDI approximately $25,000. YERARDI was associated in the bookmaking business with the Winter Hill gang. FLEMMI said that YERARDI went to ████████ for assistance in collecting the monies owed by ████████. ████████ subsequently sought assistance from FLEMMI and BULGER. A meeting was then held at the MARCONI CLUB in Roxbury. In attendance were FLEMMI, BULGER, possibly Phil COSTA, ████████, with Kevin WEEKS and ████████ somewhere in the general area of the club. According to FLEMMI, ████████ admitted owing the money, but tried to gain relief from the obligation by invoking the name of career criminal Myles CONNORS. ████████ claimed that CONNORS was ████████. FLEMMI said that Myles CONNORS subsequently spoke to ████████ and was instructed to stay out of the situation.

266. FLEMMI stated that during the meeting BULGER discussed ████████ drug business with him. ████████ claimed that he was not making any money in the drug business and therefore could not make any extortion payments. FLEMMI stated that ████████ was never assaulted during the meeting, although a fake gun was displayed during the extortion. FLEMMI initially was not sure as to how much he and BULGER extorted from ████████, because according to FLEMMI, BULGER handled the money pickups. At first FLEMMI recalled an initial payment of $25,000. However, he later indicated that the group received approximately $250,000, FLEMMI admitted that he received some $50,000 out of the ████████ cash. FLEMMI further stated that as far as he was aware, Attorney Richard Egbert never received a car from Winter Hill as any compensation for representing ████████ after ████████ arrest on federal drug trafficking charges.

Ray SLINGER extortion (03/87)

267. FLEMMI stated that Kevin O'NEIL had arranged some legitimate real estate transaction with Ray SLINGER, but the deal fell through when SLINGER reneged. O'NEIL then advised BULGER about SLINGER's

action, and it was decided to pay SLINGER a visit. FLEMMI said that he, BULGER, O'NEIL and possibly Kevin WEEKS went to SLINGER's office in South Boston. At the visit, BULGER advised SLINGER that he had been involved in the real estate deal with O'NEIL, and to work out the problems so that the transaction could proceed. SLINGER was told that O'NEIL would re-contact him at a later date to finalize the deal. FLEMMI stated that SLINGER called Boston City Council President Jimmy KELLY to complain about BULGER.

Jimmy Kelly, Boston city councilor, the gang's man at City Hall.

KELLY, an old friend of the South Boston mob, told BULGER about SLINGER's complaint. SLINGER was then called down to a meeting at Triple O's.

268. FLEMMI stated that he was not present for the Triple O's meeting with SLINGER but was later advised about its details by BULGER and WEEKS. SLINGER was threatened by BULGER during the meeting. BULGER spread a large trash bag on the floor of his office and then ordered SLINGER to step inside the bag. He was then told by BULGER that if they shot him in the top of his head that there wouldn't be much blood spilled, and that what little that did would drain into the garbage bag.

269. FLEMMI stated that SLINGER was also told at the meeting that he owed O'NEIL and BULGER a substantial amount of money. FLEMMI also recalled some discussion by BULGER with SLINGER about an alleged plot by a third party to hire someone to kill SLINGER. As usual, the "plot" had been concocted by BULGER, but SLINGER began to make payments to BULGER in order not to have the false murder contract carried out by the gang. FLEMMI received a few thousand dollars from this latest "contract."

270. FLEMMI said that a sister of SLINGER's convinced him to go to the FBI, which he eventually did. FLEMMI learned directly from S/A CONNOLLY that John NEWTON (whom BULGER called "Agent Orange" because of his red hair) and another agent had randomly been assigned to interview SLINGER. FLEMMI added that he later learned that the other agent involved in the interview was Rod Kennedy. BULGER advised FLEMMI that CONNOLLY told him that S/A's Kennedy and NEWTON interviewed SLINGER, but nothing came of the investigation. FLEMMI said that the group decided to back away from the SLINGER extortion, and no further payments were collected. FLEMMI did not recall speaking directly with S/A NEWTON about the SLINGER situation.

██████/Carmen TORTORA "beef"

271. FLEMMI stated that during the mid-to-late 1980's, ████████, a LEPERE associate and Roxbury native, had a problem he ████████ needed assistance with. According to FLEMMI, ████████ had a beef with LCN associate Carmen TORTORA. (TORTORA had recently been released from

Carmen Tortora, Mafia soldier, once left a death threat on a voice mail.

Carmelo Merlino ran his gang out of a Dorchester auto body shop.

prison after being convicted in an extortion plot; the main evidence against him had come from a recorded death threat he had left the victim on a telephone-answering machine.) The problem escalated to the point where ▆▆▆▆▆▆ attempted to put out a murder "contract" on TORTORA through an associate of Carmelo MERLINO. FLEMMI said that word got back to TORTORA, and plans were made by the LCN to kill ▆▆▆▆▆▆ . FLEMMI and BULGER also heard about the situation and confronted ▆▆▆▆▆▆ about the "contract" on TORTORA. ▆▆▆▆▆▆ subsequently admitted his involvement, and as a result FLEMMI and BULGER had a meeting with Jerry and Nicky ANGIULO and convinced them not to kill ▆▆▆▆▆▆ . After FLEMMI and BULGER's intervention, ▆▆▆▆▆▆ was fined $400,000, half of which went to ANGIULO. The remainder was retained by FLEMMI and BULGER.

FLEMMI and SALEMME's cooperative criminal ventures

272. FRANK SALEMME was released from state prison in 1989 after serving 17 years for the John FITZGERALD car bombing. FLEMMI stated that by the early 1990's, he and SALEMME consolidated and controlled all of the remaining numbers business in Boston. FLEMMI said that ▆▆▆▆▆▆

Steve Puleo handled numbers for
Stevie Flemmi.

Tommy Ryan, biggest bookie in
Cambridge, died 2012.

and Steve PULEO were merged in with SALEMME's side of the business, and the entire organization was grossing approximately $120,000 per week. FLEMMI added that the manager of the ████████ ran the numbers business for him and SALEMME. FLEMMI noted that he didn't make much money from this business, and at some point tried to sell the entire enterprise to Dick O'BRIEN and or Tom RYAN. FLEMMI speculated that ████████ is probably still running this numbers business to this very day. FLEMMI stated that after a dispute was settled which had pitted Winter Hill associate Chico KRANTZ against LCN-aligned bookmaker, ████████, he allowed SALEMME to take over a portion of the payments from KRANTZ. FLEMMI also recalled splitting with SALEMME a $7,500-a-year payment from ████████ for keeping bookmakers away from ████████ FLEMMI added that this payment began with ████████. FLEMMI speculated that ████████ may also still be receiving this money.

273. FLEMMI stated that he was told by SALEMME, and later confirmed by S/A CONNOLLY, that SALEMME had a chance meeting with CONNOLLY at the Prudential Center, where CONNOLLY had his Boston Edison office. CONNOLLY had worked there since retiring from the FBI in 1990. SALEMME told CONNOLLY that he had no hard feelings about his New York arrest. During the conversation CONNOLLY explained that he wanted an interview with SALEMME for a book (according to other accounts, a Hollywood screenplay) he was writing. CONNOLLY promised that he would portray SALEMME in a favorable light. FLEMMI said that he did not tell SALEMME about his own informant relationship with CONNOLLY at this point, and that it was not revealed until the pair was together in jail in Plymouth in 1997. FLEMMI added that SALEMME and CONNOLLY had a second meeting in CONNOLLY's office at the Prudential Center. FLEMMI said that he felt that it was a bad idea for SALEMME to meet with CONNOLLY. FLEMMI said that he told BULGER, and believes that BULGER complained to CONNOLLY about the meetings with SALEMME. FLEMMI stated that he did not make a $5,000 payment to CONNOLLY, which originated from SALEMME. FLEMMI acknowledged that the only type of payments FLEMMI made for SALEMME since

SALEMME's release from prison in 1989 was the $5,000 bribe for the entertainment license for the Channel, and $1,000 of that went to SCHNEIDERHAN, the corrupt MA state trooper.

John MARTORANO and alleged Laval Canada murders

274. FLEMMI stated that at some point in the late 1980's, John MARTORANO contacted George KAUFMAN and asked if KAUFMAN could obtain a clip for an Uzi machine gun. FLEMMI was also aware from KAUFMAN that during this time period MARTORANO was friendly with an individual from Laval Canada named "Andre" LNU (last name unknown). KAUFMAN asked FLEMMI for assistance in obtaining the clip, and FLEMMI told KAUFMAN to advise MARTORANO that he could not locate one. FLEMMI later heard from KAUFMAN that MARTORANO had secured a clip on his own. FLEMMI acknowledged that at no point did MARTORANO nor KAUFMAN say that he had killed anyone in Canada or in any other location at this time period. FLEMMI added that the possibility that MARTORANO had killed someone in Canada was broached during his defense in an attempt to discredit MARTORANO's potential testimony.

Tim CONNOLLY extortion (08/06/89)

275. FLEMMI stated that in the late 1980's Jimmy BULGER called Tim CONNOLLY down to the liquor store over some problem with a real estate transaction with former professional boxer Johnny Pretzie. FLEMMI was present when Tim CONNOLLY arrived at the store and was spoken to by BULGER in the business' store room. FLEMMI said that Tim CONNOLLY was assessed a fine of $50,000 for the problem he had created with PRETZIE. (BULGER repeatedly called CONNOLLY a "fuckster" while stabbing an empty box during the heated, extortionate discussion.) Tim CONNOLLY was clearly frightened by BULGER's out-of-control demeanor. Tim CONNOLLY returned to the store with at least one payment, which FLEMMI was again present for. FLEMMI recalled that Tim CONNOLLY only paid approximately $25,000, and that his share of the payment was about $5,000.

Johnny Pretzie, Boston prizefighter whose travails led
to another Whitey shakedown.

276. FLEMMI stated that Tim CONNOLLY came down to the liquor store
at another time after the first $25,000 payment on the extortion had been
made. FLEMMI was told by BULGER that during this trip to the liquor
mart, Tim CONNOLLY wore an FBI body wire. At first, FLEMMI could
not recall where this information on the body wire came from. At a later
debriefing interview FLEMMI remembered that BULGER told him that
he got this information from S/A John CONNOLLY. FLEMMI advised
the group to avoid Tim CONNOLLY. BULGER chose not to take FLEM-
MI's advice and sent Kevin WEEKS over to speak with Tim CONNOLLY.
WEEKS was told about the wire, and to craft his answers to Tim CON-
NOLLY's questions accordingly. WEEKS controlled the conversation with
Tim CONNOLLY and asked CONNOLLY a series of questions that elic-
ited answers tending to exonerate BULGER and the other gang members.
FLEMMI noted that Pat LINSKEY may have been present with WEEKS
during this conversation with Tim CONNOLLY. FLEMMI did not recall
any information that the body wire that Tim CONNOLLY wore was in a
cast on his hand. FLEMMI was present when S/A CONNOLLY advised
BULGER what was contained on the tape from this time when WEEKS had

been recorded with Tim CONNOLLY. (PRETZIE, the ex-boxer whose dispute with CONNOLLY had led to the extortion, was shot to death outside O'Leary's Pub in South Boston in July 1989. His murderer was sentenced to life in prison.)

Mickey DWYER extortion

277. FLEMMI stated that some time in the early 1980's, he, BULGER and WEEKS extorted bookmaker Mickey DWYER for $25,000. FLEMMI said that one day BULGER and WEEKS picked up DWYER, a one-time member of the old Mullens gang. The pair told DWYER that a contract had been put out on his life by some unknown party. The gang advised DWYER that they could take care of this problem for $25,000. To add credence to the fabricated murder contract, the group drove by DWYER's Quincy home late one night and fired several shots at the windows of his residence. DWYER produced the money and later was forced to pay "rent" in order to con-

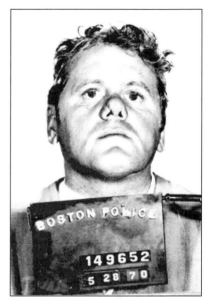

Mickey Dwyer, former Mullen, another extortion victim.

tinue his bookmaking activities. FLEMMI received approximately $5,000 from the initial DWYER payment. FLEMMI noted that he was present when the "rent" conversation took place with DWYER. FLEMMI added that DWYER paid $500 a month in "rent," and this extortion money was collected up until his arrest in 1995. FLEMMI further noted that he was the one who picked up DWYER's "rent" money for the group.

Things Fall Apart. . . .

S/A John CONNOLLY's retirement and the aftermath (12/03/90)

278. FLEMMI stated he was surprised when John CONNOLLY retired suddenly in December of 1990, after getting a good job offer from Boston Edison, where he would succeed another retired Boston FBI agent as director of security. FLEMMI added that he never heard that CONNOLLY left the FBI because of some investigation into his conduct. FLEMMI said that the FBI wanted FLEMMI and BULGER to be handled by S/A Mike BUCKLEY after CONNOLLY's retirement, but that he was not interested in continuing the relationship. FLEMMI noted that he was advised via telephone by CONNOLLY that CONNOLLY was still in touch with S/S/A Ed QUINN and S/A Mike BUCKLEY should anything important arise that FLEMMI wanted to pass on to the FBI.

Pat NEE's arrest on the attempted armored-car robbery (01/09/91)

279. FLEMMI stated that he did not recall getting any law-enforcement information regarding Pat NEE's involvement with a group of bank and armored car robbers. FLEMMI did not remember meeting with either

Billy Bulger and Zip Connolly at Zip's farewell dinner
from the FBI, December 1990.

David Ryan, the rat in the Jazzbo
Joyce armored-car-robbing gang.

Pat Nee, looking at serious time,
asked Whitey where one of the
bodies was buried.

John NEWTON or John CONNOLLY over this matter or for any other reason during this time period. FLEMMI did have a memory of NEE being warned by BULGER to stay away from David RYAN, who had been a law-enforcement informant in the past. FLEMMI does not remember exactly where the information regarding RYAN originated, but believes that it may have come from one of his Boston Police sources from the 1960's. In spite of the warning NEE still went along on the robbery and was subsequently arrested in Abington. FLEMMI also indicated that BULGER was concerned about NEE getting arrested because of the potential fallout should he cooperate with the authorities. FLEMMI recalled that BULGER had wanted to kill NEE in the past, and had attempted to get WEEKS to do the murder. FLEMMI felt that BULGER wanted NEE killed because of "old wounds" dating back to the Mullens/Killeen gang war. FLEMMI said that BULGER often denigrated NEE and would refer to him as "Cement Head".

Jimmy SIMS disappearance (02/05/91)

280. FLEMMI stated that he is not sure what exactly happened to his old Winter Hill partner Jimmy SIMS. FLEMMI added that SIMS had a falling out with his long-time partner Joe MCDONALD in the late 1980's. FLEMMI recalled that MCDON-ALD and his brother Leo tried to kill SIMS at SIMS' apartment during this time frame. FLEMMI said that SIMS had told him about the attempt on his life by the MCDONALD brothers. FLEMMI was also aware that SIMS owed ████████ between $10,000 and $15,000 in gaming money at the time of SIMS' disappearance. FLEMMI was advised by Howie WINTER that SIMS had written a letter that alluded to his

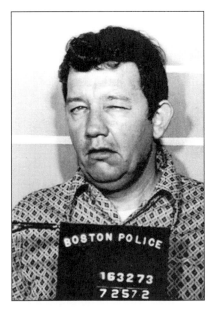

Jimmy Sims vanished after a violent dispute with Joe McDonald.

plan to commit suicide, but that SIMS' body was never found. FLEMMI stated that he believes that if SIMS is alive he may be in Florida ▉▉▉▉ ; FLEMMI further noted that ▉▉▉▉ had once turned in ▉▉▉▉ into law-enforcement authorities in the past, ▉▉▉▉ .

Massachusetts State Lottery win (07/26/91)

281. FLEMMI stated that he has mixed feelings as to whether the Mass. Millions Lottery ticket was legitimately won by Jimmy BULGER, Kevin WEEKS and Pat LINSKEY. (Actually, it was Michael Linskey who posed with the winning ticket for the media.) FLEMMI said that he first learned about the Lottery win from a girl at the variety store, who announced that Pat LINSKEY had a winning ticket. FLEMMI felt that if LINSKEY had hit, then he might be in line for a piece of the winnings. FLEMMI spoke with BULGER and WEEKS about the lottery and they never directly told FLEMMI how it was won. FLEMMI recalled that BULGER and WEEKS

Whitey Bulger (white cap) shows up at Lottery headquarters in Braintree to claim his $14 million prize in 1991.

Southie mobster hits $14M lottery jackpot

Whitey's number comes up – and elusive gangster cashes in!

By ERIC FEHRNSTROM

Reputed South Boston crime boss James "Whitey" Bulger, a trusted deputy, and two associates hit the Mass Millions for $14.3 million, embarrassing state Lottery officials and shocking federal agents who have pursued the elusive Irish mobster for more than two decades.

The big score — destined to go down in criminal and political lore — was revealed yesterday when lottery officials divulged that Bulger and three pals held the lucky 8-15-32-35-40-42 ticket.

"My understanding is that it is him, yes," said Thomas O'Heir, the lottery's executive director.

Aides to state Treasurer Joseph D. Malone were chagrined by Bulger's windfall, noting people will assume the drawing was fixed before.

Turn to Page 17

PAYDAY: Michael C. Linskey of South Boston shows off the first installment check of the $14.3 million lottery jackpot he won along with reputed mobster James J. "Whitey" Bulger, inset, Kevin J. Weeks of Quincy and Linskey's brother Patrick of Hanover.

Pat Linskey's brother Mike got to hold the winning
ticket for the front page photo.

planned to take the Lottery check, and then give Pat LINSKEY the money after it was cashed. BULGER and WEEKS were going to use the winnings to establish that they both had legitimate incomes. When FLEMMI asked to be included on the list of partners on the ticket, he was told that by adding yet another person, especially an organized-crime figure, the situation would appear totally unbelievable. FLEMMI admitted that he was upset by being left out of the arrangement. FLEMMI added that BULGER, WEEKS and LINSKEY each were paid $89,000 a year after taxes from the lottery winnings.

The Channel night club, and Steven DISARRO's murder (05/10/93)

282. FLEMMI stated that he met DISARRO on two or three occasions prior to DISARRO's murder. FLEMMI added that DISARRO was usually hanging

around with Frank SALEMME Jr. Along with SALEMME Sr., they were attempting to renovate the Channel night club in South Boston. FLEMMI recalled that he was interested in the project as a business venture. FLEMMI noted that he, James BULGER and Kevin WEEKS had also been promised a small percentage of the business. In fact, FLEMMI stated that SALEMME told him that prior to DISARRO's disappearance/ murder that they (SALEMME et al.)

Steve DiSarro's last driver's license.

had been skimming approximately $30,000 a week from the club. FLEMMI also remembered that his son, Billy HUSSEY, worked at the site during the construction phase. FLEMMI added that lumber and other supplies for the renovation were given free of charge by individuals from Rhode Island with building supply contacts. FLEMMI also added that ▮▮▮▮▮, a close friend of the SALEMME's, was also involved in the construction and management of the club. FLEMMI said that ▮▮▮▮▮ had been in state prison with SALEMME Sr. FLEMMI also added that ▮▮▮▮▮ had some type of managerial position with the business. FLEMMI noted that he was visiting the club on a nightly basis during this period.

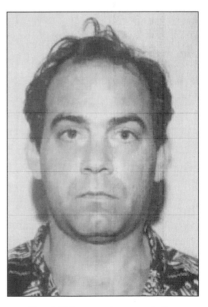

Frank Salemme Jr., soon to be dead of AIDS.

283. FLEMMI stated that SALEMME Sr. approached him about the club having trouble obtaining an entertainment license for the club. SALEMME Sr.

then gave FLEMMI $5,000 cash to bribe Boston City officials in hopes of securing the license. FLEMMI spoke with BULGER and WEEKS who in turn, possibly with or through Kevin O'NEIL, visited with Boston City Council President Jimmy KELLY from South Boston. FLEMMI noted that WEEKS advised him that the $5,000 had been passed to KELLY. FLEMMI was of the understanding from WEEKS that KELLY went to fellow Boston City Councilor Albert "Dapper" O'NEIL, a former member of the Boston Licensing Board, over the matter. FLEMMI noted that the club received its liquor license a short time later.

City Councilor Dapper O'Neil arranged for the Channel's liquor license.

284. FLEMMI stated that during the construction phase, and after the club opened, he learned that a federal grand jury investigation had begun into the Channel's operation. FLEMMI indicated that SALEMME Sr. and the others discovered that DISARRO had problems with the IRS. SALEMME Sr. told FLEMMI that DISARRO was meeting with IRS and possibly Department of Labor investigators, and may even have been interviewed by them at the club. FLEMMI noted that DISARRO was a very talkative fellow who drank heavily and was clearly becoming a liability to the group. SALEMME Sr. was concerned about legal problems DISARRO could give both SALEMMEs if he began cooperating with law-enforcement. SALEMME Sr. was also worried about DISARRO's prior business relationship in some type of fraudulent real estate deals with LCN associate ▮▮▮▮▮▮. FLEMMI also learned from SALEMME Sr. that DISARRO had also been friendly with ▮▮▮▮▮ who was cooperating with federal authorities at that time, and who could potentially corroborate ▮▮▮▮▮ testimony. FLEMMI recalled that SALEMME Sr. mentioned ▮▮▮▮▮ name during the discussions regarding DISARRO. For all these reasons, SALEMME Sr.

and the rest of the group at the Channel were clearly concerned about DIS-ARRO. FLEMMI admitted warning his son Billy HUSSEY (now known as Billy ST. CROIX) to stay away from DISARRO, SALEMME Jr. and ███████ . FLEMMI stated that based upon the way SALEMME had been talking he deduced that DISARRO was going to get "clipped." FLEMMI remembered SALEMME discussing a ruse story of letting DISARRO think that he would be going on the lam for awhile. FLEMMI said that this was often done to lull the victim into a false sense of security, in order to have the victim cooperate with his future killers voluntarily prior to the actual murder.

285. FLEMMI stated that at that point, in spite of his participation in other criminal activities with SALEMME Sr., he did not want to be involved in any murders with the LCN. FLEMMI said that one morning during this time period he was looking for the elder SALEMME, and drove to ██████ . FLEMMI noted that, ███████ . Upon arriving at the ███████ , FLEMMI saw SALEMME Jr. and DISARRO walking into the back of the home. FLEMMI remarked that only SALEMME Jr.'s car was visible at the residence. FLEMMI initially denied any other direct observations regarding the murder, but quickly admitted that he had in fact walked into the home as the murder was occurring. FLEMMI stated that he entered the house in order to ask SALEMME Jr. where he could find his father.

286. FLEMMI stated that as he walked into the kitchen area of ███████ , he observed SALEMME Jr. standing behind DISARRO with SALEMME Jr.'s arm around the victim's throat, lifting DISARRO off the ground and choking him. FLEMMI also observed ███████ grab DISARRO's legs, holding them off the ground so that the victim couldn't support himself. FLEMMI also viewed SALEMME Sr. and a third person who FLEMMI believed was ███████ standing in the rear of the room where the murder was taking place. Due to the assembled cast of characters and their activities, FLEMMI claims he quickly decided to leave the residence. FLEMMI noted that DISARRO was still being strangled, but was probably still alive when he left the home.

287. FLEMMI stated that in a later conversation with SALEMME Sr. FLEMMI learned that the third person at the scene had actually been ▓▓▓▓▓▓. FLEMMI also learned from SALEMME Sr. that later that afternoon or early evening, the body was placed in the trunk of SALEMME Sr.'s car and driven to a Rhode Island construction site. FLEMMI noted that SALEMME Sr. had advised him that the body had been wrapped up in some fashion. FLEMMI speculated that the likely location for the burial site was a construction project operated by SALEMME associate ▓▓▓▓▓▓. FLEMMI learned from SALEMME Sr. that a backhoe had been used to dig a 20-foot hole, and the body was placed inside and covered over. FLEMMI also learned from SALEMME Sr. that ▓▓▓▓▓ was present during the burial. SALEMME then left the area driven by ▓▓▓▓▓ who had followed the body from Sharon to the burial site in a separate vehicle.

288. FLEMMI stated that he was told by SALEMME Sr. that shortly after the murder, SALEMME Jr. and ▓▓▓▓▓ left the ▓▓▓▓▓, and went to a public place where they could be seen, in order to establish an alibi. FLEMMI noted that this was done because SALEMME Jr. was the last person to be seen with DISARRO before DISARRO's disappearance. FLEMMI also mentioned that to the best of his knowledge, ▓▓▓▓▓ was not ▓▓▓▓▓ during DISARRO's murder. FLEMMI stated that prior to the murder, he told BULGER that DISARRO was in trouble with SALEMME Sr.'s group. FLEMMI added that it was likely BULGER mentioned this information to CONNOLLY, but he has no actual knowledge whether this data was in fact passed on. FLEMMI also stated that he has no memory of telling his son, Billy HUSSEY, that he had a role in DISARRO's death. FLEMMI added that after DISARRO's murder the club's assets were looted in a typical "bust out" scenario.

Other SALEMME/LCN murders and criminal activities in the 1990's

289. FLEMMI stated that he was aware that Frank SALEMME was involved in several other homicides while leading the New England LCN in the early 1990's. SALEMME told FLEMMI that he, Richie DEVLIN and ▓▓▓▓▓ killed Bobby DONATI (09/24/91). FLEMMI recalled that DEVLIN had

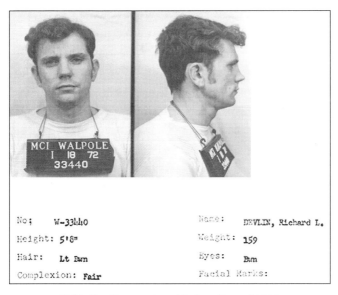

Richie Devlin, murdered Robert Donati 1990,
murdered himself in 1994.

hidden himself in a tree and jumped out on top of DONATI when DONATI was killed. FLEMMI added that the murder took place on the front lawn of DONATI's home. FLEMMI remembered that DONATI was suspected by the LCN of being an informant for some law-enforcement organization. FLEMMI also said that he once gave ▮▮▮▮▮▮▮ a pistol with a silencer on it, but that ▮▮▮▮▮▮ accidentally shot himself in the hand with the weapon. FLEMMI was also aware that ▮▮▮▮▮▮ had been made a member of the New England LCN by SALEMME, and became a caporegime.

▮▮▮▮▮▮ had asked FLEMMI's advice on whether to join the Mafia, and was told the benefits and drawbacks of membership. FLEMMI noted that while in Plymouth, ▮▮▮▮▮▮ had asked SALEMME to remove him from the active rolls of the LCN (i.e., to be put on the shelf) and the request was granted.

FLEMMI and BULGER's pre-indictment travels

290. FLEMMI stated that he remained friendly with Frank LEPERE even after LEPERE's 1984 arrest by DEA and incarceration on federal drug

charges. According to FLEMMI, in the fall of 1994, while anticipating an indictment, both he and BULGER traveled extensively, but not in each other's company. This frequent travel was intended to make surveillance and possible arrest by law-enforcement of the pair more difficult. FLEMMI referred to this pre-indictment travel as being "on the mini-lam." FLEMMI said that he spent some of this pre-indictment time period with Frank LEPERE on LEPERE's ranch in Florida.

Conversations with Dick O'BRIEN and other bookmakers during the grand jury investigation (1991-1995)

291. FLEMMI stated that he attempted, occasionally with success, to stymie the federal grand jury investigation that was conducted in the early 1990's by AUSA Fred Wyshak and the MA State Police. FLEMMI said that after he and BULGER became aware that local bookmaker Burton "Chico" KRANTZ had begun cooperating with the State Police, he contacted several other Boston area bookmakers and advised them to either flee the area, lie to the grand jury, or to take civil contempt charges. FLEMMI recalled speaking with bookmaker ███████ of Newton. ███████ had paid $1,000 in "rent" every month to FLEMMI through George KAUFMAN. FLEMMI told ███████ that it would be a good idea if he was not around to testify before the grand jury. ███████ took FLEMMI's suggestion to heart, and left the Boston area permanently. FLEMMI also spoke with ███████ and ███████ and told them that Chico KRANTZ was "a rat" and that if they took contempt sentences then they would be taken care of while in jail.

292. FLEMMI stated that he also traveled to the area of Lake Okeechobee in Florida and met with South Shore-based bookmaker Dick O'BRIEN. This meeting took place at a Cracker Barrel restaurant, and O'BRIEN had been driven to the meeting by John MARTORANO. FLEMMI noted that he was already in Florida, visiting Frank LEPERE prior to the meeting with O'BRIEN. FLEMMI recalled discussing the situation involving bookmakers and the grand jury investigation with O'BRIEN, FLEMMI said that the meeting with O'BRIEN in Florida was basically an effort to see whether O'BRIEN would truthfully testify about paying "rent" to FLEMMI and BULGER.

FLEMMI added that he was satisfied with O'BRIEN's answers at the meeting. FLEMMI said that he really didn't entertain any serious thoughts about killing O'BRIEN, and felt that Newton-based bookmaker Joe YERARDI posed a greater problem to the gang. FLEMMI and MARTORANO discussed YERARDI's pending legal problems and the fact that YERARDI was going to go "on the lam" prior to his indictment (10/14/93). FLEMMI admitted that he and MARTORANO also discussed killing YERARDI, but that he finally decided that it wasn't necessary. FLEMMI stated that he was more concerned with

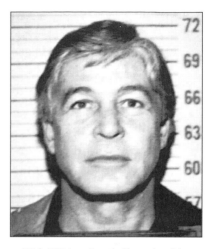

Dick O'Brien, South Shore bookie, took a contempt sentence rather than testify before the grand jury.

another Newton-based bookmaker ▬▬▬ testifying against the gang than O'BRIEN. FLEMMI remembered asking O'BRIEN about ▬▬▬ at the Lake Okeechobee meeting, and requesting that O'BRIEN find out whether ▬▬▬ was going to testify truthfully in front of the grand jury.

293. FLEMMI stated that George KAUFMAN also spoke with other bookmakers about protecting the gang while other bookies did not have to be talked to. FLEMMI said that everyone knew that Tommy RYAN would refuse to testify and thus be found guilty of civil contempt, which would mean a prison sentence. FLEMMI elaborated that RYAN knew without being told that the consequences for testifying truthfully in this matter could be death. FLEMMI concluded that RYAN understood that doing 18 months for contempt was just part of the job of being a bookmaker. FLEMMI added that ▬▬▬ was spoken to by John MARTORANO, and counseled on what ▬▬▬ options were. FLEMMI noted that John MARTORANO also spoke with North Shore bookmaker Charlie RASO about the situation. FLEMMI said that after Dick O'BRIEN was placed in jail for contempt, he discussed the situation with O'BRIEN prior to going back before the grand jury. FLEMMI recalled telling O'BRIEN to name KAUFMAN

as the individual from Winter Hill that he dealt with. FLEMMI believed that KAUFMAN had passed away by the time this conversation with O'BRIEN had occurred, and that it would be easy to "blame the dead guy."

Hidden FLEMMI money and plans to "go on the lam"

294. FLEMMI stated that when he had sold his interest at the ROTARY VARI-ETY store he took the cash and hid it in a gym bag behind an access panel to a crawl space in the upstairs closet of his mother's home in South Boston. The bag contained approximately $550,000 in cash, which was from the sale of the ROTARY VARIETY and other ventures. FLEMMI planned to take this gym bag full of money with him and flee to Canada to avoid the pending extortion and bookmaking indictments. FLEMMI also had an apartment in the Mount Royal section of Montreal

Whitey's Irish passport photo.

to live in when he arrived in Canada after going "on the lam." FLEMMI acknowledged having a bank account at the Bank of Montreal on St Catherine's Street, which was set up under the alias Clifford Beauleau. FLEMMI noted that this account only contains about $500 and was opened in 1994. FLEMMI also maintained a post office box under the same alias at the McCormack Courthouse in Post Office Square in Boston. FLEMMI obtained that post office box for handling bank statements from the Montreal account, and possibly for communicating with others in the Boston area. FLEMMI's escape plan was foiled when DEA and MA State Police investigators arrested FLEMMI outside his sons' new restaurant, Schooner's, on Jan. 5, 1995. He has been imprisoned ever since.

295. FLEMMI stated that he had secreted a plastic tub inside a hollowed-out spot in a chimney, also at his mother's home. The tub contained $500,000

cash and approximately $200,000 in gold coins. The money was intended to pay future expenses FLEMMI or his family had. The cash and coins in these two locations represented proceeds from FLEMMI's illegal ventures. FLEMMI stated that his mother, Mary FLEMMI, knew about the money he had hidden in the chimney, as well as the cash contained in the gym bag in the upstairs bedroom closet. FLEMMI did not tell his brother Michael about either of the hidden caches of cash, but Michael did have access to an additional $5,000 in the residence, as well as still another $22,000 from the sale of a six-carat diamond ring belonging to Mary FLEMMI, his mother.

296. FLEMMI stated that he learned from his mother that she had told her son Mike about the money inside the chimney. FLEMMI's son Stephen was notified of the secreted money in the chimney, but never admitted to his father that he took the cash. FLEMMI said that during the hearings in front of Judge Wolf, Stephen HUSSEY told him that the chimney hide containing the secreted money was intact. FLEMMI is now aware from testimony at Mike FLEMMI's federal trial that the money from the chimney has been split by Billy HUSSEY, Stephen HUSSEY and Marion HUSSEY. FLEMMI said that he had originally hidden money inside the window sills in the cellar at the mother's South Boston home, but had removed it and added that cash to the money within the gym bag.

297. FLEMMI stated that he had spent another $990,000 to $1,200,000 on prior real estate transactions. FLEMMI estimated that this property was now worth approximately $1,500,000. FLEMMI said that he had used $200,000 from a bank account at Braintree Savings Bank to provide the money that Billy and Stephen HUSSEY used to buy and remodel their restaurant on State Street in Boston. FLEMMI spent $120,000 on legal fees and for private investigators. FLEMMI claimed to have paid another $15,000 for Stephen HUSSEY's legal fees in his son's federal trial for obstruction of justice and perjury. FLEMMI additionally claimed to have paid yet another $11,000 in attorney's fees for family members who appeared before various grand juries.

298. FLEMMI stated that he also lost another $20,000 in a business venture with ▇▇▇▇▇ and Attorney Richard Egbert involving imported Italian business suits. FLEMMI stated that the real estate holdings and the hidden cash amounted to all that remained from all of his illegal ventures over some 40 years. The rest of FLEMMI's money has been used for living expenses for himself, his three families, and cash lavished upon his many girlfriends. FLEMMI also claimed to have spent substantial amounts of money paying various local, state and federal taxes, so as not to be susceptible to any criminal charges for income-tax evasion.

299. FLEMMI stated that he didn't keep money in safe-deposit boxes in this country or other countries because of an incident that happened in the late 1960's. FLEMMI said that he had opened up a safe-deposit box at the State Street Bank on Congress Street in Boston under an assumed name, and placed $100,000 inside. FLEMMI said that the bank was planning on moving, and he only found out about the change by chance, after which he was able to successfully remove the money. FLEMMI added that because of the inability to control the money under the assumed name in the safe-deposit box, and the possible criminal exposure it could bring, he stopped using this method to secure his funds.

300. FLEMMI stated that he maintains no property overseas and only had a small bank account in the Cayman Islands. FLEMMI acknowledged that he had originally planned to hide money in this Cayman Island account, but found that physically transporting the cash to the country was much too hazardous and so the idea was scrapped. The account was maintained in the islands after this only as a convenience when traveling in the Caribbean. The account, which is under the name "Three Island Reality Trust," currently contained only a few thousand dollars when last checked. FLEMMI added that when he attempted to open this off-shore account, he set it up through ▇▇▇▇▇ , and used a financial institution without ties to the United States. FLEMMI stated that he placed the money in the Cayman National Bank.

301. FLEMMI stated that after his experiences with safe-deposit boxes and off-shore accounts, his preferred method of concealing his money was the use of homemade and professional hides. FLEMMI said that in addition to the ones at his mother's residence, he also had one built at his Marconi Club in Roxbury. FLEMMI was questioned about jewelry and gold that he had been observed with. FLEMMI responded that he had a blue Crown Royal Whisky bag that contained some 30 to 40 rings in it. FLEMMI said that he purchased the stolen jewelry for $4,000 or $5,000 from someone who had robbed a store in the 1960's. These rings were eventually sold off.

302. FLEMMI stated that according to WEEKS, after his arrest, Jackie BULGER came over to his mother's house with $30,000. Additionally, FLEMMI admitted to collecting "rent" and tribute monies from various gaming and shylock operations that he controlled after his 1995 arrest and incarceration. These monies were collected by Phil COSTA until his death (05/02/99) and Kevin WEEKS. FLEMMI also acknowledged that

Jackie and Billy Bulger leaving federal court.

his police-officer brother Mike collected $750 a month from ███████ as part of the money from the sale of the Rotary Variety Store. These cash payments from ██████████ continued up until the spring of 1997 when FLEMMI was outed as an FBI informant.

James BULGER's money

303. FLEMMI stated that BULGER and Kevin O'NEIL had a friend at the ████████ . FLEMMI believes that BULGER and O'NEIL may have invested ██████████ at some point. FLEMMI admitted that he was offered

Mike Flemmi, not happy, would soon be convicted.

the chance to invest ██████████ , but declined the proposal. FLEMMI also said that BULGER use to bring cash to Canada, and would give it to Chris NILAN for safe keeping. Nilan was a West Roxbury native who was then playing for the Montreal Canadiens NHL hockey team and was at the time married to the daughter of Whitey BULGER's girlfriend, Teresa Stanley. FLEMMI said that BULGER usually brought approximately $50,000 at a time. FLEMMI estimated that the total amount of money BULGER smuggled into Canada was about $200,000. FLEMMI said that this money transfer ended when BULGER and Teresa STANLEY were stopped at Logan Airport in 1987 and written up by MA state trooper Billy Johnson. (The next day, the political appointee of Gov. Michael DUKAKIS who ran the airport, David W. DAVIS, appeared at the airport barracks and demanded that Johnson hand over all copies of the incident

Chris Nilan, professional hockey player, once married to one of Teresa Stanley's daughters.

Dave Davis, boss of Logan Airport,
tried to confiscate Johnson's
embarrassing police report
on Whitey's attempt to smuggle
$50,000 cash out of the country.

Billy Johnson, hounded out of the
State Police for standing up to Whitey.

report on BULGER. Johnson refused unless he was given a receipt for the reports, and DAVIS stormed out. A few days later, Johnson was transferred from Troop F at the airport to a much less prestigious, and lucrative, posting. Johnson, a decorated Vietnam War veteran, later committed suicide. Until his death in 2012, DAVIS never revealed who at the State House had ordered him to obtain the embarrassing reports on BULGER.) FLEMMI was also of the opinion that Jackie BULGER held some of Jimmy BULGER's illegal monies. (Jack BULGER was later convicted of perjury after telling a federal grand jury he had never visited one of Whitey BULGER's safe-deposit boxes in Clearwater FL.) FLEMMI said that unlike himself, BULGER liked to put his money in banks and safe-deposit boxes.

304. FLEMMI stated that he also remembered traveling with BULGER to southern New Hampshire, possibly Derry, where both purchased some $200,000 worth of gold coins. FLEMMI believes these trips to New Hampshire occurred in 1981 or 1982. FLEMMI said that these gold coins

included Chinese Pandas, South African Krugerrands, Mexican Coronas, and American Eagles. FLEMMI said the coins were newly minted and that he only purchased South African Krugerrands. FLEMMI noted that the coins were purchased with cash and that no paperwork was filled out. FLEMMI added that the purchases at the New Hampshire store were made by appointment only.

Winter Hill/South Boston guns

305. FLEMMI stated that Winter Hill's collection of firearms was picked up from many different sources over the years. FLEMMI said that some of the weapons were inherited from other members or gangs and some had been collected for the IRA but never sent over to Ireland. FLEMMI noted that the weapons were gathered in case of a new gang war, and also as a potential bargaining chip with law-enforcement. FLEMMI said that everyone in the criminal element knew that Winter Hill would buy quality firearms, and consequently thieves were constantly bringing them by for the gang to examine. FLEMMI recalled that the .45 caliber "grease guns" had been stolen years earlier by longshoremen in Everett MA from a shipment intended for Vietnam. Nick FEMIA brought these weapons to Winter Hill, and they were purchased for $600 apiece. Other weapons like the high-powered hunting rifles were stolen in house breaks and brought to Winter Hill by Jimmy SIMS.

306. FLEMMI stated that BULGER acquired the automatic carbines for the group, and that the Mach 10 machine gun came from a drug dealer in Florida, probably through ▬▬▬▬. FLEMMI said that the German World War II-vintage machine guns came separately. One of these weapons was owned by Bobby LABELLA, and was given to him by ▬▬▬▬ upon LABELLA's death. FLEMMI said that BULGER had obtained the chromed model, and also secured a Thompson submachine gun. FLEMMI said that the silencers were homemade and were built by a friend of "Wimpy" BENNETT's. FLEMMI added that he had custody of the gang's weapons from the time they were moved from KAUFMAN's Brookline house until his arrest. FLEMMI said that he offered to give up the Winter Hill arsenal

to law-enforcement shortly after his arrest in 1995. The offer was made to Attorney Richard Egbert who notified ████████. FLEMMI said that ████████ approached someone within the Department of Justice but the offer was declined.

████████ *attempted extortion of FLEMMI (January 1997)*

307. FLEMMI stated that while he was incarcerated at Plymouth House of Corrections, ████████ attempted to extort $1,000,000 in return for refraining from testifying against him. FLEMMI indicated that this information was turned over to ████████ defense attorney, ████████, who in turn notified the government. FLEMMI also reported that ████████, which he subsequently bought, was not part of any extortion involving him.

Epilogue—Where Are They Now?

STEVIE FLEMMI is serving his life sentence in parts unknown. As a co-operating witness, his location is not listed on the Bureau of Prisons' website—"not in BOP custody," the website says.

Estimated release date: "Unknown." Translation: "Never."

A few years ago, FLEMMI sent now-retired Tulsa Police Detective Mike Huff a Christmas card from the federal penitentiary in Otisville, NY. FLEMMI is expected to be a major witness against Whitey BULGER at his upcoming trial. FLEMMI is 78 years old.

JAMES J. "WHITEY" BULGER was captured in June 2011 after 16 years as a fugitive. In his apartment in Santa Monica CA police found more than 20 firearms and $822,000 cash in an old-fashioned Boston wall "hide." BULGER is currently incarcerated at the Plymouth County Correctional Facility. In February 2013, BULGER wrote to one of his old friends from Alcatraz: "This is the end of the trail for me." At press time, BULGER's federal trial on various murder and racketeering charges was expected to begin on June 6, 2013. BULGER is 83 years old.

CATHERINE E. GREIG, Whitey BULGER's girlfriend, was captured along with him in 2011. She pleaded guilty in 2012 to conspiracy to harbor a fugitive and to conspiracy to commit identity theft. She is currently incarcerated in the low-security federal prison for females in Waseca, MN. Her current release date is scheduled for June 10, 2018. She is 61 years old.

MICHAEL FLEMMI, Stevie's younger brother and corrupt ex-Boston police officer, finished his federal prison sentence on Sept. 2, 2011. He is 75 years old.

JOHN "ZIP" CONNOLLY, the corrupt FBI agent, was convicted of second-degree murder in Florida in 2008 in the 1982 slaying of former World Jai Alai executive John Callahan. He finished his federal racketeering sentence in June 2011 and immediately began serving his 40-year state sentence in Florida. CONNOLLY is 72 years old. He will be eligible for parole at age 84.

JOHN MARTORANO is living as a free man in Boston after his release from prison in 2007. He has sold his life story to Hollywood producer Graham King, who has already made one acclaimed movie loosely based on Whitey Bulger, "The Departed." MARTORANO is also expected to be a major witness against BULGER. He is 72 years old.

Howie Winter, in court charged with attempted extortion at age 83, 2012.

HOWIE WINTER is living in Millbury MA, facing trial on state charges involving an alleged extortion attempt that took place at the Sons of Italy Hall in Medford in 2012. WINTER was recorded by the State

Police telling his alleged victims, "You don't know who I am? I'll tell you something. You're full of shit. There's no one in the fucking country who doesn't know who I am." WINTER is 83 years old.

WILLIAM M. BULGER, retired from the Commonwealth of Massachusetts in 2003 with a $900,000 severance payment and is currently collecting an annual state pension of $198,205.92. BULGER is 79 years old.

JOHN "JACKIE" BULGER: Stripped of his state pension after federal conviction for lying to a grand jury, released from prison on April 1, 2004. BULGER is 74 years old. Visits his brother Whitey at the Plymouth jail "once or twice" a week, told a reporter in February 2013 that he doesn't think Whitey is being treated very well.

"But I don't want to get into it," he said.

Whitey in custody, leaving helicopter for trip to federal court, 2011.